LITERATURE AND REALITY, 1600–1800

LITERATURE AND REALITY
1600–1800

C. N. MANLOVE

ST. MARTIN'S PRESS   NEW YORK

Printed in Hong Kong
Library of Congress Catalog Card Number 78–6934
ISBN 0–312–48747–9

First published in the United States of America in 1978

Library of Congress Cataloging in Publication Data

Manlove, Colin Nicholas, 1942–
    Literature and reality, 1600–1800.
    Bibliography: p.
    Includes index.
    1. English literature—Early modern, 1500–1700—History and criticism.
2. Realism in literature. 3. English literature—18th century—History
and criticism. I. Title.

PR438.R42M3   820'.9   78–6934

ISBN 0–312–48747–9

Contents

vi *Contents*

Preface

The primary purpose of this book is to establish new approaches to works by a range of the main English literary figures of the seventeenth and eighteenth centuries. Critical orthodoxy in the interpretation of the works of these writers has sometimes come to an unwarranted degree of complacency; and denial of an author's manifest weaknesses has often exhibited itself in excessive scholastic ingenuities. The interpretations given here are offered not as final ones, only as possible stimuli to further thought.

The theme of the book emerged in writing: all the interpretations are concerned with how much of reality, at a time when 'reality' was being reinterpreted and vastly extended, the writers of these centuries found it possible to include in their work, and how the character and amount of their inclusiveness alters over the period. This theme has not been widely pursued before in relation to the literature: the nearest work is Erich Auerbach's *Mimesis: The Representation of Reality in Western Literature* (1946), which, while it deals with this period, is concerned more with the mode in which reality is represented than with the degree.

The choice of the dates 1600 and 1800 is not wholly arbitrary. The execution of Giordano Bruno in 1600 for his promulgation of the very theories concerning the universe which deeply affected the minds of the next centuries was an obvious starting point; the death of Cowper, the last writer considered, in 1800, provided a more *ad hoc* terminus. On the other hand, the limits are not absolute: Marlowe's plays anticipate some of the character of Jacobean dramas, such as Shakespeare's *Coriolanus*, Jonson's *Volpone* or Webster's plays, in their inability to reconcile admiration of amoral energy (*Tamburlaine*) with its condemnation (*Dr Faustus*); and the self-divisions evident in eighteenth-century writers are also present in the succeeding centuries. What is roughly delimited here is a single period, a kind of spiritual interregnum, falling between one intuitive approach to understanding the universe and, in the Romantics, another, if frailer, one. The problems faced and the methods employed by the writers in this period are not, of course, unique to them: but they are here dominant and besetting to a degree not evident before or since. Thus, for example, no claim will be made that the so-called 'dissociation of sensibility' which T. S. Eliot located in the seventeenth century is a wholly novel phenomenon, resulting in the binary fission of perfectly unified medieval psyches:[1] it will only be argued that the suppression of alternative views which generally produces the appearance of monolithic certainty in the medieval mind and its theocratic extension is steadily eroded throughout this period.

The many debts of this book are gratefully acknowledged in the notes. I am also grateful to Mrs Sheila Campbell, for her patience and efficiency in typing the manuscript; and to my wife, for reading and correcting the typescript, and for constant help and encouragement.

C. N. M.

List of Editions Used

Unless otherwise stated, place of publication is London.

Donne   *John Donne: The Complete English Poems*, ed. A. J. Smith (Harmondsworth: Penguin Books, 1971).

Marvell   *Andrew Marvell: The Complete Poems*, ed. E. S. Donno (Harmondsworth: Penguin Books, 1972).

Jonson   *Ben Jonson: The Complete Poems*, ed. George Parfitt (Harmondsworth: Penguin Books, 1975).

Herrick   *The Poetical Works of Robert Herrick*, ed. L. C. Martin (Oxford: Clarendon Press, 1956).

Milton   *The Poems of John Milton*, ed. John Carey and Alastair Fowler (Longmans, 1968).

Dryden   *The Poems and Fables of John Dryden*, ed. James Kinsley (Oxford: Clarendon Press, 1958).

Chaucer   *The Works of Geoffrey Chaucer*, ed. F. N. Robinson, 2nd edition (Oxford University Press, 1957).

Defoe   *The Life and Strange Surprizing Adventures of Robinson Crusoe of York, Mariner*, ed. J. D. Crowley (Oxford University Press, 1972).
     The Fortunes and Misfortunes of the Famous Moll Flanders &c., ed. G. A. Starr (Oxford University Press, 1971).

Wyndham   *The Day of the Triffids* (Michael Joseph, 1951).

Pope   *The Poems of Alexander Pope*, ed. John Butt (Methuen, 1963).

Swift   *The Prose Writings of Jonathan Swift*, ed. Herbert Davis: vol. II, *Bickerstaff Papers*, and vol. XII, *Irish Tracts, 1728–1733* (Oxford: Basil Blackwell, 1939 and 1955).

Thomson   *The Complete Poetical Works of James Thomson*, ed. J. Logie Robertson (Oxford University Press, 1908).

Fielding   *The History of the Adventures of Joseph Andrews and of his Friend Mr. Abraham Adams, and An Apology for the Life of Mrs. Shamela Andrews*, ed. Douglas Brooks (Oxford University Press, 1970).

Fielding —(Cont.)	*The History of Tom Jones, A Foundling*, the Wesleyan Edition, ed. M. C. Battestin and F. Bowers, 2 vols (Oxford, 1974).
Gray and Goldsmith	*The Poems of Thomas Gray, William Collins, Oliver Goldsmith*, ed. Roger Lonsdale (Longmans, 1969).
Johnson	*Samuel Johnson: The Complete English Poems*, ed. J. D. Fleeman (Harmondsworth: Penguin Books, 1969). *The History of Rasselas, Prince of Abissinia*, ed. Geoffrey Tillotson and Brian Jenkins (Oxford University Press, 1971).
Crabbe	*George Crabbe: Tales, 1812, and Other Selected Poems*, ed. Howard Mills (Cambridge: Cambridge University Press, 1967).
Cowper	*The Poetical Works of William Cowper*, ed. H. S. Milford (Oxford University Press, 1934).

Note. Throughout this book, all page references are prefixed 'p.' or 'pp.'; line references (principally to poetry) bear no prefix.

I Introduction

The general background to this period has been thoroughly documented[1] and here may be outlined briefly. Notions of what constituted reality, and the extent of that reality, were vastly altered from 1600 onwards. Giordano Bruno's doctrine of the decentralised, infinite, and infinitely populous universe[2] gradually took away man's ability to see himself and his history as unique, and his capacity to conceive of the universe in neat, concentric and, above all, picturable terms. Such formal proportion and universal symmetry as had been held to have survived man's fall were now lost: only the idea of the ladder of being, now increasingly emphasised, provided even a concept of universal organisation; and, since that ladder was conceived as having an infinite number of links, many of them in other stellar systems, man could conceive only a tiny part of it.[3] Renaissance wonder at man shifts to wonder or terror at the magnitude and variety of nature.

Phenomena lose their symbolic roles in a teleological scheme and are increasingly seen simply as phenomena. The new scientific interest in the world for itself and the stress on the doctrine of universal plenitude present a universe far more full of data, observed or inferred, than ever before. The old network of universal analogy, by which all things could figure one another, is sustained for a time by the metaphysical conceit[4] and the enclosed worlds of Christian symbolist poetry, but soon collapses. The previously-held belief in the relation of mind and body is undermined by discoveries such as Gilbert's concerning the magnetic properties of the earth (1600) or Harvey's of the principles behind the circulation of the blood (1628), which make the actions of the human and terrestrial bodies mechanistic rather than 'sympathetic', organic or mentally-informed. This mechanistic approach to the universe reaches its fullest scientific formulation in Newton, and its philosophic one in Hobbes; the rationalism of Descartes, on the one hand, and the empiricism of Locke and Hume, on the other, express the new oppugnancy of mind and matter.

Man becomes less the focus of the creative act and of eschatology, more only one link in an infinite chain of being, in which he can be seen as differing in degree rather than in kind from the creatures immediately below him, and also as not the only or the most intelligent being in the universe. Hierarchy is challenged, and a king is executed by his subjects. Truth, no longer a monopoly, grows multiple. The tendency of the age may be described as a movement of conflict inwards: divided along national lines between Protestants and Catholics in the sixteenth century, Christianity subdivides to produce rival Protestants and civil war in the seventeenth; and, in the eighteenth, self-division becomes characteristic within the mind of the individual. It grows steadily less possible for a man to feel that his view of reality is one endorsed and sustained by a whole society: at best he can appeal to like-minded men, but often has to fall back on his friends or himself.

Literature reflects these changes in several obvious ways. For example, a glance at the repertoire of almost any seventeenth-century poet compared to that of one from the sixteenth century will show an increase in the range of subjects, moods and attitudes, together with a proliferation of literary kinds: quite simply, there is more to write about, and there are more ways of writing about it. Again, writers deal far more directly with contemporary events, from panegyrics to satires on named individuals or on religious and political issues of the day: indeed, the rise of satire itself is partly attributable to this cause.

But our primary concern in this book will be with how much of the manifold and diverse character of this new reality the writers of the time admitted into their work, and with the way in which literary reactions to reality change over the period. The cultural and intellectual background provides explanation for the results of literary analysis, but is not itself a tool of investigation. Central to this investigation is the degree to which literature could contain the dialectical character of reality; but there are other, closely related issues, such as the changing nature of the unity of the literary work, the growth of 'unconscious' aims and tensions, relative consistency and logicality.

We begin with Donne, who may well have read Bruno's theses,[5] who had a profoundly adventurous mind and who was a constitutional rebel, whether against literary convention or against God himself; and yet who shows in his poetry the anxiety of a mind burdened by the knowledge it has gained concerning the incoherence of reality[6] and the alien character of fact.

2 Donne and Marvell

In much of his poetry Donne is in flight from uncouth fact, to the extent that the point of his poetry is often how far we can give credence to his 'fancy'.[1] The famous 'Flea' is an instance: Donne is trying to persuade his lady into his bed by arguing that the flea, having bitten both of them and sucked their blood, has mingled them inside itself so that, thanks to it, 'we . . . more than married are'; with this accomplished, why delay further? To the notion that the flea can thus alter their lives the lady replies by killing it, and by then triumphantly saying that, since its death has not altered them in the least, why then should its life? Donne now turns the tables by responding, 'Just so much honour, when thou yield'st to me, / Will waste, as this flea's death took life from thee.' Wit has succeeded in neutralising fact and manipulating it to its own advantage. But the argument is not thereby convincing: it is only a convincing argument. The lady might doubtless be entertained, and therefore a shade more pliant, but the efficacy of the poem in this direction is clearly minimal: what it is bent on doing is forming a crystalline intellectual sphere cut loose from the earth. The same is true of 'The Sun Rising', 'A Valediction: of Weeping', 'Air and Angels', 'Lovers' Infiniteness' – most, indeed, of Donne's secular lyric output.

Donne is a one-sided poet: if, as in 'The Flea', a fact opposed to his argument is introduced, he does not incorporate the contradiction and let it modify his approach, but simply denies that it is a contradiction at all. Much of his love poetry depends on making recalcitrant facts appear to serve his own ends, or in colonising reality with mind, as, for example, when he makes the sun minister to love in 'The Sun Rising' or a jet ring figure his love in 'A Jet Ring Sent'. He rarely builds a poem out of the dialectic of opposed views, but argues extreme positions (a symptom of this is his liking for the motif of 'all' and 'nothing'). In one poem he can maintain that absence is not a grief ('A Valediction: forbidding Mourning'), and in another that it is ('A Valediction: of Weeping'); in one that union in love is total ('The Ecstasy'), and in another that the gulf between the sexes cannot be bridged ('Air and Angels'); in one that love can grow ('Love's Growth'), and in another that it is above time and unalterable ('The Sun Rising'). He will not take a middle ground on which to give weight to the impulses behind both points of view.

For Donne the extremism and the narrowness are often the point. The creative urge behind most of his poems is a delight in constructing ingenious witty universes and giving credibility to diverse moods and points of view. Irrespective of any possible sincerity behind Donne's poetry, he is also a consummate actor who takes pleasure in throwing himself into different roles, from fidelity to libertinism, and from impudence to gravity. And it is on this level that his poetry is most to be enjoyed: he is more a fantasist than a realist.

When, rarely, two opposed points of view are present in a Donne poem, the presence of the second is neither intentional nor catered for. 'A Valediction: forbidding Mourning' begins assuredly enough:

> As virtuous men pass mildly away,
> And whisper to their souls, to go,
> Whilst some of their sad friends do say,
> The breath goes now, and some say, no:
>
> So let us melt, and make no noise,
> No tear-floods, nor sigh-tempests move,
> 'Twere profanation of our joys
> To tell the laity our love.

The first six lines say they should go quietly and without fuss (a point enacted by the suspended syntax). Then Donne asks himself – why? His first answer is that they would thereby be letting the intensity of their private love be dissipated in an ignorant public world. His next answer, in the third stanza, is, if by a smaller grief they raised tear-floods and sigh-tempests, they would cause harm and grief to others, thus proving their love earthly and corruptible; but the far greater character of silent grief goes unnoticed. All this fits with the implicit notion of detaching their love from all contact with publicity, externality or physicality (continued in the next two stanzas), but does not agree with the notion at the outset of the poem and in stanza 5 that they are not grieved because they are not really parted – 'Inter-assured of the mind, / Care less, eyes, lips, and hands to miss'. Nor does the assertion that their love is above the material world fit easily with the admission that they can be even partially divided. Lines 5–19 are all on the subject of their transcendent love: theirs, we are told, is of the spheres, not of earth or the entire mutable order beneath the moon, because they are 'Inter-assured of the mind'. Logically therefore, they should not 'Care *less*, eyes, lips, and hands to miss' (20): they should care not at all. But this is one poem of Donne's in which the mental realities woven by wit gave way a little to acknowledgement of fact. Perhaps this was because it was made at least partly out of real pain, perhaps because Donne is never entirely easy with the Platonic direction he tries to give many of his poems (consider the lurch to the body two-thirds through 'The Ecstasy'). He has to have two attempts at an image which will define their union-in-dissolution, because fact makes him admit an element of absence which wit would not. First he says that their souls are one, and, though their receptacles are distant, they

> endure not yet
> A breach, but an expansion,
> Like gold to aery thinness beat.

But, we must ask, if their souls are one, how can the separation of bodies *at all* affect that – especially in view of his previous separation of their love from all considerations physical and earthly? We recall too how in 'The Ecstasy' Donne could speak of souls coming out of bodies and joining outside the flesh (13–17). The next attempt, the famous compass image, is a wider allowance of division: now Donne says of the souls 'If they be two'; now they are joined more in sympathy than fused – stiffly disjoining, hearkening after one another, one circling round the other and growing erect, or more their true selves and stature, at return. The reluctant sequence of these images increases the admission of separation as stiffly as the compasses themselves: that Donne has to use two of them is some index to the fact that he, and the poem hitherto, would prefer to use neither.

Attempts have been made to personalise the 'Valediction', to see it as a unified and consistent portrayal of a shifting sensibility rather than as an uncertain argument. An example of this is Wilbur Sanders, in his *John Donne's Poetry*, pp. 83–9. He says of the fourth stanza,

> Half-jocularly, Donne moves on to 'arguefy', gently parodying the sense of superiority with which they are supporting their resolution not to make a scene: 'Dull sublunary lovers' love, compared to our pure super-celestial love . . .' (one can't *say* this, of course, and both of us understand that we can't, but your part in me and in my feelings makes it possible for me to say it at least to you – for between us it has a certain kind of truth). . . .' 'Dull sublunary lovers' love

> > (Whose soul is sense) cannot admit
> > Absence, because it doth remove
> > Those things which elemented it.

But *we*. . . .' It's not so much that he wants to impose the neo-platonic fiction of the union of two souls upon her – the tone is much too wry for that ('a love, so much refin'd, / That our *selves* know what it is') – as that it is a necessary fiction if they are not to pro-fane their joys.   (p. 84)

There simply is no evidence that Donne is half-jocular here: the claim he makes is not an unusual one in his love poetry (for example, the 'Nocturnal'); there is not the least tonal or other handhold for the cult of personality in this stanza. Where Dr Sanders says the tone 'is much too wry' for Donne to be meaning exactly what he says, the line he cites is from the next stanza (and is misquoted: it should read 'know not'). His

'Surely,' Donne says, and with a kind of urgency presses it upon her, 'surely we . . .'

> Inter-assured of the mind,
> Care less, eyes, lips, and hands to miss   (ibid.)

is mistaken: there is not a trace of urgency here; rather the reverse, calm assurance – precisely the same certainty that Donne is asking of his lady. Dr Sanders puts into the poem just what suits his case. He goes on to tell us that in the image of 'gold to aery thinness beat' 'this argument for *firmness* declares itself as a beautiful but flimsy thing' (p. 85). One could see that, if the poem had been specifically about firm-ness till now, this question just might have relevance; but in fact it has been asking quiet acceptance, for melting into separation, not firmly re-sisting it. Similarly, remarks like 'notice how aptly the mere logic is, pointing, in the word "expansion", to painful enlargement, distension (tantamount, in point of feeling, to the anguish of constriction), thus setting up a tension against the hypothesis' (ibid.) are going to be made by no one else.

This refusal to take concepts at all at face value in Donne's poetry is what leads Dr Sanders to ignore (pp. 68–75 and 115–20) the meta-physical framework of development which makes 'The Sun Rising' more than exclusively a poem of tones, and the 'Nocturnal' as much concerned with a mystical journey from all to absolute nothing, and thus to absolute 'something', as with human loss. The weakness of his method comes home to roost in his account (pp. 96–104) of 'The Ecstasy', where he objects to what he cannot dismiss, the fact that the poem is so plainly, and to him, therefore, coldly, intellectual and doctrinal on the subject of love: he flits about, forcing uneasy tones of self-mockery on the poetry where he can, but ends dissatisfied, attributing his own uncertainties to Donne. Certainly some of Donne's poems seem to centre on the speaker's tone; but some are as much concerned with something else; and some have no *personal* tone at all. To attempt to apply a single notion of 'feeling' to the idea that Donne 'felt his thoughts' is inadequate.[2]

There has also been a recent attempt to prove the 'Valediction' dialectical. Murray Roston, in his *The Soul of Wit: A Study of John Donne*, is more ready than Dr Sanders to accept that Donne's poetry is concerned with metaphysics, but he sets out to clear up the apparent inconsistencies of the poetry by arguing the existence therein of ironies, dramatised narrators and structural tensions (based, he argues, on Baroque precendent). With 'A Valediction' he argues that the initial image of death in the poem ('As virtuous men pass mildly away . . .') is there to provide a counterpoint of *memento mori* to the confident assertions of the poem, a counterpoint which becomes conflict in the different images of the last two stanzas. Donne, we are told, is full of fears about the parting and what may happen to him on his sea-journey, yet struggling to calm his lady. Dr Roston has to admit, however, that this theme of 'the dread of a fatal ending to his journey abroad' is 'submerged, almost unacknowledged' (p. 123). Since it is nowhere said in the poem that Donne is taking ship and going abroad, 'submerged' seems an understatement. The image itself no more necessarily connotes fear of disaster *during* parting than it does death *at* parting, or, as George Eliot has it, the idea that 'In every parting there is an image of death.' In support of his case, Dr Roston cites the 'tear-floods' and 'sigh-tempests' of the second stanza as storm imagery; but these are images often used by Donne in quite unaquatic contexts – for instance, in 'A Nocturnal' and 'A Valediction: of Weeping'. At the end of his account, Dr Roston is reduced to finding the compass-image a deliberately too-facile ordering of the chaos of experience:

> Animate and inanimate cannot be so easily equated. The predictable movements of a scientific instrument which will, under given circumstances, return precisely to its point of departure offer no real parallel for a vulnerable human being embarking on the perilous sea voyage of Donne's day; and at a subdued level we are aware that the lady's firmness, be it ever so perfect, will prove but poor protection against drowning should the ship founder in mid ocean.   (p. 125)

It seems hardly worth saying that Donne frequently uses comparison of the animate to the inanimate with serious intent in his poetry (chaoses, alchemical retorts, planets, sun-dials). But Dr Roston's basic assumption here is that, whenever an image in Donne's poetry is single and precise in effect, it thereby reveals its falsity, because experience is always chaotic and multiple. He also claims that Donne meant us to feel uneasy. (Thus he reads 'Good Friday, 1613. Riding Westward' in terms of a dramatised narrator whose initial apparently organised imagery and sensibility gradually break down in the poem (pp. 205–9).) Neither assumption is any more than an assumption.

In 'A Valediction: forbidding Mourning' Donne oscillates between an ideal of absolute painlessness in parting and one which admits pain. This is conveyed by the death image of the first stanza: it asks resignation and grace, but the plea is weakened by the harsh fact of the image. After this the assurances of mutuality leave the world of fact and death, and can become absolute; but when that world is returned to there is again contradiction – 'Care *less*, eyes, lips, and hands to miss'. To claim, as Dr Roston does, that at the end, as Donne 'shifts to a different image, he discards the proof with a casual "If they be two . . .", as though admitting with an unconcerned shrug that rational consistency is nugatory beside the emotional reality' (p. 124), is to make no more than an unsupportable claim. And, if one considers the whole fabric of Donne's lop-sided poetry, this claim of intentional irony may be disproved.

In his devotional poems Donne shows a one-sided approach to the central issues of sin and spiritual regeneration, shuffling off personal responsibility and seeing the whole process in terms both of determinism and of administered grace from God rather than as the partial product of voluntary acts on his own part (see, for example, Holy Sonnets I, II, V, IX, XIV, XVI, XVIII, and 'Hymn to God the Father'). Here again, however, in the occasional poem the frailty of the assumptions and argument is thrown into particular relief. An instance is 'Good Friday, 1613. Riding Westward'.

> Let man's soul be a sphere, and then, in this,
> The intelligence that moves, devotion is,
> And as the other spheres, by being grown
> Subject to foreign motions, lose their own,
> And being by others hurried every day,
> Scarce in a year their natural form obey:
> Pleasure or business, so, our souls admit
> For their first mover, and are whirled by it.
> Hence is't, that I am carried towards the west
> This day, when my soul's form bends towards the east.

The lines seem to run with all the confidence of a geometrical proposition, and in a poem where lack of confidence and self-justification become the central feature this is revealing. For what Donne is saying is that it is part of the natural order of things that he should be moving away from his God: just as the stars are dragged out of their courses by alien gravitational pulls, so too his proper devotion is wrested from its centre. When we come to the last two lines of the passage we suddenly realise the evasion of the entire figure, which so confidently seemed to make sin an inevitability, a natural law, to delude by making a pattern out of that which defies pattern.

The poem then proceeds to give a series of further justifications for this truancy – while additionally operating as panegyric on the ways of God. Thus the poet argues that he is going west, that is, away from Christ's crucifixion in the east, partly because

> Who sees God's face, that is self life, must die;
> What a death were it then to see God die?

As an argument this is specious: the reference to Exodus 32:20 is to God made manifest in his transcendent supernatural person, not to God made man; Christ demands contemplation on the Cross (Sonnet XIII). And death is seen in naive terms: it is the business of the Christian to die, whether it be into faith or out of mortal life. The picture is largely one of a man (as man) created unable to look on the face of God. At the end, in moving from excuse to invocation, the poem contradicts this by saying that it is man's sin, his 'rusts' and 'deformity' rather than his inherent nature, which thus turn his gaze. It closes, however, as it began, evading responsibility:

> I turn my back to thee, but to receive
> Corrections, till thy mercies bid thee leave.
> O think me worth thine anger, punish me,
> Burn off my rusts, and my deformity,
> Restore thine image, so much, by thy grace,
> That thou mayst know me, and I'll turn my face.

If it is argued that there is personal responsibility in the poem in the words 'obey' and 'admit' of lines 6 and 7, and in the way the 'deformity' of line 40 takes us back to the perverted 'natural form' of line 6, it can be replied that the contexts are deterministic, in as much as like the planets the soul is *created* the involuntary subject of 'foreign motions'; on just the same lines the poet argues his inability to look on God. If it be argued, too, that we have to be ironically distant from the speaker, seeing his excuses as excuses and his determinism as determinism, the performance could hardly be a very edifying one: he undergoes no spiritual development, and we would be left to construct the correct lines for ourselves. It seems that the arguments of the poem are meant to be taken seriously: they are not denied, only inadvertently contradicted; there is no question of the kind of increasing intellectual frailty before collapse into true awareness that we see in Holy Sonnet IX. Donne means us to accept that he cannot help himself, that he is justified in not turning to look on Christ, that God should do the work; this line of argument is echoed throughout his divine poems.

This is not to deny that Donne seems to feel uneasy with his argument here: witty analogies have been employed to falsify spiritual fact; and it is quite possible that the breakdown from the prim neatness and decisive rhythm of the first ten lines into a list of questions mirrors this sense of strain. But that he has done this shows how he is so continually determined to modify fact with mind as to attempt to do so even with the most intractable of facts.

The extent of Donne's refusal to accommodate to hard fact, and the strength of his predilection for making mental worlds or heterocosms divorced from external reality, are highlighted in two poems where he shows himself prepared even to make assertions about the world which are demonstrably false, and to try to deny by mere intelligence the hardest fact of all – death.

In the *First Anniversary, An Anatomy of the World*, the attempt is made to show that the death of Elizabeth Drury has caused the destruction of the world through the removal of all value: 'thou wast / Nothing but she, and her thou hast o'erpast' (31–2). Faced not least by the contradiction that the world still exists, in as much as he is alive to write its anatomy, Donne is first defensive:

> Let no man say, the world itself being dead,
> 'Tis labour lost to have discovered
> The world's infirmities, since there is none
> Alive to study this dissection;
> For there's a kind of world remaining still.   (63–7)

This invites a more gradual approach: the poem now explains the ruin of the world in terms of man's original sin and the consequent decay of the beauty, order and coherence of the universe, Elizabeth Drury being occasionally thrown in, at first as a paragon who in herself could have reversed the process,

> she that could drive
> The poisonous tincture, and the stain of Eve,
> Out of her thoughts, and deeds; and purify
> All, by a true religious alchemy;
> She. she is dead; she's dead   (179–83)

but more commonly as one whose death casts into relief the rottenness of the world:

She, she is dead; she's dead: when thou know'st this,
Thou know'st how lame a cripple this world is.
                    (237–8; see also 325–6, 369–70, 427–8)

The result is that, as Louis Martz has shown, the poem is broken-backed: as a devotional exercise it is divided into two unreconciled camps of 'Eulogy' and 'Meditation'.[3] *Of the Progress of the Soul: The Second Anniversary* succeeds by contrast, for there Donne centres the poem on the effect on *his* soul and *his* attachment to the world: the poem attains an acceptable universality by first and foremost being particular, by saying, not bleakly that the world is ruined by her death, but that it now seems so to him. Thus meditation and eulogy can be fused in a personalised *contemptus mundi*.

Holy Sonnet x is a striking demonstration of Donne's commitment to mind in opposition to external phenomena: here wit takes on death itself.

> Death be not proud, though some have called thee
> Mighty and dreadful, for, thou art not so,
> For, those, whom thou think'st, thou dost overthrow,
> Die not, poor death, nor yet canst thou kill me;
> From rest and sleep, which but thy pictures be,
> Much pleasure, then from thee, much more must flow,
> And soonest our best men with thee do go,
> Rest of their bones, and soul's delivery.
> Thou art slave to fate, chance, kings, and desperate men,
> And dost with poison, war, and sickness dwell,
> And poppy, or charms can make us sleep as well,
> And better than thy stroke; why swell'st thou then?
> One short sleep past, we wake eternally,
> And death shall be no more, Death thou shalt die.

If we except the perfunctory reference in line 8, the conception of death as defeated by God does not plainly enter the poem until the last couplet: Donne proposes to devalue death by purely human intelligence and argument. The arguments do not convince. Lines 5–6, which begin the justification of the opening quatrain, depend on the questionable notion that one is alive in death in the same way as in sleep. Lines 7–8 may be read either as 'the good die young' or 'the good are readiest to die'. In the case of the first it is false (a) that they all do, and (b) that of those of them who do, all go willingly; Donne acknowledges these facts in his last prose devotion, *Death's Duel*. The second meaning is highly debatable, so much so that the sense could be reversed and reduced to its arbitrary foundation – namely, the presupposition that those most willing to die are good.

Line 9 is saying 'You are subject to that fate which has appointed the due time of every living thing; and your action is often governed by pure accident (storms, landslides and so forth) and by men.' But in a more real sense death is fate – it is the necessary end of every created thing, irrespective of when the blow falls; and, although death may depend in part on kings and desperate men for the particular time of its harvest, in a truer sense these men are death's slaves, in as much as they, too, will fall to his scythe. Following this, line 10 says no more than that death keeps bad company, which is hardly a way to belittle. Lines 11–12, 'And poppy, or charms can make us sleep as well, / And better than thy stroke', are a claim which no living man can make; and they contradict the argument, advanced in lines 5–6, that death gives a sleep of far better pleasure than anything in life. The 'why swell'st thou then?' seems in this light not so much a triumphant sneer as a question fearfully to be asked. The last two lines contain a point that, if it had been the basis of the whole argument, might have saved it, but which, thrown in here, seems one more in a list of self-delusions; and, put as it is, it glosses over the possibility that eternal waking might be in fields not Elysian. Finally, to say that death will die is to give back to the notion of dying all the weight and meaning that the poem has tried to remove from it.

Donne took the opposite view in the 'Elegy on Mistress Boulstred':

> Death I recant, and say, unsaid by me
> Whate'er hath slipped, that might diminish thee.   (1–2)

> How could I think thee nothing, that see now
> In all this all, nothing else is, but thou.   (25–6)

Death is impervious to efforts by the merely human mind and wit to nullify it: it is only that wit which makes the fact a part of itself – that is, the divine wit that made dying the door to life – which can alter reality here; in a sense Donne's divine meditations portray a shifting awareness of that greater metaphysical wit of which his own is a pale shadow. The point needs no more labouring than a comparison with Herbert's 'Death', where the burden is not on proof but on faith, not on man, but on God, not on removal but on transfiguration:

> Death, thou wast once an uncouth hideous thing,
>   Nothing but bones, . . .
> But since our Saviours death did put some bloud
>   Into thy face;
> Thou art grown fair and full of grace,
> Much in request, much sought for as a good.

Elsewhere in his religious poetry Donne plays more safe: his conceits are used as embellishments rather than as structural arguments — for instance, when he compares the church to a wife (Holy Sonnet xviii) or pictures his heart as a usurped town at the mercy of the devil and as yet weakly besieged by God (Holy Sonnet xiv). In the devotional verse Donne is involved with external facts which cannot be conjured away; in the more mental realm of the love poetry, tears may be turned to worlds, suns to lackeys, fleas to marriage-temples or women to fish-bait, but wit alone will not turn death to sleep, sinfulness to planetary inevitability, nor the soul to water drops. To try to give the wit the status of objective rather than mental truth shatters it. But that Donne can at times try to do this shows how much he is prepared to refuse the awkwardness and the multiple truth of the real world for the singleness of a mental one in his poetry.

Marvell serves as a contrast here. That he does not so refuse the world need not argue that he is the better poet, but it does make him a more inclusive one: in his poetry we find, in Eliot's words, 'a recognition, implicit in the expression of every experience, of other kinds of experience which are possible'.[4] His 'The Definition of Love', for example, stands in marked contrast to Donne's 'A Valediction: Forbidding Mourning'. Donne is extreme: love is independent of time and space. Marvell is less idealistic and absolute: he says that his love is at once a perfect unity and a total division; fate drives 'iron wedges' between the lovers, 'always crowds itself betwixt'.

> For Fate with jealous eye does see
> Two perfect loves, nor lets them close:
> Their union would her ruin be,
> And her tyrannic power depose.
>
> And therefore her decrees of steel
> Us as the distant Poles have placed,
> (Though Love's whole world on us doth wheel)
> Not by themselves to be embraced.

Hence the mathematically neat apprehension (and dialectic, as this poem shows, can still be neat, can be part of a witty universe without ruining it):

> As lines (so loves) oblique may well
> Themselves in every angle greet:
> But ours so truly parallel,
> Though infinite, can never meet

and then the summary of this union in opposition:

> Therefore the love which us doth bind,
> But Fate so enviously debars,
> Is the conjunction of the mind,
> And opposition of the stars.

Whether or not this poem refers to any particular love Marvell experienced in the real world is unimportant: what matters is that it has the increasingly ambivalent character of reality. Wit, in short, has married, not divorced itself from, fact.

'To His Coy Mistress' shows an awareness of time that Donne's love poetry resists. The direction of the poem is not markedly idealistic: the notion that one should master time by living every instant so intensely that it seems eternal, a time out of time, is acceptable, especially when it incorporates the knowledge that nevertheless time still moves on:

> Now let us sport us while we may;
> And now, like amorous birds of prey,
> Rather at once our time devour,
> Then languish in his slow-chapped power. . . .
> Thus, though we cannot make our sun
> Stand still, yet we will make him run.

What additionally validates this conclusion is the implicit nature of its logic. If they had all time and space for their wooing, the process would sink into formality and stasis – 'this state':

> My vegetable love should grow
> Vaster than empires, and more slow.
> An hundred years should go to praise
> Thine eyes, and on thy forehead gaze.
> Two hundred to adore each breast:
> But thirty thousand to the rest.
> An age at least to every part,
> And the last age should show your heart:
> For, Lady, you deserve this state;
> Nor would I love at lower rate.

There are few verbs; the sense confines itself at most to couplets, the syntax slumping at every cadence; there is irony even at the moment of panegyric in putting a 'rate' of years to each inestimable attribute, and the sense of dislocated sensibility in the analysis of parts. Eternity, this portrait suggests, enervates, removes energy, dilutes; and the very fact that their courtship is measured in terms of years shows how such eternity leads only to a deeper slavery to time, languishing 'in his slow-chapped power'. A more limited compass of time, it is implied, will allow detachment. That more limited compass now speaks as *memento mori*, now begins to give energy to the poem even while its import is finally to take it away:

> But at my back I always hear
> Time's winged chariot hurrying near.

(The eternity here presaged is an ironic comment on the other 'And yonder all before us lie / Deserts of vast eternity.') Life is now a little room, and the poem drives towards the infinite riches therein contained. The process of unlimited expansion leading to contraction in the first section is now reversed, all under the aegis of mortality.

> Now, therefore, while the youthful glue
> Sits on thy skin like morning dew,
> And while thy willing soul transpires
> At every pore with instant fires, . . .
> Let us roll all our strength, and all
> Our sweetness, up into one ball. . . .

The run-on syntax enacts the freedom. This apprehension, that 'Things greater are in less contained' is a central one in Marvell's poetry – is indeed his ideal as poet ('Upon Appleton House', stanza 6) – but rarely is it given as much persuasive power. And it derives that power, as Donne's poetry rarely does, by its incorporation of opposites, by its marriage of idealism to fact, and by its substantiation of the one by the other.

3 Jonson and Herrick

Jonson's poetry can have some of the poise and balance that we find in Marvell's, but his conservative position limits the purview of his sympathy, the range of attitudes to which he can give equal weight and personal commitment. He could not have managed the kind of involvement with opposed political sides and figures that Marvell shows in 'An Horatian Ode'. Pushed to its limit, this is what the Roman and urbane stance behind Jonson's poetry demands; but, since it also implies the preservation of the good society in which this political and social generosity may exist, that limit is not approached. Jonson's realism lies more in the judicious precision brought to the presentation of one point of view:[1]

> Son, and my friend, I had not called you so
> To me; or been the same to you; if show,
> Profit, or chance had made us: but I know
> What, by that name, we each to other owe,
> Freedom, and truth; with love from those begot. . . .
>   ('An Epigram. To a Friend and Son')

When Jonson does write a poem dealing with opposed standpoints, the issue is moral or aesthetic rather than social or political, and the contrast in attitudes is often a matter of degree rather than of kind. 'Still to be Neat' presents differing censorious views of a woman who continually appears in elaborate dress. The first stanza runs,

> Still to be neat, still to be dressed,
> As you were going to a feast;
> Still to be powdered, still perfumed:
> Lady, it is to be presumed,
> Though art's hid causes are not found,
> All is not sweet, all is not sound.

The speaker here is polite and reticent: 'Lady, it is to be presumed, / Though art's hid causes are not found'; the 'All is not sweet, all is not sound' avoids mentioning her, and also implies that there may be sound aspects remaining. The reticence is conveyed also by the generalised form of address: the speaker never mentions his own view, but makes himself part of an imagined public – 'to dress like this must make people think like this'; and indeed he dissociates himself almost entirely in the 'Though art's hid causes are not found', suggesting that the general verdict might conceivably be wrong because it goes only by the outside. His careful decorum is suggested further by the way he advances, trying to avoid presumption: the caesura comes after the fourth syllable in the first line and after the fifth, where the syntax is paralleled, in the third; he is ruminative, deferential. Yet this decorum is equally an ironic comment on her social indecorum, her being dressed up when the occasion does not demand it. Condemnatory force comes also from the repeated 'Still' and the verbs of state ('Still *to be*') which impart a sense of inertia. These two impressions, of mannered restraint and urbane attack, are fused in an attitude at once solicitous and mocking.

In the second stanza the verbs are violent and the narrator is in the first person:

> Give me a look, give me a face,
> That makes simplicity a grace;
> Robes loosely flowing, hair as free:
> Such sweet neglect more taketh me,
> Than all the adulteries of art;
> They strike mine eyes, but not my heart.

In the first stanza what was criticised was not art simply, but art used when the occasion did not require it; the second stanza reduces the opposition to one of art versus natural simplicity, saying that to attempt grace is to be graceless. What we have in this poem is an impersonal, mannered appraisal followed by a personal and direct one: whereas the speaker in the first stanza refers the effect of the dress to a public and moral context, he of the second judges only by the effect on himself and his own sensibility ('They strike mine eyes, but not my heart'). Jonson has offered two views of one fact, neither of which has the whole truth.

Jonson's poem goes some way towards reflecting the multiple character of a reality where no one opinion is adequate. The method is like that which we shall see in Fielding, who often presents a spectrum of attitudes towards a particular person or events – introducing Sophia in *Tom Jones* (Bk IV, ch. 2) as ideal woman and then as plain Miss Western, or canvassing the range of possible opinions of Black George's theft from the hero (Bk VII, ch. 1). This encyclopaedic and additive approach, if only infrequently a moral one, to the depiction of reality is in fact characteristic of much eighteenth-century literature, and, in the additive aspect, of its Roman antecedents.

But the approach is not dynamic or synthetic: the second view does not grow out of the first, but is laid beside it, like another piece of masonry. Jonson's poetry rarely contains an argument of the thesis–antithesis–synthesis type one sees in Marvell's 'Coy Mistress' or Milton's 'Lycidas', or portrays the development of human emotion as, say, Shakespeare's sonnets do. This refusal of 'evolution' reflects Jonson's conservatism, and that of later poets: poetry exists to mirror the un-changing rather than the dynamic character of reality. The type of poetic structure preferred by such writers is a builded and linear rather than a plastic and circular one, and the type of figure the simile rather than the metaphor;[2] the analogy most frequently used by them in discussing the composition of literature is that of architecture.[3]

Jonson's poems do not show ideas being transformed; they show them being modified, or descanted upon. His comedies are 'situation' plays, characterised by the unchanging natures of his 'humorous' personages, and by the way, as Eliot puts it, in which the characters fit in with, rather than act upon, one another.[4] He is the great English writer of masque, a form concerned with presenting a series of tableaux rather than with developing plots and dramatic interaction. And his criticism recurs to the notion of poetry as architecture, carefully laid brick upon brick: 'if a man, would build a house, he would first appoint a place to build it in, which he would define within certain bounds; so in the constitution of a poem'; 'For as a house, consisting of diverse materials, becomes one structure, and one dwelling; so an action, composed of diverse parts, may become one fable, epic or dramatic' (*Timber: or Discoveries*, 3324–6 and 3453–5; the title *Timber* is itself drawn from architecture – OED, sb. 1, 7). Jonson's self-confessed practice of writing the matter of his poetry out in prose first was admirably suited to this approach.[5]

The architectural analogy is rarely applied to the overall design of a poem. What shape the finished whole has is unimportant, so long as it is a unity; what matters is that the parts do not jut out, that they make a whole by adding to and merging into one another, not that each has a role in the formation of a pattern which may be contemplated for its own sake. When Pope speaks of a finished structure (*An Essay on Criticism*, 243–52) he does so in terms of a dome, and the main interest is not the shape but the subordination of every part and the balance of opposed forces. Jonson would have had small sympathy with the formal structure of Spenser's 'Epithalamion', Donne's cyclic 'La Corona' or the fivefold pattern of Herbert's 'Aaron'. And as a neoclassic poet he had little time for art divorced from social and moral efficacy (see, for ex-ample, 'An Epigram. To William, Earl of Newcastle'). When considering the structure of a Jonson poem, what we find ourselves concerned with are the parts and the way they are proportioned and married to one another to make a seamless whole.

The correlative, if not in Jonson's case the clear cause, of this lack of formal pattern and symmetry – indeed of the 'builded' method itself – is the slowly changing view of the universe in the seventeenth century. As the cosmos ceased to be picturable in terms of the ordered and neat Ptolemaic – or Keplerian – system of concentric spheres, and the notion of the vast and varying distances of the stars from the solar system became increasingly accepted,[6] reality grew not only untidy but also uncapturable by imagery. Creation was still conceived in terms of the hierarchy of being – of which the ladder-like structure of Jonson's 'To Penshurst' is in part an emblem – but scientific discovery and stress on the fullness or plenitude of existence were, from Giordano Bruno on, making the links of that chain infinite in number and the whole beyond imaginative grasp. These views were not widely accepted in Jonson's time, and unlike Donne he does not discuss them, but we may observe that the non-formal character of his poetry matches this destructured, asymmetrical universe. Later poetry becomes much more disorganised as the idea of spatial relativity is more widely diffused.

'To Penshurst', being a description of an ideal country house, provides perhaps the fullest illustration of Jonson's method. This poem, which draws on several of Martial's *Epigrams*,[7] began a conservative country-house poem tradition which runs from Carew, Herrick and Marvell to Pope.[8] Most obviously this poetic tradition was a series of attempts, within a restricted and idealistic sphere, to shore up some fragments against the ruin in the outside world. Its concerns are both the preservation of the good society and the pleasure of retiring to it: it is at once hortatory and consolatory. Marvell caught the sense of the conservative poets of the time when he spoke of the mind withdrawing into its happiness ('The Garden', 42): a steady contraction of the Christian and Horatian ideal is to be seen throughout the seventeenth and eighteenth centuries.[9] But the appeal of the country house as an image was not only social, political, moral and emotional, but also aesthetic: as architecture it had the structural qualities to which poets responded. It was built as they saw the world built, and as they built poems.

Jonson's poem constructs a picture of a social ideal by means of a progress, in piled heroic couplets, through a hierarchy of particulars.[10] We start outside the house, with landscape and vegetation, and continue with tributary game, cattle and fish; come into the more ordered world of the orchard and the garden; then meet the country people, and enter the house with them, to be shown every aspect of its hospitality. The conceptual points made are placed like bricks upon one another. In the opening section of the poem, Penshurst is presented as the marriage of civilisation with nature:

> Thou art not, Penshurst, built to envious show,
> Of touch, or marble; nor canst boast a row
> Of polished pillars, or a roof of gold: . . .
> Thou joy'st in better marks, of soil, of air,
> Of wood, of water: therein thou art fair.

Other houses are built by civilisation and (formal) art alone, using materials whose rarity renders them unnatural, and with motives which can only be interpreted as pride: the result is that they strike the eyes, like the art of the lady's clothes in 'Still to be Neat', and raise envy through their prominence. Jonson banishes such obtrusiveness and indecorum in the first line. Through the marriage of art to the simple elements of nature, Penshurst acquires grace, imaged throughout the poem in the easy art by which the house exists and acts, and in the careless care with which the poem itself is built. (This idea is recurrent in Renaissance literature: it can be seen in the picture of Musidorus's horsemanship in Sidney's *Arcadia*, ii, 5; in Spenser's Pastorell and Colin Clout; in Shakespeare's late plays; in Marvell, Pope and Goldsmith.) Not only is Penshurst thus made gracious: it is also graced. The beholder 'reverences' the house; dryads resort to its mount, 'Where Pan, and Bacchus their high feasts have made'; and satyrs and fauns inhabit its woodlands (6, 10–11, 17–18). The theme of marriage is continued when Jonson says of the oak tree planted in Sidney's time, 'There, in the writhed bark, are cut the names / Of many a Sylvan, taken with his flames' (15–16): man and nature, name and plant become one. Similarly man joins nature by giving it his name: thus we hear of 'thy lady's oak. / Thy copse, too, named of Gamage' and of 'Ashore, and Sidney's copse' (19, 26). The method of addressing Penshurst as a person gives the point emphasis throughout the poem.

Now that man has married nature, nature marries man. First we have the provision of the landscape: the copse 'never fails to serve thee seasoned deer',

> The lower land, that to the river bends,
> Thy sheep, thy bullocks, kine and calves do feed:
> The middle grounds thy mares, and horses breed.
> Each bank doth yield thee conies; and the tops
> Fertile of wood, Ashore, and Sidney's copse,
> To crown thy open table, doth provide
> The purpled pheasant, with the speckled side.   (22–8)

We have moved up hierarchically from landscape to landscape and vegetation as suppliers. The next 'brick' in the natural fabric and the development of the poem is the animals: here the potential pathetic fallacy, on which the idea of nature marrying man is founded, becomes more overt.

> The painted partridge lies in every field,
> And, for thy mess, is willing to be killed. . . .
> Thou hast thy ponds, that pay thee tribute fish,
> Fat, aged carps, that run into thy net.
> And pikes, now weary their own kind to eat,
> As loth, the second draught, or cast to stay,
> Officiously, at first, themselves betray.
> Bright eels, that emulate them, and leap on land,
> Before the fisher, or into his hand. (29–30, 32–8)

We return to vegetation with the orchard, but now we are more aware of the organising hand of man; and it is now that we meet man, in the form of the country people visiting the house to offer gifts out of the same spontaneous love that has been seen in the orders of being below them.

Thus the points are laid one upon another, as in the construction of Penshurst itself. The wedding of Penshurst to nature is the keystone on which nature, in ascending series, offers itself back. And to the picture of Penshurst in hierarchic terms is now added one of equality between different ranks (also founded on the notion of marriage): to this house

> comes no guest, but is allowed to eat,
> Without his fear, and of the lord's own meat:
> Where the same beer, and bread, and self-same wine,
> That is his lordship's, shall be also mine. (61–4)

The communion reference[11] is gently implied; Jonson recurs to the idea of Penshurst as a church at the end of the poem, where he says of other houses 'their lords have built, but thy lord dwells' (102). Here, Christian social equality does not conflict with the notion of rank, partly because Jonson never makes the possible clash explicit, but also because the equality portrayed here would have no reality were there no separation into social classes to renounce. In the companion poem, 'To Sir Robert Wroth', he is more bold: 'Freedom doth with degree dispense' (58); but this is absolute, implying dismissal, where in 'To Penshurst' the distinction of lord and vassal is still a real one while it is denied by the acts of generous love which characterise the house. The two concepts here depend on one another, like each half of an arch.

As the people from all around come to Penshurst with their offerings in pure generosity, so the house, since it is so rich already that it has no need of their gifts, is generous in return through its hospitality to them: again the theme of marriage-in-giving is touched, now in human terms. Jonson proceeds to give a builded picture of Penshurst's hospitality. There is not only social equality at table, but also proximity – 'I not fain to sit (as some, this day, / At great men's tables) and yet dine away'. There is no calculation or meanness ('Here no man tells my cups', 'The tables hoard not up for the next day'), nor envy, because all are supplied liberally ('nor, standing by, / A waiter doth my gluttony envy'), nor need, because all needs are supplied by a true sympathy, so that each man finds that Penshurst fits him like a glove, and that he does not have to make his wants intrusively explicit:

> Nor, when I take my lodging, need I pray
> For fire, or lights, or livery: all is there,
> As if thou, then, wert mine, or I reigned here:
> There's nothing I can wish, for which I stay. (65–74)

The 'or I reigned here' prepares us for a further addition to the theme of hierarchy. Every guest, of whatever station, is treated like a king: the equality he enjoys with all other guests is not the result of any condescension or patronage on the part of the lord and lady of the house, but the expression of the honour in which they hold each of their fellow-men. Thus King James himself, when he came unannounced to Penshurst, found the house more than fit for a king's entertainment (76–88).

Having built so far, Jonson can cap off the edifice that is Penshurst and his poem with a final addition:

> These, Penshurst, are thy praise, and yet not all.
> Thy lady's noble, fruitful, chaste withal. (89–90)

He proceeds to an account of the children of the house, and their education in religion, virtue and 'The mysteries of manners, arms, and arts' (98). The children will ensure the continuance of Penshurst, and their education will ensure its continuance in its existing form and, it is to be hoped, the construction of more such Penshursts – until the whole country may express the society of the house. Meanwhile we are left with this one, and with the poem which has imitated its construction: we look out with some assurance on a hostile world:

> Now, Penshurst, they that will proportion thee
> With other edifices, when they see

Those proud, ambitious heaps, and nothing else,
May say, their lords have built, but thy lord dwells. (99–102)[12]

We have looked at the arrangement of the bricks of the poem: there
is also the way in which they are bonded together. One of Jonson's
linguistic ideals was 'the well-joining, cementing, and coagmentation of
words; when as it is smooth, gentle and sweet; like a table, upon which
you may run your finger without rubs, and your nail cannot find a
joint; not horrid, rough, wrinkled, gaping, or chapped' (*Discoveries*,
2559–64). He said of the sentence, 'The congruent, and harmonious
fitting of parts in a sentence, hath almost the fastening, and force of
knitting, and connection: as in stones well-squared, which will rise
strong a great way without mortar' (ibid., 2447–52); and of the plot of
a poem, 'being composed of many parts, it begins to be one, as those
parts grow, or are wrought together' (ibid., 3405–7). To talk of a poem
as a union of parts implies an analytical, agglomerative method of
building poetry, and thus one to which Shakespeare, Donne or Herbert,
say, would not have assented. It is the classical approach, but it also
prefigures the Newtonian view of the universe as a harmonious aggrega-
tion of atoms; and it is central to the eighteenth-century view of art.[13]
It is one explanation for the insistence on grace, proportion and decorum
over other possible forms of unity in literature. As one object the poem
must harmonise with its cause, and the stylistic 'height' be matched to
the subject. The poem must also fit in with the literary expectations of
its polite readership, avoiding technical, foreign or archaic terms,
roughness of metre, obscurity, violent metaphor, periphrasis or 'affec-
tation' – by which last is meant anything which is not lucid and the product of good, and common, sense.[14] Within the poem, this matching of
item and item relates both to the proper marriage of parts to one another so that none juts out (thus, for example, the governing hierarchic
pattern in 'To Penshurst'), and to the way parts slide into one another
without sharp transitions as one ends and another begins – or, as Pope
puts it, 'Parts answ'ring parts shall slide into a whole.'[15] The emphasis
on art as a conscious activity and on the work as a series of analysed
and precast sections means that the only way in which a poem can
avoid looking like an agglomerate is by melting the outer limits of each
part into the one preceding and following.

Jonson sounds this point at the beginning and end of 'To Penshurst',
where he banishes the disproportion and pride of other country houses.
The opening lines of the poem, where he describes the elemental materials 'of soil, of air, / Of wood, of water' from which the house is made,
prepare us for the subsequent account of the landscape and vegetation
of Penshurst's grounds. With this movement established, the hierarchic
progress from landscape to man takes over. But this hierarchy is not

rigidly traced. At the point where what the landscape does for the house is to turn into what the animals do, we are told how 'The painted partridge lies in every field, / And, for thy mess, is willing to be killed' (29–30): mentioning the field still keeps us partly with the offerings of the land even as we move on to the creatures. Further, we go back to the topography for a moment after this:

> And if the high-swoll'n Medway fail thy dish,
> Thou hast thy ponds, that pay thee tribute fish,
> Fat, aged carps, that run into thy net.   (31–3)

The last line keeps the idea that the ponds supply the fish, while also sounding the theme of the fish offering themselves, which is to be the subject of succeeding lines. Similarly, when we meet the country-people, we have not left the vegetables or animals behind, not only because the people bring capons, cakes, nuts and apples as gifts, but also in that some of the humans are seen in terms of these presents:

> some that think they make
> The better cheeses, bring them; or else send
> By their ripe daughters, whom they would commend
> This way to husbands; and whose baskets bear
> An emblem of themselves, in plum, or pear.   (52–6)

The arrival of the king is anticipated in the pheasants which 'crown thy open table', and in the hospitality of the house, which is such as would be given to someone who 'reigned' there; and Penshurst itself is prepared for the king by treating every guest like one. The personification of Penshurst throughout makes every item in the hierarchy of being portrayed more plastic and congruous by being part of a humanised fabric. And one of the functions of the picture of an ascending scale of creation in the first half of the poem is to make nature itself into a building, so that the architecture of Penshurst is anticipated in its surroundings; thus, when we enter the house we have in a sense already entered it. The point behind this is that, when an artefact is in the proper relation to nature, nature will form itself into a similar order about it.

Perhaps the most subtle and daring use of decorous transition is seen in Jonson's placing of himself in Penshurst and his poem. In a poem which is ostensibly an objective account, this could be felt intrusive, the poet making himself the assertive centre of his charmed circle: but the stages by which it is done are almost imperceptible, and the presence of the poet may be argued as a function of showing how capacious is Penshurst. Jonson is introducing the hospitality of the place in general terms when he first uses the personal pronoun: the house is one

> Where comes no guest, but is allowed to eat,
> Without his fear, and of the lord's own meat:
> Where the same beer, and bread, and self-same wine,
> That is his lordship's, shall be also mine.   (61–4)

The 'mine' here can be read as 'any guest's'. The next lines become more specific ('And I not fain to sit . . . and yet dine away'), and the next more immediate, changing 'where' to 'here' ('Here no man tells my cups . . . / But gives me what I call, and lets me eat'). There is no further development, though 'I' recurs (72–5). The personal pronoun thus never becomes fully singular: it is both one and representative. This technique of introduction of the self, potentially the most indecorus and disproportioned of parts, into the whole of a neo-classical poem, is brought to virtuosity by Pope in his 'Epistle to Miss Blount, on her Leaving the Town, after the Coronation'.

There is fluency of transition in the form of the poem also, particularly in the use of rhyme. Jonson, who in his 'Fit of Rhyme against Rhyme' jokingly termed rhyme 'the rack of finest wits, / That expresseth but by fits', takes pains, while he willingly employs them, to reduce the possible insularity of his couplets and the tendency of couplet rhymes to force the pace and amass attention to themselves.[16] Throughout he uses run-on syntax, frequent pauses within lines, and half-rhymes. Sometimes he ends a sentence with the first rhyming word and swallows its partner in another:

> Fat, aged carps, that run into thy net.
> And pikes, now weary their own kind to eat   (33–4)

or,

> There's nothing I can wish, for which I stay.
> That found King James, when hunting late, this way. . . .   (75–6)

Sometimes one of the rhyming words is of less significance than the other, so that it is not emphasised to the same degree. Thus,

> They are, and have been taught religion: thence
> Their gentler spirits have sucked innocence   (93–4)

or,

> Now, Penshurst, they that will proportion thee,
> With other edifices, when they see
> Those proud, ambitious heaps. . . .   (99–101)

In the first half of the poem, where we ascend the hierarchy of being in approaching the house, the rhyme is slightly more emphatic, to give the sense of a series of steps, even where the interweaving of the sense turns the steps into something nearer a gentle slope. Jonson both retains the formality of rhyme and is informal with it, just as 'To Penshurst' emphasises hierarchy and equality alike. In a similar manner, we enter the house approximately, but not exactly, half-way through the poem. Above all, the seemingly relaxed, conversational style is also highly compressed and organised, the realisation of Jonson's poetic aim, 'a diligent kind of negligence' (*Discoveries*, 2804).

All Jonson's poems are similarly constructed, if not always so highly wrought: fine examples are 'A Hymn to God the Father', 'An Epistle to a Friend, to Persuade Him to the Wars', 'An Elegy' ('Though beauty be the mark of praise'), 'An Epistle to a Friend' ('Sir, I am thankful, first to heaven, for you'), 'Fair friend, 'tis true, your beauties move', 'Truth is the trial of itself', 'Stay, view this stone', 'Ode Enthusiastic' and 'It was a beauty that I saw'. And neo-classical poetry throughout the late seventeenth and eighteenth centuries follows the same pattern. Exploration of every aspect of a subject, in Jonson's case to come to an exact definition, in that of others to produce coverage of all areas in support of a general point, is set in a fabric where each brick of sense is proportioned and moulded to fit the next. Used incisively the method can produce poetry of a highly woven, if 'linear' unity. In Pope's *The Rape of the Lock*, Belinda, in journeying from the sylphs to the nymphs, gnomes and salamanders, in that order, journeys in behavioural terms from coquetry, through submission and prudery, to termagancy; and, in terms of the four elements, which occur serially in the imagery of the poem, in a pattern of fall and rise from air to water to earth to fire. There are five cantos, in the last of which Belinda's lock finally flies above the world and the realm of the elements into the immutable beauty of a constellation. But in much literature of the eighteenth century this encyclopaedic aim often leads to the absence of a unifying pressure. A work can appear a list from which terms could be deleted or to which others could be added, as in Johnson's *The Vanity of Human Wishes* or *Rasselas*; or may seem repetitive, as in Pope's *Moral Essays* or Fielding's *Joseph Andrews*, which make the same points in a variety of portraits; or capable of admitting almost any topic, when the subject is so general, as in Thomson's *The Seasons*, or unspecific, as in Cowper's *The Task*. Indeed, where Romantic poets often ended their poems too soon, many eighteenth-century poets arguably did so too late.

With Herrick, who saw his poetry as an attempt to continue Jonson's mode, we find the other side of the accretive, 'truth-through-coverage' method. Herrick's poetry is frequently centrifugal in structure: the poet becomes fascinated by particulars for themselves, to the exclusion of the conceptual or moral point he intends to make through them.

In his 'Delight in Disorder', Herrick imitates revealingly Jonson's 'Still to be Neat':

> A sweet disorder in the dresse
> Kindles in cloathes a wantonnesse:
> A Lawne about the shoulders thrown
> Into a fine distraction:
> An erring Lace, which here and there
> Enthralls the Crimson Stomacher:
> A Cuffe neglectfull, and thereby
> Ribbands to flow confusedly:
> A winning wave (deserving Note)
> In the tempestuous petticote:
> A carelesse shooe-string, in whose tye
> I see a wilde civility:
> Doe more bewitch me, then when Art
> Is too precise in every part.

The poem is framed by a generalisation which does to some extent emerge from its parts, but as it proceeds it develops a quite different interest. Herrick intends to build up, through a portrayal of her dress, the character of the lady he prefers; and he follows the ordered procedure of a Renaissance blazon, starting at the shoulders and ending at the feet.[17] However, his poem shows a fascination with items of clothing for themselves, and this works against any larger purpose. The articles of clothing come to independent life – 'An erring Lace . . . / Enthralls the Crimson Stomacher', 'A Cuffe neglectfull', 'Ribbands to flow', 'the tempestuous petticote', 'A carelesse shooe-string' – and the relation to a mind which has made them grows more and more tenuous. The suspension of the syntax for so long allows the separate garments to wander off on their own, while Herrick's mind is driven all ways with them. This disintegration is portrayed also in the multiple verb-forms throughout – 'Kindles', 'thrown', 'Enthralls', 'to flow', 'I see'. Most of the items are singular, suggesting an obsessional concentration, even some kind of fetishistic sexual displacement.[18] 'Wilde civility' may be portrayed at a superficial level, but at any other there is plain wilderness.[19] Where Jonson, subduing every part of 'Still to be Neat' to ethical perception, can produce a judicious balance, Herrick's sensibility, losing touch with concepts, simply fragments.

Herrick's 'A Panegeyrick to Sir Lewis Pemberton', which imitates Jonson's 'To Penshurst', also fails almost entirely to put over the moral and conceptual aspects of its original. For much of the poem Herrick gives most detail to accounts of what Pemberton's house is not (indeed, he never gives the house a name): for example,

> thou no Porter keep'st who strikes.
> No commer to thy Roofe his *Guest-rite* wants;
> Or staying there, is scourg'd with taunts
> Of some rough Groom, who (yirkt with Corns) sayes, Sir
> Y'ave dipt too long i'th' Vinegar;
> And with our Broth and bread, and bits; Sir, friend,
> Y'ave farced well, pray make an end;
> Two dayes y'ave larded here; a third, yee know,
> Makes guests and fish smell strong; pray go
> You to some other chimney, and there take
> Essay of other giblets; make
> Merry at another's hearth; y'are here
> Welcome as thunder to our beere. . . .   (18–30)

This is in striking contrast to Jonson's far less circumstantial negative picture, which is set amid a portrayal of what Penshurst *is* ('To Penshurst', 65–8, 71–3); Herrick becomes so interested in the scene of the waiter's importunity that he goes into details of its cause ('yirkt with Corns') which blunt the moral point.

At the end of the poem Herrick argues that the strength of the house depends not on its material construction, but on the virtues it contains:

> Comliness agrees,
> With those thy primitive decrees,
> To give subsistance to thy house, and proofe,
> What *Genii* support thy roofe,
> *Goodnes* and *Greatnes*; not the oaken Piles;
> *For these, and marbles have their whiles*
> *To last, but not their ever:* Vertues Hand
> It is, which builds, 'gainst Fate to stand.   (95–102)

Thus, where Jonson locates the virtues of Penshurst *within* the materials, the simple elements of wood and water, of the building, Herrick makes his pile stand by concepts alone. The result is that when he comes, as once again he does, to describe the materials of which Pemberton's house was *not* built, we are left without any sense at all of the house as a place:

> Safe stand thy Walls, and Thee, and so both will,
> Since neithers height was rais'd by th'ill

Of others; since no Stud, no Stone, no Piece,
  Was rear'd up by the Poore-mans fleece:
No Widowes Tenement was rackt to guild
  Or fret thy Seeling, or to build
A *Sweating-Closset*, to annoint the silke-
  soft-skin, or bath in *Asses milke*:
No *Orphans* pittance, left him, serv'd to set
  The Pillars up of *lasting Jet*,
For which their cryes might beate against thine eares,
  Or in the dampe Jet read their Teares.
No *Planke* from *Hallowed* Altar, do's appeale
  To yond' *Star-chamber*, or do's seale
A curse to Thee, or Thine; but all things even
  Make for thy peace, and pace to heaven. (115–30)

(This passage is clearly derived from the first scene of Jonson's *Volpone*.) 'All things even' – what things? one is left to ask. Once again we see a division in Herrick, this time between concepts and objects. And the objects have the field:[20] most of what we hear is of the gastronomic pleasures offered by the house (the first eighty-eight of the 135 lines of the poem); and it is because he realises that these sensuous pleasures contain no more than satisfaction of the senses that Herrick veers to the totally conceptual from lines 89 to 115.

The fascination with phenomena, the frequent inability to make concepts speak through particulars, that we see in Herrick becomes a besetting feature of much eighteenth-century literature. In Defoe or Crabbe or Cowper we see minds oscillating between the bare presentation of scenes and events and the attempt to make moral significance out of them; in writers such as Dryden and Pope, minds which steadily reject those aspects of the world which run counter to the systems of meaning to which they have committed themselves. And, throughout, the groundswell of empiricism and a continual increase in the data and complexity of the known world are together the main cause.

4 Milton

Milton's early poems 'L'Allegro', 'Il Penseroso', *Comus* and 'Lycidas' belong within the older Christian and symbolist tradition which dies out in the seventeenth century. In poetic strategy, inclusiveness and allegorical or symbolic reach they are reminiscent of the poetry of Spenser, to whom Milton looked so often as 'a better teacher than Scotus or Aquinas'. Both poets write under the aegis of the inclusiveness of the Christian faith: Milton is able to harness the opposites of life and literature into a *concordia discors*, a unified vision of truth within a faith which sees the marriage of opposites – of God and man, nature and supernature, heaven and earth, flesh and spirit – as the fundamental character of reality. When this view of reality disappears, it is no longer possible to sustain the reconciliation of such metaphysical opposites in literature.

Nevertheless, Christianity is as much concerned with divorce as with marriage. There are certain opposites, like good and evil, false and true, which are radically opposed: the Christian has to be morally absolute. In Milton's early poetry we see both strands. In 'L'Allegro' and 'Il Penseroso' there is an easily-handled comprehensiveness, whereby each poem celebrates the opposite of the other, and yet both are married in a final aim. In *Comus* the magician is shown as utterly opposed to the Lady, to the point of non-communication; but she reconciles in her God-given temperance the claims of reason and passion, nature and grace. In 'Lycidas' despair is shown as the way to hope, and the process is itself subsumed in the acts of Christ, by which fallen nature is joined to supernature.

Further, the balance of 'L'Allegro' and 'Il Penseroso' is not like that which we can see in Marvell's poetry. Milton is not concerned with the judicious weighing of pros and cons which comes from an impartial understanding of the complexities of human life: Mirth and Melancholy are in their own terms absolute, not partial values. This concern with essences is of course central to the Christian and Platonic tradition in which Milton was writing. What happens is that in each poem Milton finely realises an absolute by indirection, and each absolute, though sufficient in itself, is shown to be one of two roads to a common goal.

'L'ALLEGRO' AND 'IL PENSEROSO' (1631?)

What will be suggested here is that these two poems present the two mystic ways: 'L'Allegro' the *via positiva*, or Way of the Affirmation of Images, and 'Il Penseroso' the *via negativa*, or Way of the Rejection of Images.

That their objects are alike mystical is clear. Both use the Orphean metaphor. In 'L'Allegro' this closes the poem, as the speaker asks to be 'Married to immortal verse' which may untwist 'all the chains that tie / The hidden soul of harmony' (138, 143–4), so that

> Orpheus' self may heave his head
> From golden slumber on a bed
> Of heaped Elysian flowers, and hear
> Such strains as would have won the ear
> Of Pluto, to have quite set free
> His half-regained Eurydice.   (145–50)

And the speaker in 'Il Penseroso' wishes that Melancholy (Euphrosyne)

> Might raise Musaeus from his bower,
> Or bid the soul of Orpheus sing
> Such notes as warbled to the string,
> Drew iron tears down Pluto's cheek,
> And made hell grant what love did seek.   (104–8)

The object in this poem is likewise the piercing through to the mystery of things: the speaker asks the spirit of Plato to reveal to him

> What worlds, or what vast regions hold
> The immortal mind that hath forsook
> Her mansion in this fleshly nook.   (90–2)

He looks for the high melancholy of a religious service to 'bring all heaven before mine eyes' (166) and hopes that at last 'old experience do attain / To something like prophetic strain' (173–4).

The initial 'travesties' of each poem also play a part in linking them. The Melancholy banished at the beginning of 'L'Allegro' is not the contemplative Melancholy of 'Il Penseroso' but the Galenic Melancholy of stupidity and despair; and, similarly, the Mirth banished at the beginning of 'Il Penseroso' is not the substantial pleasure portrayed in

'L'Allegro'.[1] The effect is first to divide the poems, in as much as one apparently banishes the other, and then, on closer inspection, to see that they may not be so opposed after all, since what is banished in each case is not an accurate picture of the other. The very banishments may, in fact, be an encouragement to the reader to pull together rather than apart. Thus, even while the natures of the poems are different, their false rejections of one another may be seen as a way of showing us that their differences are not the whole truth about them.

The primary contrasts between the two poems have been frequently pointed out: for example, that 'L'Allegro' is concerned mainly with the active, and 'Il Penseroso' with the contemplative life; and that, in keeping with this, the first has far more mention of daylight than the second, which is set mainly in shade or darkness. But there are many other features which fill out this basic opposition. The speaker in 'L'Allegro' is constantly flitting from place to place, on one level of existence, in a random, experience-devouring fashion:

> To hear the lark begin his flight . . .
>
> Then to come in spite of sorrow . . .
>
> Oft list'ning how the hounds and horn . . .
>
> Sometime walking not unseen . . .
>
> Straight mine eye hath caught new pleasures . . .
>
> And then in haste her bower she leaves . . .
>
> Or if the earlier season lead . . .
>
> Sometimes with secure delight
> The upland hamlets will invite . . .
>
> Then to the spicy nut-brown ale . . .
>
> Towered cities please us then . . .
>
> Then to the well-trod stage anon . . .

In 'Il Penseroso', however, the speaker is engaged in a search for places sufficiently isolated for contemplation to occur; movement is continually directional, and intensity deepens:

> Or if the air will not permit,
> Some still removed place will fit. . . .
>
>   me goddess bring
> To arched walks of twilight groves. . . .

> let my due feet never fail
> To walk the studious cloister's pale. . . .
>
> And may at last my weary age
> Find out the peaceful hermitage. . . .

The syllables of 'L'Allegro' are lighter and crisper than those of 'Il Penseroso', which are far more sonorous and open; and, whereas in the former the syntax is most frequently confined to single lines and couplets, loosely linked by conjunctions, in the latter it can be much longer-breathed. Thus, from 'L'Allegro':

> While the ploughman near at hand,
> Whistles o'er the furrowed land,
> And the milkmaid singeth blithe,
> And the mower whets his scythe,
> And every shepherd tells his tale
> Under the hawthorn in the dale.   (63–8)

and from 'Il Penseroso':

> Come pensive nun, devout and pure,
> Sober, steadfast, and demure,
> All in a robe of darkest grain,
> Flowing with majestic train,
> And sable stole of cypress lawn,
> Over thy decent shoulders drawn.
> Come, but keep thy wonted state. . . .   (31–7)

Even the introductory 'banishments' are in keeping more with the poems in which they occur than with their subjects: that of Melancholy in 'L'Allegro' has a jerky rhythm and syntax, whereas 'Il Penseroso' is flowing and smooth (the words 'smoothing' and 'smooth' are used only in this poem, at lines 58 and 66).

There is a further syntactic contrast between the two poems. In this passage from 'L'Allegro',

> Sometime walking not unseen
> By hedgerow elms, on hillocks green,
> Right against the eastern gate,
> Where the great sun begins his state,
> Robed in flames, and amber light,
> The clouds in thousand liveries dight,
> While the ploughman near at hand,
> Whistles o'er the furrowed land   (57–64)

the verb never arrives: we are with the man walking, first vaguely amid hedgerows and hillocks, then precisely, 'Right against'; but then we leave him altogether to consider the sun thus introduced, and when we return, to the ploughman, we have almost lost the speaker. This sense of dislocation, of never being able to unite things seen, is exactly what the poem wants to produce, partly because no single item or personal experience is the key to Mirth. 'Il Penseroso', concerned as it is much more with a specific type of place or direction, has also a much more 'purposeful' syntax: passages are far longer and subjects are not lost. These are some of the reference points in an extended section:

> And when the sun begins to fling
> His flaring beams, me goddess bring
> To arched walks of twilight groves . . .
>
> There in close covert by some brook,
> Where no profaner eye may look,
> Hide me from day's garish eye,
> While the bee with honied thigh . . .
>
> And let some strange mysterious dream . . .
>
> And as I wake, sweet music breathe. . . .   (131–51)

'L'Allegro', we may say, moves through the Many to the One; 'Il Penseroso' rejects multiplicity: the one spreads, the other concentrates to transcend. The sense of plurality in 'L'Allegro' comes not only from the greater variety of scenes, but from the fact that Mirth is to be found among 'elms', 'hillocks', 'lawns', 'fallows', 'Mountains', 'Meadows', 'brooks' and 'rivers'. Melancholy, however, is solitary, and her resorts are usually singular: in 'L'Allegro' we have 'Towers, and battlements' (77) and in 'Il Penseroso' 'some high lonely tower' (86).[2]

The speaker of 'Il Penseroso' is far more passive than the one of 'L'Allegro', who does not ask Mirth to direct him so constantly; and in 'L'Allegro' the delights are actually being experienced – 'Straight mine eye hath caught new pleasures' (69) – where in the companion poem each scene is not so much experienced as envisaged, and Melancholy is continually *invoked*: 'Come . . . Come . . . bring . . . let my lamp . . . me goddess bring . . . Hide me . . . let some strange mysterious dream . . . let my due feet never fail . . . let the pealing organ blow . . . Dissolve me . . . bring all heaven before mine eyes'. Indeed, in 'Il Penseroso' the speaker, as part of the contemplative process, is trying to lose identity, die out of self: 'Forget thyself to marble' (42), 'Dissolve me into ecstasies' (165).

Things are clearly seen in 'L'Allegro', but 'Il Penseroso' has 'dim religious light' (160), avoiding as it does 'day's garish eye' (141). The speaker, too, is visible in the former: 'Sometime walking not unseen' (57); but not in the latter: 'I walk unseen / On the dry smooth-shaven green' (65–6), 'Where no profaner eye may look' (140). In 'L'Allegro' the speaker is frequently in society, but in 'Il Penseroso he is solitary: 'Some still removed place will fit' (78). Mirth is asked 'admit me of thy crew' (38); but Melancholy, whose 'saintly visage is too bright / To hit the sense of human sight' (13–14), throughout the poem is sought rather than found.

Things are often close to in 'L'Allegro', as they are not in the companion poem: thus, 'Right against' (59), 'near at hand' (63), 'Hard by' (81), as opposed to 'I hear the far-off curfew sound' (74), 'Far from all resort of mirth' (81). 'Il Penseroso' makes time and place vague by its frequent use of 'some': 'some wide-watered shore' (75), 'Some still removed place' (78), 'some high lonely tower' (86), 'Sometime let gorgeous Tragedy' (97), 'some brook' (139), 'some strange mysterious dream' (147), 'something like prophetic strain' (174). The Orpheus image in 'L'Allegro' ends as 'to have quite set free / His half-regained Eurydice' (149–50); in 'Il Penseroso' with the more general 'And made hell grant what love did seek' (108).

Mirth is a given quantity, seen through different images, in 'L'Allegro'; but Melancholy is being wooed throughout the companion poem, 'missing thee', and is to be found only by passing beyond the images and scenes themselves, which provide only starting-points for meditation (85 ff., 155 ff.). Typical is the way a scene is used to 'Entice the dewy-feathered Sleep' (146). There is a sense of marriage between man and his environment in 'L'Allegro': the apparent shift from rusticity to 'Towered cities' (117) is eased by the presence of the light frolic of Mirth in the descriptions of both contexts; and in the country scenes themselves an image such as 'Hard by, a cottage chimney smokes, / From betwixt two aged Oaks' (81–2) furthers the sense of continuum in the picture of trees and habitation joined. Indeed, there is here even in the sense that opposites come together in this radiant flux of phenomena:

> Mountains on whose barren breast
> The labouring clouds do often rest. (73–4)

The clouds lose the pains of their labour and the mountains their emptiness in this meeting.

Taken all together, these various contrasts between the two poems are a complete poetic rendering of the positive and negative ways of mystical experience.

Thus one portion of being is the Prolific, the other the Devouring: to the Devourer it seems as if the producer was in his chains; but it is not so, he only takes portions of existence and fancies that the whole.

But the Prolific would cease to be Prolific unless the Devourer, as a sea, received the excess of his delights.   (Blake, *Marriage of Heaven and Hell*)

This explains the need for the introductory banishments in each of these poems: their dialectical relation in part depends on the desire of each pole to claim sole authority. The mystic journey has one aim, but can take opposite directions: through immanence, as Mirth is immanent in 'L'Allegro', and via transcendence, as the speaker penetrates beyond the world to a Melancholy 'too bright / To hit the sense of human sight' in 'Il Penseroso'. Neither has the whole truth: it is not the business of deities properly conceived to be wholly within or without the world. Nor is the truth of each specifically a Christian one: Orpheus is Orpheus as much as a prefiguring of Christ; we may as readily call the poles of the poems Aristotelianism and Platonism as put the opposition in Christian terms. But experience of the truth of both together is possible only within a faith which at once embraces and renounces the world, and in and through an incarnate god.

'COMUS' (1634)

Comus shows us what happens in an early Miltonic poem when the opposition is one between good and evil. There is no 'balance' here: the good aggregates to itself all substance, and the evil becomes mere shadow.[3] The premises of the magician Comus are steadily reduced to the point of nonentity. Comus in the end not only has no case: he has no relation to reality at all. At first he poses as the voice of nature, anxious at the unnecessary privations of the ascetic soul, but in his debate with the Lady shows that his blandishments are in reality those of a nature perverted into the unnatural and the monstrous. In short, Comus the humanist becomes Comus the fraud, and the Lady, painted by him as world-denying, replies with an ideal of temperance, an ideal in which the categories of flesh and spirit are both allowed place. The poem is concerned with bringing out the absolute moral schism between Comus and the Lady, while at the same time portraying the Lady as the balance and marriage of the opposed realities of reason and passion, spirit and matter, in the golden mean of temperance.[4] But she is ultimately given the means to be that marriage not by adherence to any merely Aristotelian ethical tenet but through the reconciliation of flesh and spirit in Christ; and without the direct assistance of grace she is powerless to enact it.

When he has bound the Lady in his enchanted chair, Comus offers her

> all the pleasures
> That fancy can beget on youthful thoughts,
> When the fresh blood grows lively, and returns
> Brisk as the April buds in primrose season.
> And first behold this cordial julep here
> That flames, and dances in his crystal bounds
> With spirits of balm, and fragrant syrups mixt.   (667–73)

The 'April buds in primrose season' introduce a sense of the simple and natural, which is at odds with the unnatural, exotic or quaint julep, balm and syrups: Comus's spiritual ignorance is highlighted by the fact that he can equate the one with the other without any sense of the discord between them. We sense too the limitation of the 'crystal bounds', perhaps partly reminiscent of the frail flesh, the confining 'pinfold' (7) of the spirit, but certainly recalling contrastively the bounds which cannot contain the Lady's spirit:

> Thou canst not touch the freedom of my mind
> With all thy charms, although this corporal rind,
> Thou hast immanacled, while heaven sees good.   (662–4)

Now Comus turns to the old utilitarian argument that the Lady should use, not waste, the gifts of nature. He argues first that she is doing wrong to herself ('Why should you be so cruel to yourself' – 678), and then, changing the insulted god to nature, maintains:

> you invert the covenants of her trust,
> And harshly deal like an ill borrower
> With that which you received on other terms,
> Scorning the unexempt condition
> By which all mortal frailty must subsist.   (681–5)

Comus is accusing her of the pride of detachment while at the same time tempting her with the pride of life. In arguing too that her refusal to drink his potion is a refusal to quench the thirst which is man's natural condition he is further giving himself away: just because poison is liquid does not make our refusal of it a too dainty resistance to the promptings of thirst. The other self-defeating point here is that Comus makes nature his god, which in itself is bestial idolatry, quite part from the fact that it is inconsistent with his having tried to make the Lady herself her god a few lines earlier, and with his speaking later of her refusal as a violation of God's trust, not nature's (719–26). The involvement that Comus asks of the Lady is of course in reality no 'Come down, O maid', but an invitation to wallow like a beast, blind to all but sensual fact – as the Lady is to point out:

> swinish gluttony
> Ne'er looks to heaven amidst his gorgeous feast,
> But with besotted base ingratitude
> Crams, and blasphemes his feeder.   (775–8)

In her first answer to Comus, the Lady lays bare the fact that, far from being the minister of the natural that he pretends to be, the magician is unnatural, with all the seventeenth-century force of that word:

> Was this the cottage, and the safe abode
> Thou told'st me of? What grim aspects are these,
> These ugly-headed monsters?   (692–4)

The cottage is to the brutes what the April buds were to the julep. However, the Lady does not know whether the potion Comus is offering her is in itself good or not, but has to judge its worth by her knowledge of him:

> Were it a draught for Juno when she banquets,
> I would not taste thy treasonous offer; none
> But such as are good men can give good things,
> And that which is not good, is not delicious
> To a well-governed and wise appetite.   (700–4)

The last point allows that she has the appetites from which Comus has argued she is claiming exemption, but states that they are governed by moral choice: she will not be indiscriminate.

But Comus simply fails to grasp this point, and thinks she is recommending abstinence: for the Devil there can be no mean – 'O foolishness of men! . . . / Praising the lean and sallow Abstinence.' He now mounts a major assault in which he shifts from nature to God as the prompter of right conduct, and back again.

> Wherefore did Nature pour her bounties forth,
> With such a full and unwithdrawing hand,
> Covering the earth with odours, fruits, and flocks,
> Thronging the seas with spawn innumerable,
> But all to please, and sate the curious taste?   (709–13)

The suspended syntax, in which the Creator's generosity expands into vast and variable being, is suddenly shut (or 'bounded') in the last line, driving home the anti-climax and the pettiness. The word 'sate' indicates the stasis of repletion, utter loss of the energy predicated in the previous lines; and 'curious' had for the seventeenth century very definite overtones of an impertinent reaching for forbidden knowledge, and of perversity.

But this last word prepares us for Comus's resort to the exotics of nature, not 'plain' nature, as temptation of the Lady. He speaks of the 'millions of spinning Worms' nature has set to make silk (the materialist argument implicit here is that the millions or the spawn innumerable should deny the resistance of one); and says how,

> that no corner might
> Be vacant of her plenty, in her own loins
> She hutched the all-worshipped ore, and precious gems
> To store her children with.   (716–19)

Nature's generosity, so the implication runs, is the character of reality, and the Lady is denying what she was made by not herself being generous (and going out of herself). The simple fact is that such natural prodigality is not available to every man: only a few are rich, and the rest downtrodden – a point the Lady is to emphasise. But then it is Comus's part to tempt with nature's rarities, while pretending that they are typical of the natural order.

Now Comus shifts the argument back to the ingratitude theme, and, to fit with his attempt to make *her* appear unnatural, perverts what the Lady means by temperance:

> if all the world
> Should in a pet of temperance feed on pulse,
> Drink the clear stream, and nothing wear but frieze,
> The all-giver would be unthanked, would be unpraised,
> Not half his riches known, and yet despised,
> And we should serve him as a grudging master,
> As a penurious niggard of his wealth,
> And live like Nature's bastards, not her sons.   (719–26)

That the 'all-giver' might be better thanked by men not absorbed in his creation, men able to look up to him, is, as the Lady is to say, past Comus's comprehension. Not only this: Comus is presuming to judge God by his own terms, as someone who wants an adequate return for his outlay – and as someone to be thanked for earthly pleasures. Again that God may be better thanked for other than material advantage, that man might delight in his creation as an image of his overflowing love and his endless plenitude, is beyond Comus. As Comus's 'nature' is perversity, so are his arguments perverted: having argued that God would be ignored by the temperate, he then twists this into a claim that he would be actively despised – 'And we should serve him as a grudging master, / As a penurious niggard of his wealth'. This simply ignores his just-given picture of men choosing to be temperate. (Though there may be psychological truth in the notion, not implied here, that the ascetic may come to make God in his own image.) If we did all this, says Comus, changing the standard from God back to nature, we would 'live like Nature's bastards, not her sons'. The unnatural magician is here raising hands in horror at what he himself is: the argument flies back in his face.

He now moves, still raising these pious hands, to an apocalyptic vision of plenitude gone mad, of nature run to chaos:

> Who would be quite surcharged with her own weight,
> And strangled with her waste fertility;
> The earth cumbered, and the winged air darked with plumes,
> The herds would over-multitude their lords,
> The sea o'erfraught would swell, and the unsought diamonds
> Would so emblaze the forehead of the deep,
> And so bestud with stars, that they below
> Would grow inured to light, and come at last
> To gaze upon the sun with shameless brows.   (727–35)

The notion of man as nature's only secateurs ignores God's providential ordering; the picture as a whole is not real enough to be comic. As for the gazing on the 'sun with shameless brows', we know that it is shame and the need for concealment that make Comus hide himself from 'the tell-tale sun' (141); and, if the last of these lines refer to the monsters and devils beneath the earth, then Comus is one himself. And the violation of hierarchy implicit in the image is what Comus himself commits in turning man to beasts. As for the pious horror at blasphemous pride, the irony needs no pointing.

At this point he turns to a specific argument against virginity. The irony of the opening 'List Lady be not coy, and be not cozened' is telling. Once more he invokes nature, 'Beauty is Nature's coin', 'Beauty is Nature's brag' (738, 744). The Lady is to spend herself like money; solitariness and hoarding of the self are unhealthy. The image in

> If you let slip time, like a neglected rose
> It withers on the stalk with languished head   (742–3)

runs counter to previous suggestions, in which neglect led to excess growth. When Comus says,

> Beauty is Nature's brag, and must be shown
> In courts, at feasts, and high solemnities
> Where most may wonder at the workmanship   (744–6)

we sense the irony of nature set beside courts, the idea that she is properly viewed and handled only by those cut off from her.

Comus has not only exposed his own arguments: he has built up by implication an impression of what the Lady is. It is therefore wrong to say that she is simply negative, a datum. Now she turns to answer him, admitting that to do so is, as we have already realised from Comus's own words, a waste of time:

> Fain would I something say, yet to what end?
> Thou hast nor ear, nor soul to apprehend
> The sublime notion, and high mystery
> That must be uttered to unfold the sage
> And serious doctrine of virginity,
> And thou art worthy that thou shouldst not know
> More happiness than this thy present lot.   (782–8)

But the answers are offered in the hope of ears more receptive than those of Comus. The Lady denounces his view of nature's supposed injunctions ('do not charge most innocent Nature' – 761), restates her temperate position (763–6), exposes, with the fact of human poverty, the fallacy of his argument concerning nature's riches –

> If every just man that now pines with want
> Had but a moderate and beseeming share
> Of that which lewdly-pampered Luxury
> Now heaps upon some few with vast excess,
> Nature's full blessings would be well-dispensed
> In unsuperfluous even proportion,
> And she no whit encumbered with her store   (767–73)

– and explodes his argument that God is properly thanked only by our partaking in his creation:

> And then the giver would be better thanked,
> His praise due paid, for swinish gluttony
> Ne'er looks to heaven amidst his gorgeous feast,
> But with besotted base ingratitude
> Crams, and blasphemes his feeder.   (774–8)

She ends by saying that should she really try to convince Comus, she would be wrought to 'such a flame of sacred vehemence'

> That dumb things would be moved to sympathize,
> And the brute Earth would lend her nerves, and shake,
> Till all thy magic structures reared so high,
> Were shattered into heaps o'er thy false head.   (794–8)

Nature would rid itself of the unnatural which has falsely tried to pass itself off, like Spenser's False Florimell, as the natural order of things. More than this, nature would sympathise: the Lady's is a higher Orphean magic requiring no conjurations or interference, a magic founded on the secret unity of all things in God. Her magic would raise 'dumb things' and the 'brute Earth' to voluntary act; his would reduce free men to the bondage of bestiality. It is a complete answer, if answer it cannot; Comus senses at least the greater power of her magic (799 ff.).

This mention of the magical powers behind the Lady's arguments shows that what guarantees the truth of her case, and makes it more than one philosophy in opposition to another, is the fact of Christianity, and the reconciliation of nature and supernature, reason and passion, flesh and spirit accomplished in the being and acts of Christ. In further witness of this, the Lady remains imprisoned by Comus's charms until, like Spenser's Guyon, she is released by an agent of divine grace – here arising from within nature in the form of the river nymph Sabrina. Unaided, the poem tells us, humanity cannot enact the *concordia discors* which Christ alone is and sustains.

'LYCIDAS' (1637)

'Lycidas' also operates within the Christian scheme of spiritual paradox, whereby opposites are joined in and through Christ. Here, however, this is not only demonstrated but enacted. The spiritual movement of the poem is founded on the idea that 'the way down is the way up', that descent is necessary to ascent: it partakes in the central Christian fact of fall and return. This primal spiritual rhythm would not have been activated had man not fallen; but, within the context of a fallen state, it is the measure of truth. Therefore Milton can show a descent into the depths (literally, in the sea in which King is drowned) as a stage on a journey upward. Founded as it is on eschatology, 'Lycidas' is an example and survival of that circularity – or, more properly here, spirality – of form and movement which was at this time disappearing from literature.

The poem develops other orders of 'marriage'. At the end nature is joined to supernature through the incarnational fact, and the cyclic movement of the sun becomes apocalypse. Similarly, the use of imagery from the beginning points to an answer before it has been found: time and the eternal contemporaneity of heaven are conjoined. By virtue of Christ's inclusiveness, the poem is enabled to be as much a re-enactment of his life as a literary commemoration; and the poet, through the 'pastoral' metaphor, himself can be seen as the Great Shepherd. The process works 'backwards' too: pagan myth and Old Testament Law are hallowed by Christ's coming into anticipations and prefigurings; the act of incarnation is not only single and historical, but eternally recurrent.

Milton uses traditional pastoral elegy in 'Lycidas' partly because it enables his mourning to become communal: he joins with – in a sense *is* – Theocritus, Moschus, Virgil, Petrarch or Spenser; and King, in being metamorphosed to Lycidas, becomes one with Daphnis, Bion, Gallus, or Dido. This guarantees the universality of the poem: it is not Milton, but all men from all times and places who utter this lament;[5] not King, but Lycidas, type of all that is best in mortality, who is lost; and thus the issues raised can be both perennial and ultimate. The way that Milton's grief is thus caught up in a larger pattern of grief, the way pastoral elegy transforms what would have been the incongruities and limitations of personal lament into a universal mourning, prefigures the spiritual transformations of the poem, the change from despair to hope. So too does the name 'Lycidas': as King is made Lycidas, so Lycidas will be metamorphosed in and through Christ, and translated to heaven.

This universalising process must break down the distinctions between mourner and mourned, in so far as both are shown as types of all men. 'Poets themselves must fall, like those they sung; / Deaf the prais'd ear, and mute the tuneful tongue' (Pope). Hence the double reference of the opening image:

> Yet once more, O ye laurels, and once more
> Ye myrtles brown, with ivy never sere,
> I come to pluck your berries harsh and crude,
> And with forced fingers rude,
> Shatter your leaves before the mellowing year.
> Bitter constraint, and sad occasion dear,
> Compels me to disturb your season due:
> For Lycidas is dead, dead ere his prime.

The shattered leaves are those of both Lycidas's life and Milton's poetic development: as the need to mourn has broken into, and bleeds or maims, Milton's aesthetic growth, so too has Lycidas's death destroyed his own. That death is not only the physical fact, but also its effect on the living; and the spiritual death of corruption in which the world (here specifically the Church) is either plunged by such loss or is revealed in its true colours (compare Donne's *Anniversaries*), is one of the bases on which this poem is founded.

This mingling of living and dead (perhaps, in this poem, prefiguring Christ, who came to life out of death) goes further. The speaker's reluctance to begin his lament arises from more than the sense of a shared predicament: it comes from the sense that, in his poem, he will have spiritually to journey through the utmost of the loss that Lycidas has experienced. The muse is reluctant, as she often is in pastoral elegy, because the generous sympathetic involvement required will be extremely painful. There is going to be no facile laying of a vexed ghost by the comfortable living: the choice of the community of pastoral elegy ensures that. Before he begins, the poet gestures humbly to that community:

> Begin, and somewhat loudly sweep the string.
> Hence with denial vain, and coy excuse,
> So may some gentle muse
> With lucky words favour my destined urn,
> And as he passes turn,
> And bid fair peace be to my sable shroud.
> For we were nursed upon the self-same hill,
> Fed the same flock; by fountain, shade, and rill.

'Bear ye one another's burdens' says Christ in the Gospel: we are to become little Christs. This can be and has been taken literally.[6] It may be that by entering into the fullness of the loss of Lycidas, and by virtue of Christ's redeeming power, the speaker of this poem is portrayed as removing that loss. The words have to be 'lucky', they have to make the sable shroud peaceful; Christ's life and death were, if true, the ultimate in miracle and human good luck: we may thus be meant to see the speaker as graced through Christ's blood to remove Lycidas's pain, and, in so doing, his own.

The speaker follows the primal spiritual rhythm that Christ enacted: that descent into the uttermost deep which is the only route to ultimate ascent.[7] The Arcadian vision of lines 25–36, of man in fruitful union with nature and time –

> Together both, ere the high lawns appeared
> Under the opening eye-lids of the morn,
> We drove a-field, and both together heard
> What time the grey-fly winds her sultry horn,
> Battening our flocks with the fresh dews of night,
> Oft till the star that rose, at evening, bright,

Toward heaven's descent had sloped his westering wheel.
Meanwhile the rural ditties were not mute   (25–32)

– gives way to 'the heavy change' of 'wild thyme' and 'gadding vine'
(38, 40). The loss is like a blight on nature, 'As killing as the canker to
the rose, / Or taint-worm to the weanling herds that graze, / Or frost
to flowers' (45–7): this begins the facing of nature's and man's frailty.
The speaker asks why the nymphs of nature were not there to save
Lycidas, but knows this is false surmise: 'Ay me, I fondly dream!' Even
the muse of Orpheus could not save him; here, in lines changed from
the original draft, the harshness and disgusting meaninglessness of loss is
pointed:

> When by the rout that made the hideous roar,
> His gory visage down the stream was sent,
> Down the swift Hebrus to the Lesbian shore.   (61–3)

Faced by this, why do anything, if doing may be destroyed (64–76)?
The speaker is answered by Phoebus, who touches his 'trembling ears',
that man's true worth receives its reward in heaven, by the 'perfect witness of all-judging Jove' (82). But this intimation of immortality can
remain only a postulate at this stage. The poet (continuing the notion of
justice) turns to ask of nature whether there was any good reason for
Lycidas's death – 'What hard mishap hath doomed this gentle swain?'
(92) – and whether nature was in any way responsible. Nature exoner-
ates herself: 'The air was calm, and on the level brine, / Sleep Panope
with all her sisters played' (98–9) says Hippotades; and the speaker concludes,

> It was that fatal and perifidous bark
> Built in the eclipse, and rigged with curses dark,
> That sunk so low that sacred head of thine.   (100–2)

In a poem of the metaphysical reach of this one, this must be read not
as an account of some obscure and meaningless act of malignancy, but
as a reference to the frailty of man in his fallen condition.[8]
Now the speaker goes on to question the order of society exempli-
fied in that which should be its highest and most loving form – the clergy.
Here too he finds no justice on earth, only in heaven, 'that two-handed
engine at the door, / Stands ready to smite once, and smite no more'
(130–1). Twice now he has looked to heaven and (as it did in its beginning, in the undying evergreens whose berries alone are subject to
the process of the 'mellowing year') the poem has prefigured its
end.[9]
We have moved through deepening cycles in a spiral mode: together-

ness, loss, helplessness, fundamental question and partial solution circle back and downwards. After the vision of the 'two-handed engine' the speaker recalls nature to offer what it may to Lycidas's laureate hearse (132–53). The comment here, 'For so to interpose a little ease, / Let our frail thoughts dally with false surmise' (152–3), recalls the 'Ay me, I fondly dream!' of line 56, where similarly the helplessness of nature was the subject. Here, however, nature is not simply helpless: she is, far more poignantly, helplessly sympathetic. And the 'frail thoughts' now break into a further awareness: not only is the laureate hearse a fiction, since Lycidas is lost at sea, but, in addition, the ocean has in it the monstrous, the unnatural, which is as much a part of existence as creaturely sympathy:

> Ay me! Whilst thee the shores, and sounding seas
> Wash far away, where'er thy bones are hurled,
> Whether beyond the stormy Hebrides
> Where thou perhaps under the whelming tide
> Visit'st the bottom of the monstrous world. . . .   (154–8)

That 'Visit'st', with its connotation of social life, is, as Rosemond Tuve has pointed out, perhaps the darkest irony of the poem.[10] Even the certainty of so monstrous an end is denied: the speaker has to allow loss itself a final ambiguity:

> Or whether thou to our moist vows denied,
> Sleep'st by the fable of Bellerus old,
> When the great vision of the guarded mount
> Looks toward Namancos and Bayona's hold;
> Look homeward angel now, and melt with ruth.
> And, O ye dolphins, waft the hapless youth.   (159–64)

It is another surmise which knows its own frailty. The speaker can go no further into loss than this, with himself and Lycidas whelmed in the random: as he has plumbed the depths of the ocean, so he has come to spiritual bedrock.

At this point, with this depth reached, the dynamic of ascent is activated. It is done in a particularly significant mode:

> Weep no more, woeful shepherds weep no more,
> For Lycidas your sorrow is not dead,
> Sunk though he be beneath the watery floor,
> So sinks the day-star in the ocean bed,
> And yet anon repairs his drooping head,
> And tricks his beams, and with new spangled ore,

Flames in the forehead of the morning sky:
So Lycidas sunk low, but mounted high,
Through the dear might of him that walked the waves. . . .   (165–73)

The image of the sun here has two functions. In the first place it points
to that renewed marriage with nature which is contained in God's gift
of himself, while at the same time also pointing out how he transcends
what he includes. Just as the sun sets before rising, so Christ set (died,
harrowed hell) before his ascension: the rhythm of nature is one with
the primal spiritual rhythm. Yet at the same time Christ's ascension is
permanent, while the sun rises only to set again. Weak though it be,
nature is redeemed in the picture of a heavenly pastoral idyll, 'Where
other groves, and other streams along, / With nectar pure his oozy
locks he laves' (174–5). This transfiguration is the resolution of the
impasse to which the poem had come. The second purpose of the sun
image is to emphasise cycle turning into apocalypse – which is the movement of the entire elegy. The sun image used at exactly the same distance from the beginning of the poem as this from the end was merely
cyclic (25–31): that one ended with a setting (a fall), and this with a rise
(Christ the Second Adam). After the infernal circles arrive at a point,
there is purgatorial and redemptory ascent in a straight line; but the
one is necessary that the other may come to be.

   This envisaged, the speaker has propitiated the vexed soul of Lycidas,
has mediated or re-enacted his salvation, and in doing so has found his
own peace. We are distanced from him now – 'Thus sang the uncouth
swain to the oaks and rills' – just as he is now distant from his own
pain; he needs no more pastoral community to sustain his spiritual quest,
but is now a singular person, an 'uncouth swain' about to shed his
universality: 'Tomorrow to fresh woods, and pastures new.' The time
is now back in joint: 'While the still morn went out with sandals grey'.
We are back in a mutable world where the sun sets (and the poet
rises); but, like the lost Arcadian landscape shared with Lycidas, such
change is welcome, though now not in innocence, but through the pains
of experience:

> And now the sun had stretched out all the hills,
> And now was dropped into the western bay;
> At last he rose. . . .   (190–2)

'PARADISE LOST' (1667, 1674)

Milton's overt intention in *Paradise Lost* is precisely that which we saw
in *Comus*: moral absolutes are opposed, and one is to be shown as

wholly without value and insubstantial. This, we shall argue, is not what happens. Milton was a great and sensitive poet. He wrote *Paradise Lost* during the Restoration period. The Civil War had proved that without benefit of theology, truth was divided between rival camps, and that no one position was an adequate account of reality. Although this had been 'proved', it had been proved only as fact: hardly anyone accepted it, and Milton certainly did not. But one may question whether a poet of Milton's genius and sensibility was not capable of registering that fact in his poetry even while at a conscious level he refused it. We have to take into account too a far greater degree of involvement with the world on Milton's part, in terms of politics and religious dispute, than had been the case when he wrote the earlier poems we have considered. What will be argued here is that in *Paradise Lost*, a poem which at the conscious level is a renunciation, like that of *Comus*, of the Devil and all his works, at the unconscious level becomes a picture of how Heaven needs Hell for the purpose of creative interaction; in short, that dialectical warfare has become the measure of truth.

Blake's remark that Milton was 'of the Devil's party without knowing it' was made in *The Marriage of Heaven and Hell*, and his point is perhaps restricted by its having arisen out of Blake's special ontology. But the title of the work in which it appears has a further truth in it concerning Milton's poem. Simply, this is that Milton's universe and his narrative are in one way the picture of a fertilisation process. We first see the devils falling into Hell; then Satan takes on himself alone the mission of assaulting man. His journey, up into the wide concave of Hell, past the momentarily resistant gate and through Chaos, is very suggestive: in the latter –

> The womb of nature and perhaps her grave,
> Of neither sea, nor shore, nor air, nor fire,
> But all these in their pregnant causes mixed
> Confusedly   (ii, 911–14)

– Satan is tossed and battered, a tiny figure in a huge wild abyss. When he has traversed Chaos and looks on Heaven far off, and he sees

> fast by hanging in a golden chain
> This pendent world, in bigness as a star
> Of smallest magnitude   (ii, 1051–3)

the parallel with the ovum, if not biologically exact, is again very striking.

Eventually he lands on the outermost crystalline sphere concentric to the Earth, and finds that, next to the stairs let down from Heaven, there

opened from beneath,
Just o'er the blissful seat of Paradise,
A passage down to the earth, a passage wide.   (III, 526–8)

He then 'Down right into the world's first region throws / His flight precipitant' (562–3). When he reaches the Earth and approaches Paradise, the garden, typically of the *locus amoenus*, includes the suggestion of the female pudenda:

delicious Paradise,
Now nearer, crowns with her enclosure green,
As with a rural mound the champaign head
Of a steep wilderness, whose hairy sides
With thicket overgrown, grotesque and wild
Access denied.   (IV, 132–7)

Paradise also does duty as a womb – 'a circling row / Of goodliest trees loaden with fairest fruit, / Blossoms and fruits at once of golden hue / Appeared' (146–9). It is a small protected place – 'In narrow room nature's whole wealth, yea more' (207) – and 'One gate there only was' (178).[11] Satan's entry is at first by leaping over the wall, and perhaps this may be one reason for his failure. His next attempt is more 'natural', in that he enters via the river that goes under the hill of Paradise and comes up as a fountain in the middle to water the garden; and again the fountain is a resonant image here. Then he enters a serpent, taking on the image of a spermatozoon. His attempt on Eve is portrayed partly as seduction. The image of him as the city dweller taking a day trip to the country underlines this:

If chance with nymph-like step fair virgin pass,
What pleasing seemed, for her now pleases more,
She most, and in her look sums all delight.
Such pleasure took the serpent to behold
This flowery plat, the sweet recess of Eve
Thus early, thus alone; her heavenly form
Angelic, but more soft, and feminine. . . .   (IX, 452–8)[12]

His shape, we are told, is lovely and alluring (503–5);[13] he approaches her with 'tract oblique' (510) like a ship tacking about before entering the mouth of a river (513–16); he 'Curled many a wanton wreath in sight of Eve, / To lure her eye' (517–18) and 'Fawning . . . licked the ground whereon she trod' (526). He is 'erect / Amidst his circling spires' (501–2); later, 'He bolder now, uncalled before her stood' (523); and, before his final temptation speech, he 'Fluctuates disturbed, yet comely, and in act / Raised, as of some great matter to begin' (668–9). His speech itself is not so much an argument as a rhetorical rape. His words are described as penetrating her: 'Into the heart of Eve his words made way' (550); and, when she is persuaded to eat of the Tree, 'his words replete with guile / Into her heart too easy entrance won' (733–4). Frequently in the poem man is described as having been seduced by him (ɪ, 219; ɪɪ, 368; vɪ, 901; ɪx, 287, 901; x, 41, 332, 485, 577).

After the Fall, Adam and Eve are filled with a mixture of good and bad impulses: Hell has, in short, fertilised man with itself. Now Sin and Death build a bridge to Earth which confirms the same sort of junction that is entailed in the golden chain and the stairs let down from Heaven. Now the children of mankind are born into sin and death. (To restore the breach, God himself will, in the Incarnation, have to fertilise man with himself and Heaven.[14])

But the imagery must not be seen purely in the terms of sexual re-production. For one thing, the parallels are not continuous, nor even biologically exact: for instance, one might look far for Fallopian tubes, and it is not the unfertilised ovum that hangs from the womb. The question here is not really how much Milton himself knew about the process, but how far, in this the imaginative core of his poem, he is drawing on an imagery of archetypal force, which need depend on no conscious knowledge – an imagery in which the specifically biological aspect of fertilisation is subsumed and prefigured. The image in question here is that of the mandala, or circle, which from ancient times has been pictured with a serpent approaching, circling, and penetrating it, and which, with the serpent contained within it, is a symbol of psychic wholeness or totality of being.[15]

The implications of such imagery in Milton's poem are far-reaching: if, underneath, it is being suggested that what Satan carries out is a penetration and fertilisation of the mandala/world-egg which symbolises fullness of being, then it is asserting that good needs evil, that of itself it is insufficient – precisely the reverse of what Milton maintains is the case.

There are other aspects of the poem that lend force to this. One is the relative importance of stasis or flux. Milton seems to be giving rather more weight to the latter: he does not present us with Heaven plain, but always in a context of imminent change – of Satan rebelling, man falling, man about to be punished. When Heaven loses a third part of its sons (ludicrous that it could lose anything, but epically necessary), God does not create as many more angels to supply the ranks, but instead creates the universe, the Earth, and man (vɪɪ, 150–9). What God has done is create an evolutionary system: if man perseveres upright, he may rise spiritually into angelic being; if not, then, man though he remain, he will be man perverted, and that perversion and its eventual cancel-lation must work their way through long ages of serial time.

Nor is adequate reason given for the origins of evil (it matters not that to the human mind it never could be given,[16] since Milton has set out in this poem to explain all, 'to justify the ways of God to men'). C. S. Lewis argues that, in giving Satan no such reason, Milton's object was to make evil 'reasonless' (as Satan terms the paradisal prohibition at IV, 516); to make Satan's position absurd from the outset; in short, to show the Devil an ass, labouring towards a 'doom of Nonsense'[17]:

> No one had in fact done anything to Satan; he was not hungry, nor over-tasked, nor removed from his place, nor shunned, nor hated – he only thought himself impaired. In the midst of a world of light and love, of song and feast and dance, he could find nothing to think of more interesting than his own prestige. And his own prestige, it must be noted, had and could have no other grounds than those which he refused to admit for the superior prestige of Messiah.[18]

But what Milton does will not entirely fit into this scheme. Milton – whether as Arian or not is unimportant here – arranges a scene where God carries out the elevation of the Son over all the angels long after the angels have been created.[19] Thus put it might be seen as his test of *their* obedience: but this test is absurd in as much as it is not God's part to tempt his own creation; nor, however much writing an epic poem may have forced Milton into such portrayal, are events sequential or subsequent in Heaven. But Milton goes further: he makes God sound like a tyrant when he makes this demand, which in the eyes of the reader must give Satan further provocation, however much we at once condemn the motion of his will:

> Hear my decree, which unrevoked shall stand.
> This day I have begot whom I declare
> My only Son, and on this holy hill
> Him have anointed, whom ye now behold
> At my right hand; your head I him appoint;
> And by my self have sworn to him shall bow
> All knees in heaven, and shall confess him Lord:
> Under his great vicegerent reign abide
> United as one individual soul
> For ever happy: him who disobeys
> Me disobeys, breaks union, and that day
> Cast out from God and blessed vision, falls
> Into utter darkness, deep ingulfed, his place
> Ordained without redemption, without end.   (v, 602–15)

The old answer with this poem, that Milton might have brought it off if he had been prepared to veil the origin of Satan's revolt in mystery, will not do here, because in writing a poem which sets out to justify God's ways, Milton is forced into making some attempt to explain the origin of evil. And that he does, that he gives Satan cause, however small or theoretically absurd, for revolt, works against the notion that Satan is meant to appear an ass; and, of course, it also ensures the ultimate failure of Milton's attempt at justification of God. But what is more important for our purposes here is that it shows how difficult it is to show permanence becoming change. Of course Milton has his concept of perfection itself as being a continual choosing, of the angels forever free to choose God or not-God; but for the angels certainly, the choice, surrounded as they are by the joys of Heaven, and with evil non-existent, must be an unreal one: there is no razor-edge of being here. Therefore they have to be given stimulus to rebel.

Granted we are not dealing simply with Milton's poem here, but with the problem inherent in any apologetics. But perhaps we come nearer to *Paradise Lost* in Milton's *preference* for an evolutionary universe. Not one of his poems reaches a final point of rest, or contemplates a static scene. 'L'Allegro' is a poem of constant flickering from place to place; 'Il Penseroso' is a quest poem, trying to find a suitable spot to begin contemplation; 'Lycidas' enacts a whole spiritual history and then looks to 'fresh woods, and pastures new'; 'On the Morning of Christ's Nativity' spends scant time on the incarnated fact in the manger, but ranges over all space and time tracing the implications of Christ's arrival up to Apocalypse; *Paradise Regained* is conceived as Christ's winning of his spurs before the Redemption of man, and as a prefiguring of his final victory over Satan; and *Samson Agonistes* is quite simply concerned with spiritual evolution. Even in *Comus*, which as a masque might have been expected to be a fairly static and iconographic form, Milton has stripped away the element of spectacle and introduced real dramatic and dynamic interplay between the Masque (the Lady and her attendants) and the Anti-masque (Comus and his rout). As for *Paradise Lost*, as we have suggested, it is little but 'developmental': beginning, perhaps significantly, with the energy of Satan, looking at Heaven only as it considers things done and about to be done, regarding even Paradise dynamically through the approach of Satan; then proceeding to the war in Heaven, the creation (considered always as being-in-motion), the temptation, the subsequent spiritual development of man (and of Devil), and the vision, in what Lewis has called 'an untransmuted lump of futurity', of Old and New Testament history to come, before that muted anticipatory close: 'The world was all before them. . . .' And here too the oft-remarked relentless forward movement of the style embodies and enacts the evolutionary drive of the poem.

This brings us, of course, to the *felix culpa*. It is not just that Michael's words to Adam in Books XI and XII put him in possession of

'A paradise within thee, happier far', but that the poem comes down to saying that 'Without Contraries is no progression', just as Milton does again in *Areopagitica*: evil, that is, is the stimulus to a greater good (VII, 613–6). And if man had not fallen, Christ would never have become incarnated, God would never have shown that act of colossal self-denying love. If Satan had not fallen, all the variety and flux of the universe would never have come into being. Thus Adam:

> O goodness infinite, goodness immense!
> That all this good of evil shall produce,
> And evil turn to good; more wonderful
> Than that which by creation first brought forth
> Light out of darkness!   (XII, 469–73)

This may explain why the innocence of Adam and Eve means less to Milton than their readiness to fall. For one thing, they are always presented in a context of frailty and imminent doom: we see them from the first through Satan's eyes, and Eve's dream is a softening-up process. For another (to retrace well-trodden ground), they are presented as capable of failings without reference to the prohibited tree: Adam, we are told, dotes too much on Eve (VIII, 530 ff.) and fails to incline her to reason before she leaves him on the fatal day (IX, 342–75); and she, in leaving him, recklessly disobeys (IX, 376–84). In innocence, therefore, they act on those motions of the heart which are ultimately evil. Perhaps this is one reason why the temptation of Eve (as presented to the reader), and Adam's later decision to follow her, are brief.

Whatever issues this raises with reference to the justification of God's ways is not our concern here. What is, is that any portrayal of innocence becoming culpable is bound either to stress the innocence at the expense of the culpability, or *vice versa*. That Milton has chosen the latter seems a significant fact about his poem.

The point may be brought out by comparison. C. S. Lewis wrote an account of an imagined averted fall, *Perelandra*, in which a Cambridge philologist, Ransom, is sent under divine instruction to Venus (mythically conceived) to help the sole and primally innocent human inhabitants, a Lord Tor and a Lady Tinidril, to resist the eventual assaults of the Devil in the body of a former megalomaniac scientist, Weston, who also travels there. This assault at first takes the form of a three-cornered debate among the Lady, Ransom and the Un-man (Weston possessed); and during this, when the Un-man is trying to persuade the Lady to break the prohibition of Maleldil (God), it produces a point which temporarily crushes Ransom: '[Ransom] has not told you that it was this breaking of the commandment which brought Maleldil to our world and because of which He was made man. He dare not deny it' (p. 137).

Eventually Ransom recovers sufficiently to reply, 'Of course good came of it. Is Maleldil a beast that we can stop His path, or a leaf that we can twist His shape? Whatever you do, He will make good of it. But not the good He had prepared for you if you had obeyed Him. That is lost for ever' (p. 138).

That is a good answer; it is also the one Lewis tries to find in Milton in his *A Preface to 'Paradise Lost'* (1942). But, though it is said in Milton's poem that men might have ascended through time to angelic status and heavenly paradises (v, 493–500), the point lacks final weight when set in the dialectical context of the poem. If loss is to be emphasised, there must be a full portrayal of what is being lost: but Milton is concerned with process more than with what is processed. And yet, if there is such portrayal of what is being lost, the loss inevitably becomes unconvincing. Lewis spends long and loving care on the portrayal of perfect innocence, and the result is that he is quite unable to show us how such innocence could be tempted and fall. On this subject there is no compromise, no meeting-ground: one opts either for stasis or for flux, and pays the price.

There is also the question of the nature of the prohibition and human choice. Any view of goodness as being in constant crisis, in as much as it has constantly to be opting for the good rather than the bad, is, as we have seen, not correct as far as the angels go. Milton has to make God force a crisis of choice through the exaltation of the Son: otherwise the choice, if choice it be, remains formal, since there is no evil to reject. But this notion of continual crisis, as Milton would have us accept it, is not true of man either. One is not to suppose that at every moment Adam and Eve are turning away from the idea of eating of the Tree: it is not a temptation (however much the frequent admonitions to them might have made it interesting) until someone from outside makes them see it as such; it is, as God puts it, the 'Sole pledge of his obedience' (iii, 95; see also iv, 419–39, and viii, 324–30). This is not to deny that they are formally in a state of crisis, in that they may be so tempted at any time, and indeed are about to be from the first time that we see them through Satan's eyes. But their choices, until the Devil leads Eve to the Tree, are on Milton's terms quite non-moral. Just as there is but one (clear) physical way into the garden, so there is but one moral way out.

While this form of confinement – 'you may do all this, but not this one thing' (as in fairy-tale) – is generous liberty, there is a sense in which, when the crisis does come, man's capacity to resist it is more limited than it might be. For the Tree is such that it can be presented by Satan as a tree of scientific knowledge, and Adam has been created in such a way that he thirsts for knowledge to the point where Raphael has to suppress him. It follows that, when tempted with the Tree, man is tempted by that which finds most answer in himself. In *Perelandra*, perhaps feeling this problem, and freed from fidelity to the Genesis myth, Lewis makes the prohibition one whereby man, who lives on vegetated islands floating on the deeps of the primarily oceanic planet Venus, is not to sleep on the Fixed Land, the land rooted, like ours, to the planet. The Lady is never tempted by the act itself – indeed, with her preference for the islands, finds the notion of it repugnant. Milton's Tree, however, is repeatedly presented to Adam and Eve as one conferring knowledge – of whatever kind, since they know nothing of evil or death. It is therefore easy for Satan to translate 'knowledge' meaning 'experience as a consequence of disobedience' into 'sapience magically inherent in the fruit'; and to portray God's prohibition as man's inhibition. Eve is tempted by this knowledge and by the sight and smell of the fruit itself. When Satan realises what the prohibition laid on Adam and Eve is, he is amazed, and sees how God has played into his hands:

> knowledge forbidden?
> Suspicious, reasonless. Why should their Lord
> Envy them that? Can it be sin to know,
> Can it be death? And do they only stand
> By ignorance, is that their happy state,
> The proof of their obedience and their faith?
> Of fair foundation laid whereon to build
> Their ruin!   (IV, 515–22)

This is a perversion of the truth, but it is a perversion to which the truth is open. The fault derives from the myth in Genesis, but it is there as a fact in Milton's poem, as are all the other problems that are inevitable concomitants of the Christian world picture. They are there, and their effect, perhaps nowhere more pointedly than in the character of this prohibition, is to further the evolutionary bias of the poem – here, to make it more likely that Adam and Eve will fall when tempted. The questions have to be asked: how did the angels fall unless God made evil in them? Why did he make Adam and Eve as frail as he did? Why does he so load the scales against them with the prohibition? The answer is simply that Christianity – to man at least – contains an inherent dichotomy between the notions of permanence and change, and that sooner or later any apologist is bound to throw his emphasis on one or the other. Milton has opted for the latter. Perhaps it was a preference for revolution rather than conservatism that led him to this subject in the first place.

The large-scale imagery and the evolutionary character of Milton's poem thus give us a picture of the marriage of Heaven and Hell.[19] Blake sensed the truth, though his vision of Milton being simply on the side of Satan is erroneous. Repulsive God may at times be, but the picture of him throughout Book VII, as creator of the universe, is an unforgettable portrayal of the Prolific which Blake would forbid him, a sheer joy at giving of himself. Energy is struck by distance, between two poles, like an electric arc.

This unconscious meaning of the poem is sheerly in conflict with Milton's avowed purpose; that purpose did not satisfy every aspect of his being. We shall find this kind of warfare between explicit and implicit intentions in much eighteenth-century poetry: it expresses a refusal to accommodate whole areas of the world or the self which are in opposition to cherished beliefs and one-sided views.

5 Dryden

DRYDEN AND SATIRE

The emergence of satire as a dominant literary form in the latter part of the seventeenth century was certainly a result of the spirit of party and faction which characterised the time. There had been periods of satire in previous English literature, but none in which the central output of the dominant literary figures was of this character. Augustan satire is also different in kind from earlier varieties. The satire in Langland's *Piers Plowman* attacks general religious and moral abuses through typical figures; and Elizabethan satire, while similarly concerned with perennial human failings, is equally directed at portraying the satirist as character.[1] But in Augustan satire the subject is people and events of the day, however much these may be allegorised into recurrent or typical figures. Dryden speaks of contemporary political struggle; Pope of recognisable individuals; Swift of current religious, social or political issues. To this extent the Augustan satirists show a greater engagement with immediate life than had appeared in English poetry before. Yet they show that engagement with life precisely to disengage themselves from large parts of it: they speak of many local events and individuals in order to expose them. Their use of mock heroic, the Augustan version of the metaphysical conceit, is the bringing together of opposed contexts not to unite but in order to divide them: a case of *sauter pour mieux reculer*.[2] But there are retreats less deliberate. Dryden under William loses his faith in monarchic order; Pope and Swift, under the Hanoverians and Walpole, lose faith in any public order. All move back finally on their private selves: Dryden and Pope into retirement, and Swift, in the end, into madness. The Augustan satirists show that now serious poetry cannot escape being involved with the mutable world; but their work testifies to the fact that a vision of order which rejects most of that world can ultimately sustain itself only in subjective terms.

The character of Dryden as a satirist can be highlighted by comparison with Pope, who directs his verse more at morals and aesthetics than at politics. Dryden, by contrast, is far more often concerned in his poetry with national issues and matters of government – an instance being the way in which, at the beginning of *Absalom and Achitophel*, he can shuffle off the moral character of Charles before directing the poem along the lines of political analysis. The difference has of course historical explanation: Dryden wrote at a time when the scars of the Civil War were still unhealed, and rebellion was an ever-present threat; Pope wrote with the Succession fairly settled, the Union accomplished (and, after 1715, the Jacobite threat crushed), and his country generally at peace. Further, for much of his poetic career Dryden was a professional poet in the sense that he spoke, if at times with varying degrees of enthusiasm, for the monarchy, divine right, hierarchy and public order; and as Poet Laureate (after 1668) and Historiographer Royal (after 1670) was paid for doing so. Dryden saw himself as a public servant with a poetico-political mission as a propagandist. Pope, however, found in political life no correlative for his ideals: *Windsor Forest* looks hopefully to the monarchy, but the final defeat of Tory hopes in 1713, with the Whig dominance and the Hanoverian succession which followed, turned him away from specifically political concerns. Lacking this correlative, and faced by what he saw as the destruction of taste and morals all about him, Pope as satirist works from a far more negative standpoint than Dryden does.[3] But, at the same time, by being less specifically tied to a particular political programme of order, his imagination is free to range more widely; and, without having to tie his characters so insistently to a doctrine, he can give them greater creative individuality.

Dryden's satiric stance can be seen from the portrait of Achitophel in *Absalom and Achitophel*, lines 150–229. At first the picture is a balanced, urbane one (recalling the 'mannered urbanity' Dryden praised in Horace), and has life through its dialectic. We are told that Achitophel was

> For close Designs, and crooked Counsels fit;
> Sagacious, Bold, and Turbulent of wit:
> Restless, unfixt in Principles and Place;
> In Power unpleas'd, impatient of Disgrace.
> A fiery Soul, which working out its way,
> Fretted the Pigmy Body to decay:
> And o'r inform'd the Tenement of Clay.
> A daring Pilot in extremity;
> Pleas'd with the Danger, when the Waves went high
> He sought the Storms; but for a Calm unfit,
> Would Steer too nigh the Sands, to boast his Wit.
> Great Wits are sure to Madness near ally'd;
> And thin Partitions do their Bounds divide. . . .

The portrait is certainly one of a man with a detestation of fixity and stability; but it is also generous, acknowledging that such dynamism is at times essential to life and the survival of kingdoms, and admiring while lamenting the greatness of Achitophel's soul. The double attitude is a fused one: the admiration is harnessed to the sense of loss, just as Achitophel is 'fitted' to the 'unfit' ('close Designs, and crooked Counsels').

But now the method changes:

> why should he, with Wealth and Honour blest,
> Refuse his Age the needful hours of Rest?
> Punish a Body which he coud not please;
> Bankrupt of Life, yet Prodigal of Ease?
> And all to leave, what with his Toyl he won,
> To that unfeather'd, two Leg'd thing, a Son:
> Got, while his Soul did hudled Notions try;
> And born a shapeless Lump, like Anarchy.

(handwritten margin notes: "pity", "pity & contempt", "contempt & pity", "contempt")

Taking this couplet by couplet, the first shows pity, the second pity and contempt, the third contempt and pity and the last plain contempt. Dryden is moving into direct and 'unbalanced' attack on Shaftesbury:

> In Friendship False, Implacable in Hate:
> Resolv'd to Ruine or to Rule the State.
> To Compass this the Triple Bond he broke;
> The Pillars of the publick Safety shook:
> And fitted *Israel* for a Foreign Yoke.
> Then, seiz'd with Fear, yet still affecting Fame,
> Usurp'd a Patriott's All-attoning Name.

Here there is no longer any allowance, none of the previously complex attitude: Achitophel is simply damned. And if it were argued that what we have in this portrait is a process of trial before sentence, and that the above is the necessary judgment that must always, finally, simplify the complexities of the case, the word is not final: for Dryden now shifts back to making a point in Shaftesbury's favour:

> Yet, Fame deserv'd, no Enemy can grudge;
> The Statesman we abhor, but praise the Judge.
> In *Israels* Courts ne'r sat an *Abbethdin*
> With more discerning Eyes, or Hands more clean:
> Unbrib'd, unsought, the Wretched to redress;
> Swift of Dispatch, and easie of Access.

(handwritten margin note: "Fair")

In short we have moved from a single apprehension of the ambiguous moral status of Achitophel, to one of 'on the one hand this, on the other that'; and Dryden proceeds to abandon altogether the favourable side of the duality as he builds up a picture of the political menace and Satanic corruption of Achitophel (194 ff.).

Thus Achitophel is not allowed to be a creation for more than a few lines before he is made a function of the didactic purpose of the poem. The relation between being and doing, the *dulce* and the *utile*, is one of Dryden's primary problems in writing satire.[4] *MacFlecknoe* (written *c.* 1678, pub. 1682), his lampoon on Shadwell, is all creation and no significance: Shadwell is metamorphosed into a fantastic comic figure –

> A Tun of Man in thy Large bulk is writ,
> But sure thou'rt but a Kilderkin of wit.   (195–6)

But the poem has no didactic purpose: it simply says 'Shadwell is dull' in as many and various ways as possible; we are far from the apocalyptic overtones of Pope's *The Dunciad*. *The Medall* (1682), the attack Dryden wrote on Shaftesbury after the latter's acquittal by a London Grand Jury on the charge of incitement to rebellion, may be described as all significance and no creation: it is from the outset absolutely direct, hortatory and unpoetic attack. *Absalom and Achitophel* (1681) might appear to be the attempt to reconcile the two extremes, but it fails. And it fails because Dryden is finally too partisan in political satire, too earnest and strident. *MacFlecknoe*, on the other hand, fine though it is, shows a too-great detachment (and Dryden had small cause for resentment at Shadwell).

There is one exception to this general rule, and that is the portrait of Zimri in *Absalom and Achitophel*, the portrait in which Dryden comes closest to Pope, and which he himself considered 'worth the whole poem'. Dryden made this last point in his *A Discourse Concerning the Original and Progress of Satire* (1693), and the context in which he made it is a significant one: for it comes where he is distinguishing between direct and indirect attack in satire –

> How easy is it to call rogue and villain, and that wittily! But how hard to make a man appear a fool, a blockhead, or a knave, without using any of those opprobrious terms! . . . there is still a vast differ-ence betwixt the slovenly butchering of a man, and the fineness of a stroke that separates the head from the body, and leaves it standing in its place.[5]

Dryden feels that he succeeded in this with Zimri – ' 'tis not bloody, but 'tis ridiculous enough'. Clearly, his account of the problems of writing satire comes straight from his own experience. This is part of the portrait:

> A man so various, that he seem'd to be
> Not one, but all Mankinds Epitome.
> Stiff in Opinions, always in the wrong:
> Was every thing by starts, and nothing long:
> But, in the course of one revolving Moon,
> Was Chymist, Fidler, States-Man, and Buffoon:
> Then all for Women, Painting, Rhiming, Drinking;
> Besides ten thousand freaks that dy'd in thinking.
> Blest Madman, who coud every hour employ,
> With something New to wish, or to enjoy!   (545–54)

The manner, even allowing for the fact that Dryden has deliberately moved down a notch from the high style used in describing Achitophel or Absalom, is relaxed, seemingly casual: the run-on line and the weak fading rhyme of the first couplet give an air of prose rather than poetry, and the impression generally is one of the poet's being able to stand back from his character. Yet at the same time there is much more use of antithesis and balanced contrast than is usual with Dryden,[6] and the poetry is really working: the 'revolving Moon', for instance, is a description not only of the moon but also of Zimri. It was from Dryden's list of perverted hierarchy – 'Chymist, Fidler, States-Man and Buffoon' – that Pope must have constructed his own 'Puffs, Powders, Patches, Bibles, Billet-doux' (*Rape of the Lock*, I, 138). The way words are working here is in contrast to the verbose and repetitious mode in the picture of Achitophel, which is three times the length. Yet even here Dryden cannot resist the sidelong *sententia* of the last couplet.

   The picture continues:

> Rayling and praising were his usual Theams;
> And both (to shew his Judgment) in Extreams:
> So over Violent, or over Civil,
> That every man, with him, was God or Devil.
> In squandring Wealth was his peculiar Art:
> Nothing went unrewarded, but Desert.
> Begger'd by Fools, whom still he found too late:
> He had his Jest, and they had his Estate.   (555–62)

This could have been written by Pope: it has his compression and epigrammatic terseness. To describe 'Rayling and praising' as 'Theams' is to give them an order or pattern their nature denies; and similar is the description of how 'In squandring Wealth was his peculiar *Art*.' The 'Nothing went unrewarded, but Desert' is a fine *mot*. In this portrait balance is being used poetically, to damn more surely; in that of

Achitophel there was too much of a moral casting of accounts for the poetry to do its work. Zimri's portrait is both entertaining and instructive. Dryden is not striving against his will for moral generosity, nor indeed assailing major sins: 'If I had railed, I might have suffered for it justly: but I managed my own work more happily, perhaps more dexterously. I avoided the mention of great crimes, and applied myself to the representing of blindsides, and little extravagancies; to which, the wittier a man is, he is generally the more obnoxious.'[7] The method of careful detachment, of seeming to retreat where in fact one outflanks (cf. Pope's *Essay on Criticism*, 169–78, 566–77), is what makes Zimri at once a creation in his own right, and a penetrating object lesson. That lesson is the lack of fixity or stability in true value that is behind everything Zimri does; and it is precisely that unsteadiness which Dryden sees in all the would-be rebels he portrays, except Shimei, who in a sense has the stable corruption to make all the others helpless pawns. Achitophel's 'wilde Ambition loves to slide, not stand' (198). Absalom's mind cannot see right in David, only no wrong, and is fired with illegitimate ambition (his bastardy is a metaphor of his shaky moral basis); he is easily 'staggered' and overthrown by Achitophel (373–5). Corah has lost all touch with sense, possessed by 'Visionary flights' until 'The Spirit caught him up, the Lord knows where' (656–7).

   Zimri, however, is the exception. The contrast between Dryden's more usual satiric mode and Pope's may be brought out by looking at the latter's Atossa in Epistle II of the *Moral Essays*. Having reviewed a range of feminine inconsistencies Pope turns to ask,

> But what are these to great Atossa's mind?
> Scarce once herself, by turns all Womankind!
> Who, with herself, or others, from her birth
> Finds all her life one warfare upon earth:
> Shines, in exposing Knaves, and painting Fools,
> Yet is, whate'er she hates and ridicules.
> No Thought advances, but her Eddy Brain
> Whisks it about, and down it goes again.
> Full sixty years the World has been her Trade,
> The wisest Fool much Time has ever made.   (115–24)

The portrait is one, in Pope's aesthetic terms, of 'boldness' without 'regularity': it is to be contrasted with that of the reverse which follows it, Chloe. Atossa has no calm, even no private self in her continual preoccupation with society; Chloe has nothing but self. Atossa's ruling passion is, in a sense, passion (which fact assists in dissipating the notion of the 'ruling passion' which Pope has proposed as his general theme). Dryden always fits his characters into a deliberate scheme of moral and political analysis, but Pope's characters often escape such schemes, grouping themselves in patterns less consciously imposed by the poet.

The complexity of Atossa's portrait is striking. Her energy is futile in that it achieves nothing in the world. Exposing fools, she is one herself. All her loving and hating leave her only as an object of contempt. The only passion gratified is her rage; and here Pope begins to show that her obsession with the world is that not of the prolific, but of the devourer. She consumes thought (121–2); she cannot tolerate being brought into relation or comparison with someone else:

> Love, if it makes her yield, must make her hate:
> Superiors? death! and Equals? what a curse!
> But an Inferior not dependant? worse.
> Offend her, and she knows not to forgive;
> Oblige her, and she'll hate you while you live:
> But die, and she'll adore you – Then the Bust
> And Temple rise – then fall again to dust.
> Last night, her Lord was all that's good and great,
> A Knave this morning, and his Will a Cheat.   (134–42)

Death she welcomes, because death breaks relation; but then there remain wills. The suggestion is that she has a spiritual 'hole in the heart' which she strives to fill, but only enlarges, by her violent impact on the world. Cuts more grim and sad follow: whatever she has attacked has rebounded on her; with all her plenitude and force she is ultimately a barren vacancy; with all her obsession with the external world she is really a solipsist.

> Atossa, curs'd with ev'ry granted pray'r,
> Childless with all her Children, wants an Heir.   (147–8)

The complexity of the picture and the submerged character of its unity, contrast with Dryden's mode of characterisation. Pope's portraits are often fully human, exploring all the manifold impulses of humanity as it is; Dryden's are shorn for the purposes of his poems. Further, Dryden's characters often fit a traditional mould. The situation of Charles, and his promiscuousness, are compared to, and subsumed in, those of the biblical David; Shaftesbury is, in Achitophel, made a type of the ambitious rebel, and is further classified by the frequent analogies drawn between his career and methods and those of Milton's Satan. In Pope's poetry, however, such names as Atossa, Sir Balaam or Timon do little more than provide situational analogies: they are in only perfunctory degree used to define or limit characterisation.

Pope is rather more impartial than Dryden. It is the impartiality of creative delight: he stands back and admires, while in a sense the characters damn themselves. Atossa is a wonder. 'But what are these to great Atossa's mind?' She overgoes the others in the pyrotechnics of extraordinary character. So too with Wharton – modelled directly on Dryden's Zimri – 'Wharton stands confest. / Wharton, the scorn and wonder of our days' (I, 179–80). This delight can make the moral assessments more penetrating: we can feel that full justice has been done.[8] Yet at the same time the very fact of Pope's constant interest, throughout his work, in the depiction of human disproportion and monstrosity shows a more general fascination with that which he condemns: at this level, what he gains in vivacity he loses in moral efficacy. The contrast here between Dryden and Pope – the one moral only by restricting life, the other ultimately 'life-like' only by emasculating the moral – expresses the increasing gulf between a now manifold world and concepts of order or principle: the two cannot finally be reconciled in one work.

A TRANSLATION OF CHAUCER: 'THE COCK AND THE FOX' (1700)

Dryden's late translation 'The Cock and the Fox' affords a fuller picture of how as a 'public' poet Dryden felt constantly aware of his audience, and of the need for that audience to be kept within the framework of order, propriety, reason and sense.

In the preface to his *Fables Ancient and Modern* (1700), Dryden describes how, when he had completed his translations of Ovid, he happened on the idea of modernising Chaucer:

> Having done with *Ovid* for this time, it came into my mind that our old *English* poet *Chaucer* in many Things resembled him, and that with no disadvantage on the Side of the Modern Author. . . . And as I am, and always have been studious to promote the Honour of my Native Country, so I soon resolv'd to put their Merits to the Trial, by turning some of the *Canterbury* Tales into our Language, as it is now refin'd. (39–46)

But it was not only a patriotic object, but also a real love of, and kinship with, Chaucer that impelled Dryden. Chaucer, Dryden saw, had invention and understood people (245–58, 421–49); was 'a perpetual Fountain of good Sense' (309); 'follow'd Nature every where; but was never so bold to go beyond her' (328–9) – was, excepting his rough metre and rather limited sense of decency and propriety, Dryden's picture of the ideal artist. He found, too, that he and Chaucer showed many of the same attitudes: 'I found I had a Soul congenial to his, and that I had been conversant in the same Studies' (526–7). Most of all Dryden was drawn to Chaucer's sense of life. ' 'Tis sufficient to say according to the Proverb, that here is God's Plenty' (443–4).

Dryden, however, allowed himself the latitude of free translation or 'paraphrase'[9] of his source: his 'Cock and the Fox' is 821 lines in length, as against the 625 of the 'Nun's Priest's Tale'. With the example of Waller in view, Chaucer's rough metre and irregular line-lengths must be corrected and made more smooth (331–50). With his own social context Dryden must refine away the indecencies of Chaucer's poem: it is this principle that guides him away from Chaucer's more 'obscene' tales, and into omitting the prologue of the 'Wife of Bath's Tale' (449–90). Further,

> *Chaucer*, I confess, is a rough Diamond, and must first be polish'd e'er he shines. I deny not likewise, that living in our early Days of Poetry, he writes not always of a piece; but sometimes mingles trivial Things, with those of greater Moment. Sometimes also, though not often, he runs riot, like *Ovid*, and knows not when he has said enough. . . . Having observ'd this Redundancy in *Chaucer*, (as it is an easie Matter for a Man of ordinary Parts to find a Fault in one of greater) I have not ty'd myself to a Literal Translation; but have often omitted what I judg'd unnecessary, or not of Dignity enough to appear in the Company of better Thoughts. I have presum'd farther in some Places, and added somewhat of my own where I thought my Author was deficient, and had not given his Thoughts their true Lustre, for want of Words in the Beginning of our Language.   (510–24)

Here Dryden is pointing to literary rather than directly social or sexual indecorum – to a single level of style and thought, matched together.

Dryden's sympathy with Chaucer certainly qualifies him as a translator; but the differences in their approach are far larger than he realised.

In the first place, Dryden has omitted all reference to the nun's priest, the gently humorous, pedantic and unworldly cleric whom Chaucer introduces from among the Canterbury pilgrims before the tale begins. The hearty host drags him from the throng and mockingly bids him not be nervous:

> 'What thogh thyn hors be bothe foul and lene?
> If he wol serve thee, rekke nat a bene.
> Looke that thyn herte be murie everemo.'
> 'Yis, sir', quod he, 'yis, Hoost, so moot I go,
> But I be myrie, ywis I wol be blamed.'
> And right anon his tale he hath attamed,
> And thus he said unto us everichon,
> This sweete preest, this goodly man sir John.
>   ('Nun's Priest's Tale', 2813–20.)

The 'I' often used in Chaucer's tale is thus the nun's priest, but the absence of such a teller for Dryden's version makes the 'I' refer only to the artist himself; Chaucer's own attitudes are concealed from sight behind those of a dramatised narrator, but Dryden's are not. Thus we relate the discussion of predestination in Chaucer's version to the special interests of the nun's priest – as also his hesitant misogynist remarks – where in Dryden's we have only the author on whom to hang them ('Nun's Priest's Tale', 3230–66; 'Cock and the Fox', 503–72). And in Chaucer's tale we can partly refer Chauntecleer's interest in the nature of dreams to a scholarly preoccupation of the nun's priest as well as allowing its comic force in coming from a barnyard fowl. What is reduced to being straight didactic comment in Dryden is richly comic in Chaucer – for example, in this heavy *sententia*:

> evere the latter ende of joye is wo.
> God woot that worldly joy is soone ago;
> And if a rethor koude faire endite,
> He in a cronycle saufly myghte it write
> As for a sovereyn notabilitee.
> ('Nun's Priest's Tale', 3205–9; cf. 'Cock and the Fox', 467–73)

And the whole moral of the tale – that one should not trust flatterers – can be taken much more lightly in Chaucer's poem. There the artist is detached, giving autonomy to the fictional microcosm he has created; in the translation this microcosm is continually invaded by authorial commentary, and the relation of the work to life is made direct. The effect is one of stridency in Dryden's tale. Though he and Chaucer may have similar temperaments and attitudes to life, the instability of Dryden's time makes him fight more for his than the earlier poet had to. He will make us learn morally, where Chaucer allowed us to learn about humanity.

This moral emphasis in Dryden can be seen in other aspects of his poem. He often alters Chaucer's attribution of events to fate or fortune into a pattern of moral justice. When Chauntecleer is defending the veracity of dreams against Pertelote's scepticism, he cites the example of two merchants on a journey, one of whom dreamt of disaster should they take ship the next day, while the other laughed him to scorn, set sail and was duly wrecked and drowned. Dryden's version turns these events into a pattern of poetic justice, for his travellers have as the object of their journey 'the hope of Gain' (298), and the one who ignores the counsel of his friend declares, 'For me no Fears restrain, / Who follow *Mercury* the God of Gain' (321–2). Where in Chaucer the point is simply the awful veracity of dreams, Dryden obscures this with moral criteria. This imposition of causality is the major alteration he makes to 'Palamon and Arcite', his translation of Chaucer's 'Knight's Tale': where Chaucer leaves ambiguous the question of how far Arcite and Palamon deserved what they received, Dryden gives us an Arcite who usurps Palamon's prior claim on Emily (he saw her first) by making love into an anarchic absolute:

> Each Day we break the Bond of Humane Laws
> For Love, and vindicate the Common Cause.
> Laws for Defence of Civil Rights are plac'd,
> Love throws the Fences down, and makes a general Waste.
>
> (I, 331–4)

When Arcite and Palamon visit their respective shrines of Mars and Venus before the tournament, the first asks in a far simpler way than in Chaucer for victory, while the second asks only for Emily (III, 159–64, 355–6); each then gets exactly what he asks, and justice is done. At the end Arcite admits his fault (III, 806–27) and the poem concludes with the moral, 'So may the Queen of Love long Duty bless, / And all true Lovers find the same Success' (III, 1154–5).[10]

What we have in this tendency of Dryden's is not only a too-eager desire to make art teach, but Augustan antipathy towards disproportion. The idea of man suffering more or less than he deserves finds little sympathy in Dryden, Pope or even Johnson: this notion of tragedy is one alien to the eighteenth-century sensibility. This dislike in Dryden is to be explained by reference not so much simply to the value he placed on reason, as to why he felt reason so much a value in the first place: and for the answer to that one must look to his fear of moral, religious and political loss of control as so near in time to him it had been experienced, and as it might recur.

To matters left without comment by Chaucer, Dryden gives explanations wherever he may. Chaucer tells us of the boat in which the traveller recklessly set out that 'casuelly the shippes botme rente' ('Nun's Priest's Tale', 3101): that is, he says it happened by accident, and accident is here a local arm of inscrutable fate. And he adds to this inscrutability by saying that the ship went down 'In sighte of othere shippes it bisyde, / That with hem seyled at the same tyde' (3103–4). Dryden, however, raises a whole number of possible reasons for the foundering, and omits the other ships, which lessens the mystery:

> Whether she sprung a Leak, I cannot find,
> Or whether she was overset with Wind;
> Or that some Rock below, her bottom rent. . . .
>
> ('Cock and the Fox', 350–2)

Again the point about the dreadful truth of dreams, and the supernatural governance of mortal affairs is obscured.

On the subject of 'de-supernaturalisation', the earlier dream example given by Dryden's Chanticleer of two travellers on pilgrimage is also revealing. Both put up in an inn, and there comes to one of them a dream in which the other implores him three times in vain to get up and save him from murder, and then finally describes where his dead body may be found. When the sleeper wakes he finds his friend gone, and following the directions given to him in the dream, discovers his friend's corpse and arraigns the murderers before justice. The conclusion of Chauntecleer (and Chaucer's nun's priest) to this is

> O blisful God, that art so just and trewe,
> Lo, how that thou biwreyest mordre alway!
> Mordre wol out, that se we day by day.
> Mordre is so wlatsom and abhomynable
> To God, that is so just and resonable,
> That he wol nat suffre it heled be,
> Though it abyde a yeer, or two, or thre.
> Mordre wol out, this my conclusioun.
>   ('Nun's Priest's Tale', 3050–7).

(This, incidentally, is an example of a fogging of the point about dreams in *Chaucer's* poem, but here it has comic point in relation to those who give vent to it.) Here God is the agent of discovery, and, more than this, the abstract has life of its own: murder will spring out like a loose nail from a board. Dryden's stress is more on the sinner than on the sin ('Good Heav'n . . . / Abhors the Cruel' – 'Cock and the Fox', 281–3) and, in his version, murder does not come out of itself, but is dragged forth ('Murther may pass unpunished for a time, / But tardy Justice will o'ertake the Crime' – 285–6). Further, this 'Justice' is in one sense human justice, since we have just heard of 'Good Heav'n, whose darling Attribute we find / Is boundless Grace, and Mercy to Mankind' (281–2), and the generalisation about justice refers to any context. Dryden thus moves towards a picture of mundane justice divinely sanctioned, where Chaucer's nun's priest's emphasis is specifically on supernatural action – the difference being that between an 'early Augustan' conservative and a medieval Christian. Thus we find Dryden addressing 'Magistrates, who sacred Laws dispense' (274), and referring to the crowd who pursue and capture the criminals as 'The Hue and Cry of Heav'n' (288).

The moralising bias of Dryden's version can also be seen in the way he is not fully content to leave it as the tale of a cock and a fox with a lesson subjoined, but tries, with the fox at least, to give the characters an allegorical dimension. His Reynard is frequently reminiscent of his portrait of Shaftesbury in *Absalom and Achitophel*, particularly in his temptation of Chanticleer (590 ff., 790–2), but the analogy with Milton's Satan is even more overt: the reference, for example, to Satan's despair and vain resolve in *Paradise Regained* (IV, 1–24) is unmistakable – 'th' Artificer of Lies / Renews th' Assault, and his last Batt'ry tries' (776–7). Frequently, too, the fox is described as a hypocritical Roman Catholic:

> A Fox full fraught with seeming Sanctity,
> That fear'd an Oath, but like the Devil, would lie,
> Who look'd like Lent, and had the holy Leer,
> And durst not sin before he say'd his Pray'r.   (480–3)

He is 'Saint *Reynard*' (492) and has a rosary (601). Here the method and subject of *The Hind and The Panther* return with different burden, with Chanticleer as the Anglican Church. Elsewhere Dryden compares Reynard to courtly flatterers (659–64) and, though this is also done by the nun's priest ('Nun's Priest's Tale', 3325–30), it is in Chaucer's poem a joke directed at the portentousness of the teller.

This increase by Dryden of the potential allegorical significance of his characters reduces their status as cock and fox, reduces, in short, the comic mock-heroic element that arises from the disparity between, say, the fowl that Chanticleer is, and the learned and pompous debates which he gives vent. Dryden had – if we except *MacFlecknoe*, in which a high style is used for a low subject – a different notion of decorum from that of Pope, and perhaps in this sense a different satiric method: in *Absalom and Achitophel* the varying social status of the characters attacked is shown in different levels of style, ranging from heroic to directly abusive. The mock-heroic method was one to which Dryden could not give more than occasional assent. It is perhaps this which explains the oddities in his portrayal of Chanticleer. He had, presumably, the choice of considering the subject as a low or a high one, and seems from the evidence of the preface to the *Fables* to have wanted to elevate it. In so far as he was translating a mock-heroic poem, it was impossible to remove that element of comedy; yet we see him frequently giving Chanticleer greater stature than Chaucer allows him. Sometimes such elevation leads to surprising reversals, as when Dryden drops the beast-allegory and has Chanticleer, surveying the glories of nature about him, declare, in a burst of energetic primitivism:

> All these are ours; and I with pleasure see
> Man strutting on two Legs, and aping me!
> An unfledg'd Creature, of a lumpish frame,
> Indew'd with fewer Particles of Flame:

> Our Dame sits couring o'er a Kitchin-fire,
> I draw fresh Air, and Nature's Works admire.
> ('Cock and the Fox', 459–64)[11]

At this, realising how far Chanticleer is flying above the judgments
of the poem, he has to add another passage not in Chaucer, an otherwise unnecessary didactic reminder:

> The time shall come when Chanticleer shall wish
> His Words unsaid, and hate his boasted Bliss:
> The crested Bird shall by Experience know,
> *Jove* made him not his Master-piece below;
> And learn the latter end of Joy is Woe.   (467–71)

Yet he is still the 'crested Bird', at least one of nature's wonders.

Dryden's cock is more a prince among birds than a pretender: his
regality comes over rather more than his absurdity.[12] Often Chanticleer
is referred to as a 'Knight' (for example, 134, 414, 688, 705): the point
may in part be comic elevation, but the elevation sticks; as, too, when
Reynard addresses Chanticleer, 'My Lord, your Sire familiarly I knew, / A
Peer deserving such a Son, as you' (608–9). It does so because Dryden
has made the moral point about Chanticleer far more prominent and serious than it is in Chaucer: he wants to show the bird's pride to be a pride
which has something to build on. In Chaucer's version Chauntecleer is
continually deflating himself as we sense the disparity between his pretensions and his barnyard reality, but Dryden's Chanticleer is cut down
by 'Experience', not ever-present mock-heroic: with Chaucer it is pride
constantly exploding itself through over-inflation, but with Dryden the
pride comes before the fall. Thus Dryden has little of the domestic
familiarity of Chaucer's Pertelote: when Chauntecleer gasps and quakes
for fear at his dream, Pertelote chides him anxiously,

> What eyleth yow, to grone in this manere?
> Ye been a verray sleper; fy, for shame!
> ('Nun's Priest's Tale', 2890–1)

while Dryden's Partlet says, rather humbly,

> You groan, Sir, ever since the Morning-light,
> As something had disturb'd your noble Spright.
> ('Cock and the Fox', 103–4)

She advises him on a cure, where Chaucer's Pertelote takes Chauntecleer in hand. Further, Dryden omits the deflationary devices that

Chaucer inserts into Chauntecleer's lengthy monologue on dreams. Having referred to Cato's views Chauntecleer declares,

> Ther nedeth make of this noon argument;
> The verray preeve sheweth it in dede
> ('Nun's Priest's Tale', 2892–3)

before launching forth into just such an argument. Similar is the narrator's later 'What sholde I moore unto this tale sayn?' (3046).

Frequently Dryden has 'elevated' Chaucer's style with poetic diction. When the speaker of the dream vision comes to the merchant in Chaucer's version, he says bluntly,

> If thou tomorwe wende,
> Thou shalt be dreynt; my tale is at an ende   (3081–2)

but in Dryden's tale he says,

> I come, thy Genius, to command thy stay;
> Trust not the Winds, for fatal is the Day,
> And death unhop'd attends the watry way.
> ('Cock and the Fox', 312–14)

This removes from the terror conveyed by the very brevity of the words used in Chaucer. Indeed Dryden's method of embellishment frequently removes the edge of Chaucer's poem: coarse experience is made refined, and in so being loses much of its nature. When Dryden's Chanticleer escapes from the mouth of the fox, we are told that he

> stretch'd his feather'd Fans with all his might,
> And to the neighb'ring Maple wing'd his flight   (770–1)

where we hear of Chaucer's cock only that 'heigh upon a tree he fleigh anon' (3417). Dryden's lines blur the action, and make us concentrate on Chanticleer poetically flying into the tree, where Chaucer's brief statement makes the action *happen* and at the same time does not remove us from the point of the fox's mistake to look at something else.[13]

The remaining distinctions between the two poems may be described as those of social context; or, rather, of the social context which Dryden's has and Chaucer's does not. Perhaps the most striking example of Dryden's refinement is that his Partlet is made Chanticleer's wife, where in Chaucer's poem Pertelote is simply the most favoured of his mistresses ('Cock and the Fox', 56, 75–81; 'Nun's Priest's Tale', 2865–70). Where Chaucer's poem simply admits the beastly fact, Dryden's tries to turn the beastly into the human and socially acceptable. Again, faced with Chaucer's bleak description of the hens as Chauntecleer's 'sustres and his paramours' (2867), Dryden is reluctant: 'Scandal that spares no King, tho' ne'er so good, / Says, they were all of his own Flesh and Blood' (57–8). He proceeds, in a manner reminiscent of the excuses he offers for the philandering of Charles II at the beginning of *Absalom and Achitophel*, to give justifications of this possible incest to placate the ruffled sensibilities of his 'decent' readers:

> But make the worst, the Monarch did no more,
> Than all the *Ptolomeys* had done before:
> When Incest is for Int'rest of a Nation,
> 'Tis made no Sin by Holy Dispensation.   (61–4)[14]

There is intended to be an element of humour in this, but the social and aesthetic aim comes over more powerfully. In general Dryden's aims were first to make the tale decent or significant by refining the barnyard aspect and increasing the moral or allegoric overtones, and second, to make the reader smile at that which is only dressed up to be refined and meaningful; but the former impulse is dominant, and is in conflict with the latter. This can also be seen in the picture of the widow who keeps the cock and hens. For Chaucer's nun's priest she is worthy for her simple, temperate and unworldly life; for Dryden she is in a sense a natural aristocrat of Horatian good sense and taste.[15] Dryden refers to her as a 'Dowager' ('Cock and the Fox', 5) and adds such lines as

> Before the Day was done her Work she sped,
> And never went by Candle-light to Bed:
> With Exercise she sweat ill Humours out,
> Her Dancing was not hindr'd by the Gout.
> Her Poverty was glad; her Heart content,
> Nor knew she what the Spleen or Vapors meant.   (25–30)

He tells us that her temperate diet amounted to 'On Holy-Days, an Egg or two at most; / But her Ambition never reach'd to roast' (35–6). By such means the widow is made very much a 'U' person.

There are frequent sidelong remarks in Dryden's poem which further the 'social' element. After Partlet has prescribed Chanticleer her homespun medicinal remedies for his bad dreams, she declares that at least they will 'save long Bills, and a damn'd Doctor's Fees' (170); and Chanticleer utters a longer attack on doctors at the end of his answering monologue (400–7). Chanticleer gives so much pleasure to Partlet in his love-making that 'Her Sisters pin'd with Envy at the sight' (440).

When the fox describes to Chanticleer how his father's crowing attracted the 'Matrons' from all around, he comments, 'What will not Beaux attempt to please the Fair?' (624).

Generally, therefore, Dryden has set his poem in a very definite social milieu. Perhaps one factor in this was his relaxed attitude in translating the poem: it comes at the end of his life, when he was established and far more secure than thitherto. Another may have been his ignorance of the artistic function of Chaucer's 'digressions' as portrayals not only of Chauntecleer but also of the nun's priest: he may have felt encouraged to a further and less warranted digressiveness. A third source may be the increased use of *descriptio* typical of the late Renaissance (the growth of an interest in phenomena for themselves).[16] For example, Chaucer's account of the attempts of the two pilgrims, whose story is recounted in Chauntecleer's oration on dreams, to find a room for the night, is merely that the town was so crowded that they had to separate to sleep; but Dryden adds explanation of the time of day and the packing of the inns:

> It happen'd so that when the Sun was down,
> They just arriv'd by twilight at a Town;
> That Day had been the baiting of a Bull,
> 'Twas at a Feast, and ev'ry Inn so full;
> That no void Room in Chamber, or on Ground,
> And but one sorry Bed was to be found.   (213–18)

Again, in her version of the hue-and-cry after the seizing of Chanticleer, Dryden expands Chaucer's 'The dokes cryden as men wolde hem quelle' ('Nun's Priest's Tale', 3390) to

> The Ducks that heard the Proclamation cry'd,
> And fear'd a Persecution might betide,
> Full twenty Mile from Town their Voyage take,
> Obscure in Rushes of the liquid Lake.
> ('Cock and the Fox', 736–9)

Here once more Dryden pushes the human and political analogy.

This more expansive tendency in Dryden has unfortunate result in the discussion of predestination that follows Chanticleer's capture. In Chaucer's version the point of the reflections is that they express the interests of the nun's priest, and that there is comic effect in applying such weighty reflections to the experience of a mere barnyard cock. Dryden's translation, which expands Chaucer's eighteen into forty-four lines, has no such comic escape; and further, where the nun's priest keeps the rival possibilities, that God's foreknowledge may or may not

determine the actions of men, clearly in view, Dryden takes the deterministic line of thought to an extreme whereby the context of 'weighing
the possibilities' fades into what appears a direct questioning of God's
purpose:

> Some hold Predestination absolute:
> Some Clerks maintain, that Heav'n at first foresees,
> And in the virtue of Foresight decrees.
> If this be so, then Prescience binds the Will,
> And Mortals are not free to Good or Ill:
> For what he first foresaw, he must ordain,
> Or its eternal Prescience may be vain:
> As bad for us as Prescience had not bin:
> For first, or last, he's Author of the Sin.
> And who says that, let the blaspheming Man
> Say worse ev'n of the Devil, if he can.
> For how can that Eternal Pow'r be just
> To punish Man, who Sins because he must?
> Or, how can He reward a vertuous Deed,
> Which is not done by us; but first decreed?   (508–22)

The 'If this be so' of line 511, though meant to govern the remainder
of the paragraph, soon loses all power to do so, and we have what seem
direct authorial questions. After this paragraph, the return to the notion
of rival possibilities, 'I cannot boult this Matter to the Bran', comes as
a jerk. At the end of his account, Chaucer's nun's priest can dismiss
the subject simply (though the *occupatio* is ironic): 'I wol nat han to
do of swich mateere; / My tale is of a cok, as ye may heere' ('Nun's
Priest's Tale', 3251–2). But Dryden adds to this a recoil on to 'cosmic
Toryism':

> For Heav'n's unfathom'd Pow'r what Man can sound,
> Or put to his Omnipotence a Bound?
>
> ('Cock and the Fox', 544–5)

He has to do this because he has made the debate his own – not simply
that of constantly-mentioned rival clerks, as in Chaucer's account; and
because he has in himself shown rebellious and blasphemous questioning,
which have to be suppressed in scepticism. What we have in Dryden's version is in fact a dramatic conflict between his own revolution-
ary and submissive instincts – an example that the very qualities he
attacks in other poems are present in himself (which perhaps helps
explain why those attacks are so often over-violent and shrill). Clearly
his relaxation can let rather too many things slip.

Dryden's alterations to Chaucer's tale stem from a consistent view of the function of literature. As a member of the Royal Society and as a public poet he was concerned that art should be both clear in meaning and efficacious. This is doubtless part of the reason for his frequent explicit comments and for his refusal to leave the story a world of its own, a fictional microcosm referable only to the character of the nun's priest. Dryden probably also objected to the presentation of the story as an expression of the nun's priest because he and his contemporaries did not find individuals, considered only for their own sake, a proper or sufficient subject for poetry. Further, Dryden's reduction of the 'beast-fable' element and his allegorical presentation of the characters are the expression of a desire to suppress the independence of the fiction and to make the cock come nearer to being a feathered man, so that the point will not be missed. The whole nature of Chaucer's tale implies the kind of freedom of interpretation which Dryden opposed for much of his life, whether in attacking private and individual political notions, or in attacking sectarian 'spiritual' readings of the Bible. For Dryden metaphor and fable are to be strictly functional: there is to be nothing arcane, no swarms of inarticulate feelings, nothing left unexplained. Such a conscious, rationalising approach demands equally that the world mirror it: thus Dryden labours to make sense of the apparently random, and to make the seemingly arbitrary or 'supernatural' blows of fortune into deserved miseries within a scheme of cosmic justice; there is to be no 'enthusiasm' here. Lastly, he is concerned with the preservation of public morals, decency and refinement, and to this end reduces Chanticleer's sexual irregularities, removes much of the coarse detail and context of the original and elevates the style.

In Dryden's work we see fiction eroded by external fact. With Pope's we shall see fact almost wholly transformed into fiction.

6 Pope

The underlying theme and interest of much of Pope's poetry is proportion – moral, social and aesthetic. The *Essay on Criticism* is most frequently concerned with the proper harmony of parts of a poem and their
fit relation to the whole, whereby, as in 'some well-proportion'd Dome /
. . . No single Parts unequally surprize; / All comes *united* to th'admiring
Eyes' (247–50). The mock-heroic basis of *The Rape of the Lock* and *The
Dunciad* is the disproportion between the high terms used and the trivial
or vulgar reality. The insistence of the *Essay on Man* is on the need for
every being to keep to its proper station and bounds within the hierarchy
of being.

The source of this concern is most pervasively an attack on pride.
It is pride which for Pope biases critical judgment and distorts poems,
vanity which drives Belinda, ignorant egotism which makes the dunces
so self-important and active, and reasoning pride that makes man aspire
to knowledge and attributes not assigned to his rank in the scale of
creation. Pride is anathema because it challenges the settled order of
things, and puts the part, the individual, before the social, the traditional and the whole.

But the emphasis on proportion relates not only to proper size, but
also to harmonious relation among parts: not only the true dimensions
of individual particles, but also the way they slide into one another is
at issue. In the eighteenth century there was unprecedented emphasis
on the notion of 'continuity' within the great chain of being, whereby
any one creature was seen as shading into the next above or below it
rather than remaining sharply distinguished.[1] (The idea is a logical consequence of that doctrine of plenitude which states that God, being infinite, must have created a universe containing a hierarchy of being with
an infinity of links: for therefore the difference between any two con-
tiguous links must be infinitesimal. This deduction was increasingly made
both because of increased emphasis on that doctrine, and because of the
revelations of infinity which astronomic and microscopic investigation
had produced.)[2] The stress on politeness and grace of behaviour in the
Augustan period is at least a concomitant, and in Pope's poetry certainly

an expression, of this. In poetry we find a search for elegance, smoothness of transition, the melting of one item into another, which is a primary explanation for the high praise accorded Waller and Denham as reformers of English numbers.[3] In the *Essay on Man* Pope retains the notion of distinct species while emphasising continuity:

> 'Twixt that [instinct] and Reason, what a nice barrier;
> For ever sep'rate, yet for ever near!
> Remembrance and Reflection how ally'd;
> What thin partitions Sense from Thought divide:
> And Middle natures, how they long to join,
> Yet never pass th'insuperable line! (1, 223–8)

This is a metaphor for the structure and ethos of much of his poetry.

This concern with cosmic, social and aesthetic grace did not, however, spring from nothing with the Restoration: it was part of the fabric of the Renaissance humanist tradition, and can be seen in Sidney, Spenser, Jonson ('unpolished' to the Augustans) or Marvell; but with Pope it becomes central to the interest and effect of his work. Again, in much of his poetry (apart from the more discursive essays) Pope follows the 'builded' method of composition observable in Jonson's 'To Penshurst', laying couplets of meaning one upon another to a pinnacle of being or intensity, and sliding one section into the next. 'To Penshurst' is a poetic image of the great chain of being as Jonson saw it; but far more poems of Pope's can be seen in this way.

Pope also differs from Jonson in that his idealistic picture of the proportioned world is far less inclusive socially. For him the social correlative of a gracious universe is only one class, the aristocratic and polite, among whom alone are taste and elegance to be found. The more religious sense of grace, of that union between God and corruptible flesh in Christ which made disproportion a universal grace, or of that Christian charity which in Jonson's poem has 'all come in, the farmer, and the clown' receives only occasional mention in Pope's poetry. Even the upper classes offer few examples save his friends: Pope's proportioned world is narrow, and grows narrower as he writes. He can be more inclusive only from a theoretic or 'God's-eye' point of view: in the *Essay on Man* and the *Moral Essays* he argues that the disproportionate passions of men are part of a universal harmony not understood, and are necessary in a cosmic scheme where 'Whatever is, is RIGHT'; yet he is frequently disposed to slip away from this philosophic and deterministic view into a moral condemnation of all divergence from a norm.

'AN EPISTLE TO MISS BLOUNT: ON HER LEAVING THE TOWN, AFTER THE CORONATION' (1714)

This poem, which has been described as 'the finest poem Pope wrote before *'The Dunciad'*,[4] portrays the misfortunes of a girl forced to leave the delights of the town, but gradually and by almost imperceptible transitions brings in the poet in town to whom her absence is also a misery. The way in which the poet eventually identifies himself makes the poem a picture of mannered and polite courtship; but in its interwoven vertical structure it is also a universal analogy, a delicate social correlative of cosmic order. Disproportion is overcome: Teresa Blount's shrill laments are 'placed' and gently mocked; and the potentially disruptive and indecorous element in the poet's expression of his personal feeling is neutralised.

The method Pope uses in the poem might be described as one of by indirections finding directions out. The opening figure is oblique:

> As some fond virgin, whom her mother's care
> Drags from the town to wholsom country air,
> Just when she learns to roll a melting eye,
> And hear a spark, yet think no danger nigh;
> From the dear man unwilling she must sever,
> Yet takes one kiss before she parts for ever:
> Thus from the world fair *Zephalinda* flew,
> Saw others happy, and with sighs withdrew. . . .

The first function of this simile is to generalise Teresa Blount's condition: hers is no special loss, and she joins a whole army of regretful virgins. At the same time, by its complicity with what presumably is Miss Blount's shrill idiom here – 'Drags', 'dear man', 'sever' and the melodrama of 'for ever' – the simile suggests itself as Teresa's own, as her turning herself into a sentimental heroine, dramatising herself. This is perhaps reinforced by the fact that there is, if we except this aspect, hardly any gap between the comparison and what is compared – suggesting that she cannot see her plight in any but its own terms. For the reader, coming on this lack of distance in line 7, the effect is anti-climactic and politely deflationary, which is what Pope intends it to be, here and elsewhere in the poem. Then again, the way the point is dragged out finely enacts the girl's reluctance as she is being dragged to the country air in line 2, is back with her spark in lines 3 and 4, leaving him in line 5, back bidding him farewell in line 6, leaving again in line 7, and gradually withdrawing in lines 8 to 10. The simile has one further function: it enables Pope to mention himself under the guise of fiction, to smuggle himself into the poem – he being the 'spark' and the 'dear man' of the analogy. The transitions by which he effects an introduction of his actual self by the end of this poem are an image of social decorum.

In the next lines Pope is almost conspiratorially sympathetic with Teresa in the reiterated horror of

> She went, to plain-work, and to purling brooks,
> Old fashion'd halls, dull aunts, and croaking rooks,
> She went from Op'ra, park, assembly, play,
> To morning walks, and pray'rs three hours a day;
> To pass her time 'twixt reading and Bohea,
> To muse, and spill her solitary Tea,
> Or o'er cold coffee trifle with the spoon. . . .

The comic aspect of the privation, the loss of being, is finely caught in the way the aunts are collocated with halls and rooks. The third line skips rhythmically upwards through its list – mockingly, because there is no ascent in value – and the fourth, like a wounded snake, drags its slow length along. Verbs are neutralised into infinitives – 'To pass', 'To muse', '[to] trifle' – and the fact that in the fourth line the 'To' comes before a noun leads us to expect the same in the fifth and thus removes all life from the verb. The rhyme is repeated – 'play', 'day', 'Bohea', 'Tea' – adding to the sense of monotony; and its sound catches the note of over-pitched sorrow.

In the next lines the verbs change in mood, as anticipated by the omission of 'to' before 'trifle':

> Or o'er cold coffee trifle with the spoon,
> Count the slow clock, and dine exact at noon;
> Divert her eyes with pictures in the fire,
> Hum half a tune, tell stories to the squire;
> Up to her godly garret after sev'n,
> There starve and pray, for that's the way to heav'n.

By the third line here the mood is beginning to change to the imperative, and the 'her' seems slightly anomalous; and this change of mood is finalised in the last line, so that the next can go straight on to the second person pronoun: 'Some Squire, perhaps, you take delight to rack'. We have moved from Teresa Blount as the generalised 'fond virgin' of the first line of the poem, through her as the personalised but still remote Zephalinda of the seventh and as 'she' thereafter, until the she becomes 'you' and the poem begins to turn from narration to conversation. At the same time the tense has moved from continuing present to past, and through the transforming imperative mood to a localised present – and this first a frequent (the portrait of the squire) and then a more local present ('In some fair evening', 'So when your slave, at some dear, idle time'). It is a fine enactment of decorous wooing and polite, even self-depreciating approach, to which of course the squire's methods are a pointed contrast:

> Some Squire, perhaps, you take delight to rack;
> Whose game is Whisk, whose treat a toast in sack,
> Who visits with a gun, presents you birds,
> Then gives a smacking buss, and cries – No words!
> Or with his hound comes hollowing from the stable,
> Makes love with nods, and knees beneath a table;
> Whose laughs are hearty, tho' his jests are coarse,
> And loves you best of all things – but his horse.

What characterises this anticipation of Fielding's Western is his complete commitment to the physical – love to him is word made flesh: for words themselves, for any kind of linguistic delay, he has 'No words!'; not surprisingly he prefers his horse, and for the reverse of Gulliver's reasons. And this kind of crude physical jostling, this indecorous violence, runs precisely counter to the method of the poem.

The conversational 'you' of these lines has been slightly muted by the presence of a third person, but now Pope speaks to Teresa on her own:

> In some fair evening, on your elbow laid,
> You dream of triumphs in the rural shade;
> In pensive thought recall the fancy'd scene. . . .

The tautology of 'pensive thought' here nicely catches the redundancy of thoughts continually circling about themselves. 'Recall the fancy'd scene' suggests both the return to a mental picture oft enjoyed, and that the scene means so much to her that it is recalled as the memory of an actual occurrence.

> Before you pass th'imaginary sights
> Of Lords, and Earls, and Dukes, and garter'd Knights;
> While the spread Fan o'ershades your closing eyes;
> Then give one flirt, and all the vision flies.
> Thus vanish sceptres, coronets, and balls,
> And leave you in lone woods, or empty walls.

The 'imaginary sights' of the first line here would seem to substantiate what we noted about her recall of 'fancy'd scene[s]', and at the same time exposes it. The titles of the second line seem to prance in confusion. The slow syllables of the third line, and the pauses necessary to pronounce them (consider the phonetic transitions 'spread Fan o'ershades') give the sense of stretching langour, and in the next line the change of verb mood, the caesura, the alliteration on 'fl' and the terse syllables carry out the sense. The next line suggests more than gentle mockery: there is the smallest hint of a moral point, a *sic transit gloria* referring not only to the productions of the fancy; but we are returned to this point in the next doleful line.

Now the poet, the lover, Pope – call him what we will – comes forward rather more. He has been a 'spark' in a simile at first, and then has passed through the status of plain recorder, sympathiser, gentle mocker and perhaps moral tutor, to the point where he has begun a conversation with Teresa; but he has not yet taken a part in the local drama. Now he introduces himself: 'So when your slave' – the gentle mockery of that shrill 'slave' is fine –

> So when your slave, at some dear, idle time,
> (Not plagu'd with headachs, or the want of rhime)
> Stands in the streets, abstracted from the crew,
> And while he seems to study, thinks of you. . . .

The time would be 'dear' (compare 'the dear man' of line 5), but its dearness is undercut by the fact that it would also be idle, a spare moment in between the debilitating activities of having a headache or trying to devise a poem. He is not quite saying that like the squire he loves her less than these things, but he is suggesting that they have the force to drive her image out of his head – even though it is done to him (he is 'plagu'd'), it is still something that takes place. She is complimented in his regarding his fellows as 'the crew' when he thinks of her, and yet slightly taken down by the fact that this abstraction seems to others like his thinking of the next poem – or that her reality is in a way lost behind this appearance.

> Just when his fancy points your sprightly eyes,
> Or sees the blush of fair *Parthenia* rise,
> *Gay* pats my shoulder, and you vanish quite;
> Streets, chairs, and coxcombs rush upon my sight.

Now the speaker has entered in the first person; the slight surprise at the change in the third line also effects what other poetic methods had to perform in the parallel 'Then give one flirt, and all the vision flies' of line 38. There is irony in the fact that he also is fancying her, as she fancied 'Coronations . . . on ev'ry green': he is not recalling her as she is, by memory, but as an ideal; so that as 'fair *Parthenia*' she is both praised and mocked. Yet what dismisses the fancy in his case – Gay patting his shoulder – would have dismissed any thoughts of her on which he was engaged: suggesting certainly that he would not be so ready as she to dismiss the images of fancy by himself, but needs an external interruption; and that the interruption has to be more of an intrusion because it takes more to dislodge his thoughts – she, that is, is dilettante, where he is 'taking a breather'.

The main difference, of course, is that she does not think of him but of coronations and titles, while he thinks of her alone: and this gives a last turn of the screw. If we say that the account of Teresa's doings in exile is an objective one, then one can only refer this to a (however gently-implied) selfishness and ambition, like Belinda's in *The Rape of the Lock*. If, on the other hand – and this perhaps is when the simile which starts the poem has one more suggestion to make – we consider the entire description of her life in the country as one fancied for her by the speaker, then the absence of any thoughts about him would be the kind of decorous self-depreciation which we have seen running throughout the poem: in which the whole poem then becomes a fancy of a fancy. The first possibility, that the speaker in the town has only limited purview, might seem to be suggested in the last lines:

> Vext to be still in town, I knit my brow,
> Look sow'r, and hum a tune – as you may now.

He is seen, back in a specific place, speculating, as one ignorant of her rustic life as described in the first part of the poem, on what she may be doing. Yet still it is 'as you may *now* (and the tense has now finally come to a *point* in the present) – that is, 'as you may at this particular instant': nothing in the poem has claimed knowledge of her exactly contemporary activities, and therefore the uncertainty is justifiable even if all that has preceded is fancy, and if there is no difference of knowledge between the speaker of the last part and of the first. That the poem may be a fancy 'squared' is further reinforced by the transitions of the poem, whereby the speaker in the last part has been led up to by shifting verbs and pronouns throughout in such a way that he cannot be seen as a different person from the one who has described Teresa.

And as he has gradually approached her, until he reveals himself and speaks directly, so the poem ends on a note that points to a *possible* togetherness, the products of such a delicately-managed courtship – 'as you *may* now'. She may, as he is, be knitting her brow and humming at the interruption of her thoughts; she may not. This frail, half-hopeful, half-mockingly doubtful note of reciprocity, with himself and Teresa perhaps sharing the moment, but lacking one another's company, is the limited poise which the speaker has been guaranteed by the poem.

THE 'MORAL ESSAYS' (1731–5)

Pope's *Moral Essays* are, like *Paradise Lost*, an example of how conscious and unconscious aims are becoming divorced in poetry at this time, like 'judgment' and 'fancy'. In large part it is Pope's 'fancy' that gives the poem a consistency and imaginative force which any narrow conformity to a deliberate theme, or 'judgment', would have denied it. Yet Pope, like Milton, and many eighteenth-century writers, must make his meaning plain, must labour to be *utile* as well as *dulce*, instead of letting the creative imagination produce its own truths without interference. This gap between creative or imaginative response to material, and reflection upon it, is seen in nearly all the poetry of the eighteenth century.[5] Pope, however, is a great enough poet for it not finally to affect the power of his poem.

In their stated intention the four Epistles making up the *Moral Essays* are an attempt at a reconciliation of the ideal and the actual. Pope is proposing to show, along the lines of the Mandeville–Shaftesbury argument expounded in the *Essay on Man*, that the ruling passions of men, directed along whatever paths of virtue or vice, are ultimately converted by a benign providential scheme to social profit. However, his vision of man's behaviour cannot long sustain such a deterministic and optimistic view, especially in a poem concerned not with theory but with particular human examples. From the evidence of Pope's poetry it is clear that for him the corruption of society and the decay of values and coherence in the world had proceeded to a point where they must work against any *laisser-faire*, optimistic doctrine. Most of Pope's satire operates from negative examples, because negations are for Pope taking over the world: for example, where for Jonson there was still something approaching an ideal in Penshurst, for Pope the only 'objective correlative' is an anti-value, Timon's villa.[6] The result is that optimism becomes only intermittent, and determinism often disappears for a more voluntaristic, condemnatory attitude to human characters and actions. And the ideal and the actual are thus *not* reconciled: the vision is the darker one of values being overthrown by a world to which they stand in stark opposition.

The elaborate thematic prolegomenon in Epistle i, *To Cobham*, concerning the ruling passion in man, acknowledges that which the generalities of the *Essay on Man* did not mention – namely, that this passion is hard to trace. After a lengthy account of how manners, humours, tenets, principles, actions or passions and nature itself are all various or inconsistent in any man (1–173), Pope bids us (in just six lines) to search out the ruling passion as the solution, the point where alone 'The Wild are Constant and the Cunning known; / The Fool consistent

and the False sincere; / Priests, Princes, Women, no dissemblers here'
(175– 7). While we have been in suspense for the answer during all the
preceding negatives and reticences, their sheer weight forces on us the
sense that Pope is finally both baffled and fascinated by man's unclassifiable and inconsistent individuality, and that, however on the level of
conscious thought and judgment he may try to capture the creature, he
is bound on that level to fail – as, not merely rhetorically, he himself
here frequently admits, where he speaks of haste and personal bias
clouding judgment (23–34), or simply acknowledges that 'God and Nature
only are the same: / In Man, the judgment shoots at flying game'
(154–5). And we may also suppose that a man of Pope's intelligence
could not have been wholly content with a theory of human character
and action which was so nearly deterministic, allowing no final separation of reason or choice from the dictates of nature.[7]

In reading the *Moral Essays* we find the theory only intermittently
useful. Pope himself admits its limited applicability to women: it is part
of the strength of Epistle II, *To a Lady*, that the portraits bear out his
confession that 'believe me, good as well as ill, / Woman's at best a
Contradiction still' (269–70). In Epistle III, *To Bathurst*, on wealth,
we are as much concerned with the object of the ruling passion, money,
as the passion itself, indeed to such a degree that money takes on the
character of a force which preys on man; and, when the passion is considered, it is treated not so much for itself as for the portrayal, in the
miser and the spendthrift, of how 'Extremes in Nature equal good produce, / Extremes in man concur to gen'ral use' (163–4). Epistle IV, *To
Burlington*, is not at all about the idea of the ruling passion: Timon's
futile prodigality is taken for granted while his tastelessness is analysed.

But these four Epistles have an underlying unity, one of vision rather
than statement, which can be traced in every portrait. An extended instance of this is the tale of Sir Balaam in Epistle III. The opening lines
of this portrait –

> Where London's column, pointing at the skies,
> Like a tall bully, lifts the head, and lyes;
> There dwelt a Citizen of sober fame,
> A plain good man, and Balaam was his name.   (339–42)

– suggest at once Balaam's present modesty of circumstance, and, in
his proximity to the column, the blasphemous (disproportionate) pride
that is to come (and perhaps a hint of what is to come of that, in the
overtones of Babel); and the one undercuts the other. That Balaam is
the name of this 'plain good man' (the phrase likens him to the puddings
he eats) points to the 'moral vacuity', as T. R. Edwards puts it,[8] which
is at the centre of his soul. In his natural state Balaam is 'religious,

punctual, frugal and so forth': he reduces different levels of value to one plane, and the 'and so forth' also shows how he espouses these virtues not for themselves but for their social and material use. By his careful and politic management of his outward appearance, by proportioning himself to the standards of worth of his community, he is able to live in disproportion to his spiritual means: 'His word would pass for more than he was worth'; the usurious implications here are evident. He measures what should be spiritual value by material criteria: 'One solid dish his week-day meal affords, / An added pudding solemniz'd the Lord's.' Balaam is a type of the Puritan who sees worldly success so much as a testimony of election that he forgets God and concern with grace for simple capitalist self-advancement. He is 'Constant at Church, and Change' – the alliteration shows the equation of sacred and secular in Balaam's mind; and the size of his spiritual residue is measured in his charity: 'his gains were sure, / His givings rare, save farthings to the poor.'

The Devil, we are told, longed to tempt Balaam like Job, 'But Satan now is wiser than of yore, / And tempts by making rich, not making poor.' By his agency, Balaam becomes the beneficiary of 'two rich ship-wrecks' in Cornwall. Now he 'lives like other folks, / . . . takes his chirping pint, and cracks his jokes.' However, though he now drinks, he has not yet lost control: his wife tells him to 'Live like yourself', and he now lives his life to its capacity, no longer self-denying; and still there is rule, for now, instead of one, 'lo! two puddings smoak'd upon the board' (a sinister extension of the two shipwrecks which blessed the lucky shore).

The next stage in Balaam's corruption is plain swindling. He *did* nothing to profit from the wrecks, though he wished them, but now he is fence for a thief, whom he cheats. At first sight the passage des-cribing this seems completely detached from the preceding account of Balaam and the two puddings: it opens vaguely, with indefinite articles, suspended verb and a curious lyricism – 'Asleep and naked as an Indian lay, / An honest factor stole a Gem away'; here the sense of Balaam losing control even where he gains power is hinted. Still his conscience pains him, and he thinks that he can buy its silence, thinks that the spiritual may be quantified by the material:

> 'I'll now give six-pence where I gave a groat,
> Where once I went to church, I'll now go twice –
> And am so clear too of all other vice.'

The last line is yet another financial metaphor. Where number was pre-viously a sign of something done (one or two puddings), it is now used to try to stop something being done.

Not surprisingly, therefore, 'The Tempter saw his time'. He now knocks Balaam off his tiptoed feet with a profusion of wealth: 'Stocks and Subscriptions pour on ev'ry side, / 'Till all the Dæmon makes his full descent, / In one abundant show'r of Cent. per Cent.' Like the sea into which he descended and sank deep, so he descends and sinks deep into Balaam, 'dubs' him 'Director' (the modern knighthood) and possesses his soul entirely.

The rest, with Balaam now out of his cautious element, living beyond himself, is predictable. God disappears from his mind even as having contributed to his success, and he covers the fact with empty generalisation: 'Things change their titles, as our manners turn'. He spends Sunday in his counting house, not in church, to which, like things, he 'duly' sends his family and wife. His wife dying ('one Christmas-tide' – only Puritan nomenclature remains to Balaam),[9] even that last empty religious link is snapped. He is sucked into the vortex of the court, assumes its gibberish ('Nymph of Quality', 'dull Cits',[10] 'the fair'); sees his family ruined, and his new wife sunk in gambling debts; takes a bribe to save the last, is found out, sentenced, stripped of his wealth and hanged. The whole of the last section of the portrait moves at a violent jerky pace, mirroring the fact that Balaam is now totally out of control:

> He marries, bows at Court, and grows polite:
> Leaves the dull Cits and joins . . .
> My Lady falls to play; so bad her chance,
> He must repair it; takes a bribe from France;
> The House impeach him; Coningsby harangues;
> The Court forsake him, and Sir Balaam hangs.

At the last Balaam returns to God, not now to thank him for prospering his success, but to curse him for, as he sees it, engineering his defeat.

Clearly, this passage is *about* proportion: it says that the kind of empty proportion by which Balaam governs his life is fundamentally unstable, capable at any time of being knocked out of itself into destructive disproportion. We learn from the portrait that, to put it aesthetically, without content, form is weak; that without true faith and charity godliness is nothing. And it is in the portrayal of a range of types of proportion and disproportion that the local strength and overall unity of the *Moral Essays* lies. Individual pictures may subscribe to the ostensible themes of the ruling passion or of tastelessness, but their force comes through this basic dialectic.

In Epistle iv, *To Burlington*, the theme is the uselessness of art which does not marry itself to nature: Timon's villa crushes nature with art, and the result is aesthetic and moral sterility. But the theme is adumbrated through the idea of proportion. In contrast to the pompous buildings which in Rome 'were things of use', the modern designer will be found all too often to 'Load some vain Church with old Theatric state, / Turn Arcs of triumph to a Garden-gate' (29–30): here meanness is forced into grandeur and grandeur into the mean. Pope bids the designer, as the *Essay on Criticism* did the critic, to 'Consult the Genius of the Place in all' (57), and encapsulates his aesthetic norm in 'Parts answ'ring parts shall slide into a whole' (66). Timon's villa is so vast that 'his building is a Town, / His pond an Ocean, his parterre a Down' (105–6), while its master is 'A puny insect' (here all the force of the tradition of the house matched to its owner, as in Marvell's poetry, is evident). Seen plainly, all this is 'huge heaps of littleness'. Everything is done out of proportion with nature, and the result is that nature has its revenges in the 'keenness of the Northern wind', which the destruction of the trees has admitted. The dominance of art has meant that that which sets out to appear limitless defines itself by limits, 'On ev'ry side you look, behold the Wall!' (114). The notion of proportion which governs the scene is entirely formal; there is no softening for the order, no boldness to enliven its regularity: 'Grove nods at grove, each Alley has a brother, / And half the platform just reflects the other' (117–18). What the suffering eye sees is inverted nature, nature out of joint with itself in a kind of *topos* of 'upside-down':[11]

> Trees cut to Statues, Statues thick as trees,
> With here a Fountain, never to be play'd,
> And there a Summer-house, that knows no shade;
> Here Amphitrite sails thro' myrtle bow'rs;
> There Gladiators fight, or die, in flow'rs;
> Un-water'd see the drooping sea-horse mourn,
> And swallows roost in Nilus' dusty Urn. (120–6)

We move into the study, where form, as with Sir Balaam, exists at the expense of content, for Timon cares only for the outside appearance of his books. From thence we pass to the chapel, and 'all the Pride of Pray'r', where the music, 'broken and uneven, / Make[s] the soul dance upon a Jig to Heaven'; where the paintings on the ceilings are discordantly secular, and the 'soft Dean' (identified with the 'Cushion' which precedes him) 'never mentions Hell to ears polite'. We end in the enormous marble dining chamber, where the meal is 'A solemn Sacrifice, perform'd in state, / You drink by measure, and to minutes eat'; and so quickly is each course changed that one sits 'In plenty starving, tantaliz'd in state'. What Timon offers is dead art, grown monstrous at the expense of nature, and regularity without grace to make it live. 'Sick

of his civil Pride', Pope turns to offer a country-house and landscape-
garden ideal in which use and plenty, ornament and practicality, nature
and civility, are properly married (173–204).

In Epistle ɪ, the picture of Wharton is concerned with the disproportion that loses a sense of distinction (a similar point is at the root
of the picture of Flavia in Epistle ɪɪ, 95–100). Wharton's lust for praise
led him to seek it in any context:

> Women and Fools must like him as he dies;
> Tho' wond'ring Senates hung on all he spoke,
> The Club must hail him master of the joke. . . .
> Enough if all around him but admire,
> And now the Punk applaud, and now the Fryer.   (183–5, 190–1)

Wharton is indiscriminate, lacking all sense of a scale of value, and Pope,
as with Sir Balaam, points out the central instability which has caused
this: 'And wanting nothing but an honest heart'. The result of Wharton's
insatiability is disproportionately mean return:

> His Passion still, to covet gen'ral praise,
> His Life, to forfeit it a thousand ways;
> A constant Bounty which no friend has made;
> An angel Tongue, which no man can persuade;
> A Fool, with more of Wit than half mankind,
> Too quick for Thought, for Action too refin'd.   (196–201)

We are reminded again, as with Sir Balaam, of the biblical 'he that findeth
his life, shall lose it': input and return are as utterly disjoined as everything and nothing.

At the end of this Epistle, when the subject changes from the discovery of the ruling passion beneath 'puzzling Contraries' to the per-
sistence of the passion, which 'sticks to our last sand', the portraits are
all founded on disproportion: the lecherous old man still crawling 'to
his wench . . . on knocking knees'; the glutton Helluo, who, though his
greed has brought him to his death-bed, eats on; 'the frugal Crone' who
tries to save a candle-end with her last breath; the dying lady of fashion,
Narcissa, who asks her maid to dress her *à la mode* and rouge her
cheeks, for 'One would not, sure, be frightful when one's dead' (surely
one of the most grimly ironic lines in literature); the 'Courtier smooth'
whose last words are 'If – where I'm going – I could serve you, Sir?';
the miser Euclio, who to the last refuses to part with his treasures in
his will – and then, in dying, does so – ' "Not that, – I cannot part with
that" – and dy'd.' The last portrait, of Cobham himself, whose 'ruling

passion strong in death' will make his last words, 'Oh, save my Country, Heav'n!', does, of course, exemplify proportion: death is used here as a measure of life, and in this balance few objects of the ruling passion save those of a heroic and self-denying order have weight.

The reader may explore for himself in detail the motif of disproportion underlying Epistles II and III: perhaps the central contrast in the former, apart from that between the beautiful appearance of women and the coarse reality (21–8, 83–6, 181–98), is that between Atossa, who has too much love of life, and those who have too little, like Chloe, who 'speaks, behaves, and acts just as she ought; / But never, never, reach'd one gen'rous thought' (161–2). Epistle III is concerned with the disproportion between, on the one hand, the power and material equivalent of money, and, on the other, its weight and size (particularly now that it is paper credit);[12] throughout the poem Pope also proposes a well-proportioned *attitude* to wealth and its use. He surveys the different types of disproportionate attitude in the miser and the spendthrift before putting forward a temperate norm between the extremes 'Of mad Good-nature, and of mean Self-love' (228). Yet the portrait of the Man of Ross which follows offers no tepid middle path, but shows how a proper relation to nature can produce a disproportionate return on investment: the picture is of one whose temperance enables him to encompass both the miser and the spendthrift:

> Who hung with woods yon mountain's sultry brow?
> From the dry rock who bade the waters flow?
> Not to the skies in useless columns tost,
> Or in proud falls magnificently lost,
> But clear and artless, pouring thro' the plain,
> Health to the sick, and solace to the swain.   (253–8)

The Man of Ross has no part either in empty eminence or in magnificent collapse: his stream runs level, over the plain, and it imparts bounty willingly, just as at a more involuntary level nature defeats the desires of the misers by pouring their wealth abroad (again the water image is used) on their deaths (173–8). He is a type of Christ – 'Behold the Market-place with poor o'erspread! / The MAN of ROSS divides the weekly bread' (263–4) – and it may well be that the parable of the loaves and fishes came to Pope's mind here and prompted the amazed question and still more amazed answer,

> 'Oh say, what sums that gen'rous hand supply?
> What mines, to swell that boundless charity?'
>   Of Debts, and Taxes, Wife and Children clear,
> This man possest – five hundred pounds a year.   (277–80)

Bathetic perhaps, but there is real point behind it. The disproportion here is the Christian one that whoever gives shall find his gift multiplied. Equally, it is that in giving up our lives for others we shall gain them: the Man of Ross needs no pompous monuments, for he lives on in the grateful memory of the environment and the society to which he has devoted himself. We recall here the essential isolation, whether in ruin or death, of all the figures satirised in these portraits: they go alone and are instantly forgotten, like Villiers in his fall, cast on his coarse bed in 'the worst inn's worst room':

> No Wit to flatter, left of all his store!
> No Fool to laugh at, which he valu'd more.
> There, Victor of his health, of fortune, friends,
> And fame; this lord of useless thousands ends.   (311–14)

'Spirit, taste and sense' (*Epistle to Dr Arbuthnot*, 160) are the three principles on which Pope's notion of true proportion is founded. Spirit, which comes from nature, gives life; taste turns that spirit into grace; and sense weds the whole back to the lineaments of nature. Proportion, to put it in Renaissance terms, is fused with disproportion in a *concordia discors*; or, in another phrase, the *dulce* with the *utile*. In the *Moral Essays* we have seen how Pope constructs such a picture in the round, through an entire spectrum of negative examples.

What, incidentally, may lie behind the order of the four Epistles as we have them is a principle similar to that which partly governs the organisation of Spenser's *Faerie Queene* – a movement from the individual to the social. We begin with follies which affect only their owners, and move outwards – first to personal relationships (Epistle II); then to the effect, in the form of wealth, of a monomania on a wider society and on nature; and lastly, with Timon, to a form not only of artistic corruption, but of blasphemy, in as much as his villa is in many ways a perverted church. The sense of evil deepens in Epistles III and IV, as we move from greed to pride; the humanity and sympathy that are present in some of Pope's portraits in Epistles I and II are not so evident later (except, perhaps, in Villiers), where the moral lineaments of the characters are much more exclusively the central interest. This gradual widening of reference and deepening of intensity is not unlike the strategy of *An Epistle to Dr Arbuthnot*.

'AN EPISTLE TO DR ARBUTHNOT' (1735)

This poem (written 1731–4) is one of several self-justifying satires Pope wrote at this time (1731–8). It is radically different from the *Moral Essays* and *The Dunciad* in that it does not assume the values against which the vicious are to be exposed, so much as show and justify their growth; the method is here, at least in intention, *a posteriori* rather than *a priori*. It is, in a sense, Pope's *Prelude*: and it has an orientation towards private and personal springs of value that shows how Pope's 'public' certainties could narrow even beyond those of the *Moral Essays*, at a time when he was losing faith in an external social or political order which could match the values asked by his poetry. In the end, all that remain are the certainties of friendship; of familial ties; of a life founded on retirement into a world arranged as desired, in the form of a house and garden;[13] and of poetry, in which, if only in art, evil is successfully fought or circumscribed and proportion is expressed in the lineaments of finely-wrought verse. Nevertheless, this poem has a special place here, because Pope is, as it were, giving his idealism a basis in reality, arguing that his self-enclosure was not a function of native arrogance but a product of the world itself. To the extent that his justification is a convincing one, he will be able to show that his position has been earned; or, to put it another way, that he has shown the ideal developing out of the actual. Yet this must remain an exercise.

The *Epistle to Dr Arbuthnot* thus presents a different aspect of the theme of proportion which we have seen elsewhere in Pope's poetry: in this poem Pope is trying to demonstrate how the growth of his role as a satirist, an attacker of the vices of mankind, is to be explained not as the consequence of any indecorous personal animus or pride, but as the natural development of a strong antipathy of good to bad. He has to show how he became a poet in the first place; how he became a satiric poet; and how the objects of his satire widened. And he must manage the transitions so that they do not appear abrupt or violent. The technique, then, will be that of the 'Epistle to Miss Blount', and the object will be a similar depersonalisation or self-effacement; but, while there this was done to show manners, here the purpose will be to show both manners and morals.[14]

Here Pope is with us in the first person from the outset. He is besieged by scribblers and hack poets all demanding his intercession on their behalf. The first half of the poem is written in a dramatic idiom and the 'I' is as much a character as the rest: the dangers of personal animus are thereby largely removed. Further, the 'I' in the first half of the poem is conspicuous for his lack of angry passion: his judgment is reasoned and just at all times.

> Seiz'd and ty'd down to judge, how wretched I!
> Who can't be silent, and who will not lye;
> To laugh, were want of Goodness and of Grace,
> And to be grave, exceeds all Pow'r of Face.
> I sit with sad Civility. . . .   (33–7)

Yet he is also comically desperate – we have to see the spectacle of a bard almost strangled with the clamour of a mob of would-be Parnassians, and we laugh. It may not be very pleasant for the bard himself but we must find it so. These two facts – the self-control of the poet and his half-humorous predicament – further remove personal rage on Pope's part from the scene. But we are still not certain what the purpose is behind it all. We only begin to see when we look at some of the moral points being made. In the first part, Pope is exposing not only folly but also vice. The scribblers represent a kind of profanity:

> No place is sacred, not the Church is free,
> Ev'n *Sunday* shines no *Sabbath-day* to me.   (11–12)

Their flattery is seen as gross hypocrisy:

> If Foes, they write, if Friends, they read me dead.   (32)

> *Pitholeon* libell'd me – 'but here's a Letter
> Informs you Sir, 'twas when he knew no better.'   (51–2)

Their self-seeking vanity makes them stoop to any vice: Pope tells one that the price he wants from the bookseller Lintot for his manuscript is too much, but the other replies,

> 'Not Sir, if you revise it, and retouch.'
> All my demurrs but double his attacks,
> At last he whispers 'Do, and we go snacks.'
> Glad of a quarrel, strait I clap the door,
> Sir, let me see your works and you no more.   (64–8)

In fact, the poem is highly moral in purpose, like all Pope's major work – highly moral because it deepens its attacks as it continues. There are several stages of development. The first is the theme of privacy, which opens the poem. The poet is hunted down by legions of hacks – they invade his home, his dinner-hour, his garden; and this assault becomes blasphemy with their solicitations in church and on Sundays (11–12). But it is not simply the poet's environment the privacy of which they destroy: they try to invade the privacy of his personality. In their egotism they visualise Pope entirely as they want him to be; they bring their works to him to judge, and, if he is unfavourable, they render their asking a judgment futile by falling into a fury. They expect the poet to minister to their desires: they see him as someone to be used, the rubber stamp of their own wishes. Pope retains his critical faculties despite all; however, he is soon to explore his own position and responsibilities. More immediately, his responsibility rests in showing up all those who swarm around him for the fools they are, revealing 'That Secret to each Fool, that he's an Ass' (80). Pope denies that this is cruel, since all asses remain unaltered by criticism; so what, we have to ask, is the sense in attacking them? How, in any real sense, can Pope be bringing the asses to a full realisation of their foolishness if he is bound to fail to change them? As yet the answer – that the attacks on these dunces are written not for their improvement but to hold them up as *exempla* to all men – is latent. Meanwhile Pope rounds off his statement of the unalterable folly of the hacks by saying they are far less danger- ous when they are enraged by his attacks than when they 'repent'. We know what Pope means by 'repent': he has recently told us that it is impossible to correct a fool, that a fool never repents; so that by 'repent' here he clearly means become a 'false friend', a flatterer. The line 'It is the Slaver kills, and not the Bite' (106) is anticipatory of the portrait of Sporus's kind, 'mumbling of the Game they dare not bite'. Lines 109–124 exemplify the theme of flattery, which is to engage Pope's severest attack in the rest of the poem.

Having sounded this theme, Pope now turns to examine his status as a poet and as a judge. He has to dissociate himself from all the qualities of those he attacks. He explains the origin of his poetic impulse as entirely disinterested: 'I lisp'd in Numbers, for the Numbers came' (128). Further, he hurt the wishes of nobody by becoming a poet: 'I left no Calling for this idle trade, / No Duty broke, no Father dis-obey'd' (129–30; contrast 17). If Pope were saying here that his status as a poet is more virtuous than that of others merely because to become a poet he contravened nobody's wishes, while others did, then this is rather disingenuous: how, we might ask, would he have behaved if, say, his father had had other plans for him? It would seem scarcely fair to build virtue on others' failures. But Pope is making quite a differ- ent point in these lines: he is giving another touch to his disinterested- ness. He is saying that, since what one is is defined largely by what one gives up or rejects, in not rejecting anything in order that he might write poetry he cannot be labelled simply as a poet; in a sense he is fundamentally uncommitted. His becoming a poet is the adoption neither of a profession nor of a conscious role. It is another angle on the theme of privacy: since Pope's being a poet had nothing to do with society – that is, he came into conflict with no one else's desires, nor did he desire acclaim or reward from others – he cannot be 'typed'. It is thus natural for Pope to see poetry in terms of a therapy (131–2).

It is not at all inconsistent with this to publish, always accepting Pope's disinterested attitude: further, he decided to publish, not because he himself knew he was good but because the judgments of others assured him (135 ff.) – the poet is incapable of that self-confidence which implies self-consciousness and the playing of a role. What kind of poetry was he writing, at first, when he was so commendable?

> . . . who could take offence
> While pure Description held the place of Sense?   (147–8)

Again, there is no role, even inside the verse: the poet, in his unmotivated state, has not ascended the platform of moral teaching. In this condition of excellence, no responsibility whatever could be attached to him for the outbursts against him by others – Pope is generous enough, and consistent enough with the texture of the poem at this point, to see his outraged innocence in continued comic light:

> Yet then did *Gildon* draw his venal quill;
> I wish'd the man a dinner, and sate still:
> Yet then did *Dennis* rave in furious fret;
> I never answer'd, I was not in debt:
> If want provok'd, or madness made them print,
> I wag'd no war with *Bedlam* or the *Mint*.
>   Did some more sober Critic come abroad?
> If wrong, I smil'd; if right, I kiss'd the rod. . . .   (151–8)

The poet is still comically detached. The lines that follow are an attack on critics. Here the two tenses Pope is using are significant. Lines 159–72 represent his present attitude, but 157–8 represent the far less committed, less explicitly judging attitude of his early days. Lines 173–4 are again a past attitude, but we are nearer now to the present – the poet has begun to judge and attack in his poetry: 'Well might they rage; I gave them but their due' (174). Lines 175–89 represent his present ratification and elaboration of past assaults. This juxtaposition of past and present has two functions: first, it generalises the poet's judgments – what was true is true because those attacked are permanent types; secondly, it gives fluency to the transition from the poet innocently warbling his lays to the poet with the satiric axe in his hand. The gap is finally closed in lines 189–90:

> All these, my modest Satire bad *translate*,
> And own'd, that nine such Poets made a *Tate*.[15]

Past and present are now a continuum – the poet's development into a satiric method is fully rounded. The transition has been accomplished without our questioning just how far Pope's motives in changing were based on personal feeling or on outraged moral sense or on both – or on neither, since the attack so far has not been so much moral in tone as aesthetic ('all they want is spirit, taste, and sense' – 160).

In the portrait of 'One' (Addison), Pope further helps us to accept the transition from idyllic poet to satirist:

> were there One whose fires
> True Genius Kindles, and fair Fame inspires,
> Blest with each Talent and each Art to please,
> And born to write, converse, and live with ease:
> Shou'd such a man, too fond to rule alone,
> Bear, like the Turk, no brother near the throne,
> View him with scornful, yet with jealous eyes,
> And hate for Arts that caus'd himself to rise;
> Damn with faint praise, assent with civil leer,
> And without sneering, teach the rest to sneer;
> Willing to wound, and yet afraid to strike,
> Just hint a fault, and hesitate dislike;
> Alike reserv'd to blame, or to commend,
> A tim'rous foe, and a suspicious friend,
> Dreading ev'n fools, by Flatterers besieg'd,
> And so obliging that he ne'er oblig'd;
> Like *Cato*, give his little Senate laws,
> And sit attentive to his own applause;
> While Wits and Templers ev'ry sentence raise,
> And wonder with a foolish face of praise.
> Who but must laugh, if such a man there be?
> Who would not weep, if *Atticus* were he!   (193–214)

Addison did not judge the artistic works of others, but this was because he was an interested party: if he told hacks that their works were bad they would cease to worship and applaud him. Here of course, the theme of flattery is continued. Addison, like Osmond in Henry James's *The Portrait of a Lady*, rejects all others and yet at the same time needs them to minister to his own egotism – with the difference that what in Osmond is the paradox of situation is in Addison inner conflict. But the main point here is that Addison's refusal to judge others explicitly, to commit himself, is in direct contrast with Pope's openness of judgment. Addison, in doing something that might seem good to others, does so from motives of the worst self-interest; while Pope performs an objectionable activity from a position of complete disinterestedness, for the sake of truth. The portrait of Addison renders fully explicit Pope's own position by contrast: we are drawn into the contrast by the initial similarity between Addison and Pope – both are 'Blest with each Talent and each Art to please, / And born to write, converse, and live with ease'. But Addison, though a fine poet and artist, is morally corrupted. We are at a stage in the poem where the attack on bad taste and poverty of talent has shifted to a moral attack – the transition from aesthetic to ethical judgment hangs poised before us. Addison has defiled his talent in so far as he uses it to feed his pride.

Yet in so far as this portrait is internalised, in so far as we fully comprehend the motives that drive Addison, can sense the comic inner conflict of 'Willing to wound, and yet afraid to strike', so far can we see that the moral attack on him is not so intense as that on Sporus will be: Addison is at the mercy of his vice, pride; but we are to see Sporus as deliberately assenting to, allying himself with, his own evil. Here again the idea of commitment comes up: Pope, because he judges honestly and impartially, is in the most real way detached and uncommitted; Addison, because overruled by his vice, is more committed, yet rather controlled; but Sporus, because he has no inner conflict, is not intense but deliberate, is exactly at the opposite pole from Pope, absolutely committed to the world, the flesh – and the Devil. The structure of this poem is very carefully planned on the basis of a deepening intensity of attack which runs parallel to a deepening revelation of evil. In this way Pope can ensure that his strictures will not appear mere personal rancour. From his portrait of Addison Pope goes on to contrast his own position (215–30). Although his name is to be heard and seen a great deal, although he is entirely publicised, this does not mean he wishes the applause and flattery of the world of literature – in fact he rejects the swarms of hacks and the whole world of poetry (considered as a business). He leaves these poets to the great patrons – or rather, he leaves these poets (full stop).

For the portrait of Bufo which follows is the portrait of a degenerate. Pope gives a two-pronged attack – one on Bufo himself and one on those who flatter him; the implication being that the only way to gratify literary hacks is to be corrupt.

> Proud, as *Apollo* on his forked hill,
> Sate full-blown Bufo, puff'd by ev'ry quill;
> Fed with soft Dedication all day long,
> *Horace* and he went hand in hand in song.
> His Library, (where Busts of Poets dead
> And a true *Pindar* stood without a head)
> Receiv'd of Wits an undistinguish'd race,
> Who first his Judgment ask'd, and then a Place:
> Much they extoll'd his Pictures, much his Seat,
> And flatter'd ev'ry day, and some days eat:
> Till grown more frugal in his riper days,
> He paid some Bards with Port, and some with Praise,
> To some a dry Rehearsal was assign'd,
> And others (harder still) he pay'd in kind.

Dryden alone (what wonder?) came not nigh,
Dryden alone escap'd this judging eye:
But still the Great have kindness in reserve,
He help'd to bury whom he help'd to starve.   (231–48)

The portrait of Bufo is a step beyond that of Addison: Bufo is without
taste (his headless trunk of Pindar) and without talent. Like Addison,
however, his egotism (rather more flabby than Addison's) requires flattery, and for this he is prepared to pay. Bufo is morally 'more open'
than Addison, therefore. But he is similar in his precise relation to evil:
he is 'controlled' by his egotism, and again we get the sense of a being
at the mercy of his own vice, passive. Indeed, in the cases of both Addison
and Bufo we are aware of their being static: they are both seated (210,
232), and Bufo is described in passive verbs – 'puff'd by ev'ry quill', 'Fed
with soft Dedication all day long'. There are harsher cuts in Bufo's portrait at the end (247–8). The theme of flattery has now become fully
explicit: flattery is false friendship. By taking the dunces off his hands,
Bufo leaves Pope with his true friends, the Gays and Queensburys of this
world, leaves him with his private, inner world, the one to which he gives
sole allegiance. Moreover, it is wrong to see this private world as invaded by the creation of poetry, as if the poet had no other interests:

Heav'ns! was I born for nothing but to write?
Has Life no Joys for me? or (to be grave)
Have I no Friend to serve, no Soul to save?   (272–4)

It is flatterers, and those who encourage them, who thus identify the
public and the private man, the appearance and the reality.[16] The theme
of friendship versus flattery is continued (283–304). But this passage
is also a definitive statement by Pope of those whom he will attack and
those whom he will not:

A Lash like mine no honest man shall dread,
But all such babling blockheads in his stead.   (303–4)

It is a preliminary statement of the moral function of poetry. But it also
fully asserts Pope's moral stance, gives it full justification in drawing
together all the other elements of the poem that have preceded it. The
portrait of Sporus follows. The attack here has ceased to be concerned
with people in the world of letters: Sporus is a general antisocial animal.
The poem has widened out to this – we have already noticed how
aesthetic judgments became moral ones in the case of Addison: now the
aesthetic context has been entirely removed. This accounts for the non-
specific, the 'all-out' assault on Sporus as a kind of incarnation of all

vice. It accounts also for the clear linkage of Sporus to Satan: he is a classic example of all evil. Pope has now both defined and justified the breadth of his moral concern in poetry: all roads of corruption – Addison, Bufo, literary hacks and flatterers – lead finally to this, their full embodiment and nemesis, Sporus.

In this poem, as in the 'Epistle to Miss Blount', the structure is linear and vertical: each point is a base for the next, and the poem proceeds by smooth gradations, brick laid upon and cemented to brick, to build a satirist. But also, as in the 'Epistle', the method admits the poet's private self. If the fact that he is here in part imitating the treatment of the satirist's growth and role in Horace, Juvenal and Persius guarantees Pope a measure of impersonality at the outset of his poem, it is ultimately his skill in handling his theme and its transitions that enables him to put himself and his private likes and dislikes at the centre of his poem and yet sound like much more than mere self.

7 Defoe

Defoe on the one hand and Dryden and Pope on the other illustrate the more radical divisions of the Augustan period. In his novels, Defoe takes the world as he finds it, and makes only intermittent attempts to impose patterns or values upon it: he is near to being the first truly empiricist writer in English literature. He is not interested in verisimilitude for its own sake, however: the realism in his novels is to a large extent the expression of an unconscious interest, present throughout his fiction, in the idea of survival, and in putting his heroes in positions where that interest is central. This can be brought out by comparison with a genre in which the motif of survival is paramount – science fiction.

First, however, and at the risk of retracing some familiar ground, we must establish the character of Defoe's novels. It is clear that he seeks to give them themes; but the attempt has only limited success. In *Robinson Crusoe* he wants us to view Crusoe's shipwreck on the island as divine retribution for his refusal to accept his appointed station in life, whether the life of settled bourgeois respectability[1] that his father recommended, or that of successful farmer in the Brazils. From the start, however, this spiritual standard is intermingled with a more worldly one: Crusoe can say in his first storm on board ship after leaving home, 'I began now seriously to reflect upon what I had done, and how justly I was overtaken by the Judgment of Heaven for my wicked leaving my Father's House, and abandoning my Duty' (p. 8); but in the next paragraph, 'Now I saw plainly the Goodness of his Observations about the middle Station of Life, how easy, how comfortably he had liv'd all his Days, and never had been expos'd to Tempests at Sea, or Troubles on Shore; and I resolv'd that I would, like a true repenting Prodigal, go home to my Father.' (Similar mixtures may be found on pp. 15–16 and 35–6.) Indeed, we wonder how heinous rather than impractical Crusoe's truancies have been; and our impression whenever he reviles himself as a sinner is of someone making a mountain out of a molehill.[2] We may, of course, put it down to that Puritan habit (which, formally at least, is pride) of imposing patterns of sin and divine punishment and providence on the random character of the individual life, but this does not justify it; and Defoe certainly does not view the habit ironically. We must feel, then, that the spiritual significance of Crusoe's career is frailly-based.[3]

Further, the motions of conscience, or the thoughts of God and providence to which Crusoe gives utterance, alternate throughout the novel with narrative accounts in which self-help and selfishness are the dominant and uncriticised motives, and there is no sign that Defoe intends us to relate these ironically: indeed, if the general pattern of providence implied behind the action has any point, he supposes that Crusoe, who at the end is almost wholly immersed in financial considerations, has reached the heights of spiritual development and, in his escape from the island, providential favour (p. 273).

It has been argued, too, that there is a pattern of traditional Christian imagery behind the story, particularly of storms and shipwrecks, which figure man at the mercy of his unruly passions, bound to be ruined if he does not walk with God; and that this gives the narrative meaningful pattern.[4] But the island itself, with which most of the story is concerned, has no such traditional base in theological allegory, and even if it did have, it is far from being a spot simply of suffering or educative punishment. Doubtless Defoe could have made something of it: he could have made it, and Crusoe's life on it, a grimly ironic comment on the free self-sufficiency that led him to it, and the necessary self-sufficiency he is doomed to when he is on it; or he could have pointed the ironic contrast between the relative stasis of Crusoe's life there and his previous parent-defying, ocean-wandering restlessness. That he does not can only indicate a different interest in putting Crusoe there.

We must conclude, therefore, that Defoe had two, inconsistent, aims in *Robinson Crusoe*: he wanted to portray Crusoe's life simply for what it was, and he wanted to make theological sense of it; and the latter aim eventually went to the wall. In *Moll Flanders* the moral theme is more perfunctory.[5] The preface asserts that, 'To give the History of a wicked Life repented of, necessarily requires that the wicked Part should be made as wicked, as the real History of it will bear; to illustrate and give a Beauty to the Penitent part, which is certainly the best and brightest, if related with equal Spirit and Life' (p. 2). Clearly, the last point begs the question: a question which a glance at a typical passage will show is only too relevant:

I was now return'd to *London*, and tho' by the Accident of my last Adventure, I got something considerable, yet I was not fond of any more Country rambles; nor should I have ventur'd Abroad again if I had carried the Trade on to the End of my Days; I gave my Governess a History of my Travels, she lik'd the *Harwich* journey well enough, and in Discoursing of these things between ourselves she observ'd, that a Thief being a Creature that Watches the Advantages of other

Peoples mistakes, 'tis impossible but that to one that is vigilant and industrious many Opportunities must happen, and therefore she thought that one so exquisitely keen in the Trade as I was, would scarce fail of something extraordinary wherever I went.

On the other hand, every Branch of my Story, if duly consider'd, may be useful to honest People, and afford a due Caution to People of some sort, or other to Guard against the like Surprizes, and to have their Eyes about them when they have to do with Strangers of any kind, for 'tis very seldom that some Snare or other is not in their way. The Moral, indeed, of all my History is left to be gather'd by the Senses and Judgment of the Reader, I am not Qualified to preach to them, let the Experience of one Creature compleatly wicked, and compleatly Miserable be a Storehouse of useful warning to those that read. (p. 268)

The disjunction between the two attitudes to thieving could hardly be more marked than by such a lurching 'On the other hand'. The recommendation is a merely practical one, that her victims should look to themselves; when it comes to the moral of her history, she is silent. The style of that second paragraph, with its vague 'People of some sort, or other', 'some Snare or other', is an illustration of how 'the Penitent part' is certainly not 'related with equal Spirit and Life' to the accounts of her adventures; Moll specifically and continually declares as much (pp. 65, 108, 287–8, 289, 291, 339). Similar effects may be observed in *Roxana*; the heroines of both books insist that it is their business to relate facts, not offer judgments.[6] What spiritual self-analyses we have are often shrill or inaccurate.[7] The progressive substitution of physical quantities for moral qualities is the cause of such erosion: throughout *Moll Flanders* the term 'virtue' is confused – 'Thus the Government of our Virtue was broken, and I exchang'd the Place of Friend, for that unmusical harsh-sounding Title of WHORE' (p. 116); 'I should have been as faithful and true a Wife to him as Virtue it self could have form'd' (p. 128); 'you may see how necessary it is, for all Women who expect any thing in the World, to preserve the Character of their Virtue, even when perhaps they have sacrific'd the Thing itself' (p. 138).[8]

It has been argued that Defoe deliberately creates an ironic distance between the novel and the reader, and that this enables him to be critical of Moll in just the way we have been: the morality of the novel then becomes not Moll's comments but our comments upon them.[9] But, as Ian Watt has said,[10] there is as little evidence of such ironic intent as there is in *Robinson Crusoe*: however much we might care to reflect on Moll's fluctuating attitudes to her children (pp. 59, 173–6, 322), or her defences of her thefts in terms of the lessons they confer on those robbed (pp. 194–5, 225–8), or her protestations of feeling –

Nothing that ever befel me in my Life, sunk so deep into my Heart as this Farewel: I reproach'd him a Thousand times in my Thoughts for leaving me, for I would have gone with him thro' the World, if I had beg'd my Bread. I felt in my Pocket, and there I found ten Guineas, his Gold Watch, and two little Rings, one a small Diamond Ring, worth only about six Pound, and the other a plain Gold Ring (p. 153)

– such reflections are not evidently intended by either Moll or Defoe.[11] Nor may the old Moll who tells the story be viewed in critical detachment from the young and relatively innocent Moll, who gradually becomes her narrator:[12] such a distance is impossible because the young Moll is simply insufficiently distinguished from her later self,[13] whether in her continuously politic and self-seeking motivation (see, for example, pp. 25–6, 75–6) or in such lapses as

But I never once reflected that I was all this while a marry'd Woman, a Wife to Mr. ——, the Linnen Draper, who tho' he had left me by the Necessity of his Circumstances, had no power to Discharge me from the Marriage Contract which was between us, or to give me a legal Liberty to marry again; so that I had been no less than a Whore and an Adultress all this while: I then reproach'd my self with the Liberties I had taken. . . .　(p. 124; see also pp. 226–8)

First she tells us that she did not *then* reflect; but, having described what she should have reflected, the 'should have' becomes 'did' – in short, the old Moll simply breaks down the barriers of time between herself and the young.[14]

Thus, while Defoe does make some attempt to render his novels moral or thematic in intent, that intent is to a greater or lesser extent frustrated. Sometimes it can lead to plain self-contradiction: in the *Journal of the Plague Year* the narrator continually changes his mind on whether the confining of people to their houses was a good idea;[15] is confused as to how far the plague, both in its inception and cessation, was the product of the immediate hand of God, or the result of natural causes as agents of God (pp. 36, 75, 171, 193–4, 209, 244–5, 246–7); stays in London because divine providence suggests he should (pp. 10–11, 12–13), yet later says that, notwithstanding such assurances, as many others besides himself received them, and subsequently died despite them, '*the best Physic against the Plague is to run away from it*' (pp. 197–8); laughs at the notion that the plague was transmitted by invisible creatures in the air and says, 'I shall say more to this Case in its Order' (p. 75), but, when he does so, agrees with it (pp. 219–20). Clearly, any attempt to make sense of the material fails; and this inconsistency of stance must

be traced to the absence of a total vision or a settled conviction, resulting in purely local observation.[16]

It has been claimed that, lacking wider themes or consistent moral
vision, Defoe's novels may nonetheless be unified at less conscious levels,
by a single-minded portrayal, in all his protagonists, of economic individu-
alism and 'the dynamic tendency of capitalism'.[17] There is some truth
in this; but again, it is not the whole truth. The motivation of Robinson
Crusoe, for example, may be largely economic, but it is also romantic, a
Wanderlust: economic man, as Crusoe says himself, would have stayed
with his father or in the Brazils, and have made his fortune in the regular
way (pp. 194–5). Crusoe sets this 'meer wandring Inclination' (p. 4) or
'rambling Designs' (p. 40) beside sensible economic motivation (p. 4) as
'my apparent obstinate adhering to my foolish inclination of wandring
abroad and pursuing that Inclination, in contradiction to the clearest
Views of doing my self good in a fair and plain pursuit of those Prospects
and those measures of Life, which Nature and Providence concurred to
present me with, and to make my Duty' (p. 38).

Of course, the rambling instinct is not simply romantic: it is also
economic: 'this Voyage made me both a Sailor and a Merchant: for I
brought Home *L. 5. 9 Ounces* of Gold Dust for my Adventure, which
yielded me in *London* at my Return, almost 300 *l*. and this fill'd me with
those aspiring Thoughts which have since so compleated my Ruin' (p. 17).
And the voyage from the Brazils has the commercial object of securing
slaves from Guinea for sale. Clearly, though, both motives operate, not
one, and the romantic one frequently to the detriment of the economic,
in as much as Crusoe is either captured by Moors or cast up on an
island.

There is here no simple or single answer to what Crusoe is, and what
makes him act. It is wrong to say, for further example, that what we
see in Crusoe's treatment of Xury or Friday is the erosion of human by
mercantile motives. Ian Watt tells us, of Crusoe's parting with Xury the
Moorish boy, who has companioned his imprisonment by the Moors of
Guinea and his subsequent escape, that,

> when chance leads them to the Portuguese Captain, who offers Crusoe
> sixty pieces of eight – twice Judas' figure – he cannot resist the bargain,
> and sells Xury into slavery. He has momentary scruples, it is true, but
> they are cheaply satisfied by securing a promise from the new owner
> to 'set him free in ten years if he turn Christian'. Remorse later super-
> venes, but only when the tasks of his island life make manpower more
> valuable to him than money.[18]

But what this account omits is Crusoe's statement before the bargain is
struck, 'upon this, and *Xury* saying he was willing to go to him, I let

the Captain have him' (p. 34). Presumably, if Xury had not been so willing, Crusoe might not have gone ahead. Though human feeling is over-
borne by economic drives, it is not extinguished.

Much the same can be seen with the treatment of Friday. It is true,
that 'Crusoe does not ask his name, but gives him one'; not true that 'a
functional silence, broken only by an occasional "No Friday", or an
abject "Yes, Master", is the golden music of Crusoe's *île joyeuse*'.[19]
Crusoe hands out these names when he has small reason to rate Friday
high on the human scale, and Friday is in any case desperately eager
to serve him. Later, when he knows Friday better, Crusoe becomes
'greatly delighted with him', and teaches him 'every Thing, that was
proper to make him useful, handy, and helpful; but especially to make
him speak, and understand me when I spake' (p. 210): here patronage
is producing education, even if the end is selfish. Later still we are told,

> This was the pleasantest Year of all the Life I led in this Place; *Friday*
> began to talk pretty well, and understand the Names of almost every
> Thing I had occasion to call for, and of every Place I had to send him
> to, and talk'd a great deal to me; so that in short I began now to have
> some Use for my Tongue again, which indeed I had very little occasion
> for before; that is to say, *about Speech*; besides the Pleasure of talking
> to him, I had a singular Satisfaction in the Fellow himself; his simple
> unfeign'd Honesty, appear'd to me more and more every Day, and I
> began really to love the Creature; and on his Side, I believe he lov'd
> me more than it was possible for him ever to love any Thing before.
> (p. 213)

The first half of this concerns Friday's usefulness; the rest relates how
Crusoe is drawn into human affection. We do end with his calling
Friday 'Creature', it is true, and there seems egosim in the notion that
Crusoe's person is more lovable than anything Friday has hitherto met.
But once again, though human emotion is somewhat limited, any simple
view of Crusoe's motivation does not do justice to the facts.[20]

The springs of Moll Flanders's actions appear similarly mixed at this
level. Moll's romantic drives are sometimes at variance with her economic
ones, as in the cases of the young gentleman to whom she early sur-
renders that prime commodity, her virtue, and of the impoverished
highwayman Jemmy, for whom she nourishes a constant and frequently
impolitic passion. Despite her claims to the contrary, she is not a thief
by necessity, for after her first few essays in pilfering she secures an
honest sufficiency doing quilting work (pp. 199, 202). When her thieving
has gained her enough to live comfortably, she still carries on the trade
for mere love of and pride in her craft (pp. 213, 214, 220–1, 241, 262–3,
269). A similar flightiness moves the hard-headed businesswoman Roxana

to reject, for the sake of continued freedom and the necessity of living by her wits, the opportunity of marriage to a wealthy Dutchman.[21] As soon as he has gained it, Colonel Jacque forsakes his hard-won position as a Virginia gentleman for fresh adventures.[22] And the narrator of *A Journal of the Plague Year* remains in London, in the teeth of common sense, because of a supposed counsel of providence, which is really a justification of his own prior wish to stay and to take risks.

If Crusoe as economic individualist will not suffice, we have been told by Ian Watt that in *Robinson Crusoe* Defoe wanted 'to give narrative expression to the ideological counterpart of the Division of Labour, the Dignity of Labour',[23] and that this is the real reason for the isolation of his hero. But it is not the dignity of what he does that fires Crusoe, but the ingenuity with which he avoids indignity. What pride he feels in his work he feels for two reasons: it involves considerable powers of improvisation, and he feels much safer and more secure when he has done it. 'No Joy at a Thing of so mean a Nature was ever equal to mine, when I found I had made an Earthen Pot that would bear the Fire' (p. 121); 'I improv'd my self in this time in all the mechanick Exercises which my Necessities put me upon applying my self to, and I believe cou'd, upon Occasion, make a very good *Carpenter*, especially considering how few Tools I had' (p. 144); 'I think I was never more vain of my own Performance, or more joyful for any thing I found out, than for my being able to make a Tobacco-Pipe' (ibid.). There is no suggestion that work, as work, particularly manual work, is a good thing (on the subject of manual work, we may recall that Crusoe has a number of tools and supplies salvaged from the wreck, without which he would certainly have perished). As in his comments on the making of a board (pp. 68, 114–5), a spade (pp. 73, 118, 119), or the disastrous canoe which when complete is too heavy to be moved to the sea (pp. 125–8), or on the cumbrous business of trying to make earthenware pots, bread, or enclosures for goats (pp. 118–23, 144, 146–7), he is constantly portrayed as finding his work laborious, degrading or wasteful (even though he often adds the rider that none of this mattered, since, with unlimited supply of time and materials, efficiency is unimportant).

This is not to deny that being thrown largely on his own resources and overcoming the limitations of his environment is one of Crusoe's primary pleasures – and ours, in reading his story. His joy is that of the man who has turned catastrophe to advantage. To give him a chance to do this is, in short, the real reason why Defoe puts him on the island

The same motive is at work in *Moll Flanders*. Defoe is not so much interested in how or why Moll became what she is, but in what she makes of what she is. This is no sociological novel: that is made plain from the start. On the first page Moll tries to claim that her wicked life is the consequence of a wretched childhood; which childhood she blames on the absence of a system of care for foundlings in England. She compares the French system of the House of Orphans 'where they [foundlings] are Bred up, Cloath'd, Fed, Taught, and when fit to go out, are plac'd out to Trades, or to Services, so as to be well able to provide for themselves by an honest industrious Behaviour' (p. 8). Within the next page or two, however, we discover that, though Moll was abandoned by her mother at six months and had been kept with gypsies until she was three, she was then taken in very compassionate care by the magistrates of Colchester; and that when fourteen she was taken into service with one of the local ladies, where she was fully equipped to perform just the skills that she claimed her enforced wretchedness left her without. The element of social attack fails and does not return, even in the portrayal of Moll's term at Newgate, where, however horrible the place may be, she feels it a natural part of life, as crime and punishment; and accepts that she deserves execution, even though terrified by the fact itself. The emphasis on the individual is paramount: the environment may be lamented, but it is never questioned.[24]

The simple fact behind all that we have traced so far is that Defoe's novels are, unseen by their author, centrally about *survival*. This is why we find such mixed characters as Crusoe and Moll, who are bound to ruin themselves and thus have to overcome ruin. The novels cover a range of 'survival conditions': *Robinson Crusoe* explores the theme of survival in isolation from society; *A Journal of the Plague Year* examines how people inside society react when civilisation is under attack; *Moll Flanders, Colonel Jacque* and *Roxana*[25] show the individual who lives within but does not belong to society, and *Captain Singleton* the freebooter outside the social fabric, who preys on civilisation to live. The interest is always in how long the protagonist can keep the wolf from the door: every step forward is a source of vicarious satisfaction to the author and the reader, a satisfaction never complete, or the thrill of risk and possible loss would fade. The risks which the characters take or the follies to which they are liable or the accidents they suffer are means of ensuring that the struggle to survive will remain the dominant interest: the stasis of sufficiency or success is to be avoided, and yet the quest for such stasis is constantly in view; and if it is gained then it is thrown away or lost. This is why Defoe's novels do not end on a 'full close': why Crusoe cannot settle to his recovered property in the Brazils and promises more adventures; why Moll does not stay in Virginia, and Roxana speaks of 'a dreadful Course of Calamities' into which she is to fall beyond the limits of her story. The ethic of Defoe's novels seems to be one of constant forward movement, whether to one's profit or one's loss: the frequent haste of his narratives, their sheer obsession with what happens next, limits our ability to look back and make comparisons, ensures that the dominant question will always be 'And then?' In *The Farther Adventures . . . of Robinson Crusoe*, Crusoe's friend the English merchant asks, 'what should we stand still for? The whole world is in motion, rolling round and round; all the creatures of God, heavenly bodies and earthly, are busy and diligent: why should we be idle?'[26] Defoe's characters enact a ceaseless dialectic between conflicting desires: for comfort and for danger, money and love, steadiness and romance, stasis and flux; as Crusoe puts it, 'How strange a Chequer Work of Providence is the Life of Man! and by what secret differing Springs are the Affections hurry'd about as differing Circumstance present! To Day we love what to Morrow we hate; to Day we seek what to Morrow we shun; to Day we desire what to Morrow we fear' (p. 156), or, earlier, 'we never see the true State of our Condition, till it is illustrated to us by its Contraries; nor know how to value what we enjoy, but by the want of it' (p. 139).[27]

Defoe's unapprehended interest in this theme of survival may explain both the febrile nature of the moral and spiritual issues of his novels, and the uneasy mixture, in his protagonists, of economic and humane motives. The human feelings and the consciences of the characters are surrounded by economic and practical drives in just the same way as the humans themselves are surrounded by an inhospitable environment. The concern of the characters with economic self-betterment is a function of a larger concern with manipulating the external world in order to live and move; and their involvement with the external world of facts and sense-data is in conflict with their inner worlds of spiritual and moral experience.[28]

We can further validate this account of Defoe's novels by observing similar effects in other works where the primary interest and pleasure is in survival and the constant oscillation between 'comfort' and 'discomfort'. In science fiction that interest is almost always central: our concern, whether the story be one of interplanetary or time travel, invasion of earth or life after a catastrophe, is with whether or not the protagonist will survive. As a result, few works in the genre contain other themes, except in a rather *voulu* or self-conscious manner (for example, James Blish, *A Case of Conscience*, the Goldsteinian lumber in *Nineteen Eighty-Four*). Rarely does science fiction reach the dimension of myth: perhaps the symbolic narrative of Wells's *The Time Machine* is the nearest approach, and, significantly, that book is concerned not so much with surviving as with seeing and contemplating. As with Defoe, the narratives of most science-fiction stories are linear and non-retrospective; there is a sub-class which depends on the narrative 'sting in the tail'. Generally works of science fiction lack structure and artistic form. They are, like Defoe's novels, fundamentally committed to the notion of forward movement, whether that movement ends in apocalypse or in utopia;

and each moment in a given narrative tends not to exist in its own right, to be held, contemplated and remembered, but only as it occupies the space before the next.

John Wyndham's novels, particularly *The Day of the Triffids* (1951), may serve to illustrate these points. All Wyndham's novels are concerned with the theme of survival. *The Day of the Triffids* examines the effects on society when most of its members are blinded, and all are attacked by mobile armies of killer-plants; *The Kraken Wakes* (1953) describes humanity's fight for survival against attacks by armour-clad monsters which emerge from the depths of the oceans; *The Midwich Cuckoos* (1957) relates how man finally destroys the threat to him in the form of a group of children born with telepathic powers and mental control over matter – ending, 'If you want to keep alive in the jungle, you must live as the jungle does'; *The Chrysalids* (1955) portrays a post-holocaust world in which telepathic and other mutants, who are being hunted down by still 'normal' human beings, escape and organise a new society in New Zealand; *Trouble with Lichen* (1960), is about survival in another mode, through the discovery of a lichen which can produce longevity; and *Chocky* (1968) describes the attempt of an alien intelligence to alert mankind to the disaster-course it is pursuing.

In only two of these books, *The Midwich Cuckoos* and *Chocky*, do things return to normal, but in both of these that normality is by the end seen to be far frailer, far more subject to alteration at a moment's notice, than it seemed at the outset. The protagonist of *The Day of the Triffids* says, of the destruction of society, 'It was bound to happen some time in some way. It's an unnatural thought that one type of creature should dominate perpetually'; and he goes on, 'it is an inescapable conclusion that life has to be dynamic and not static. Change is bound to come one way or another' (p. 123). And the Sealand woman of *The Chrysalids* tells the children, 'The essential quality of life is living; the essential quality of living is change; change is evolution: and we are part of it. The static, the enemy of change, is the enemy of life, and therefore our implacable enemy',[29] and, earlier, 'The idea of completed man is the supreme vanity: the finished image is a sacrilegious myth.'[30] The point in relation to the restlessness of Defoe's heroes needs no labouring.

In *The Day of the Triffids* moral issues are given about the same scope as they receive in *Robinson Crusoe*, though in Wyndham's book they are *deliberately* tried and found a hindrance to the survival of man. With most of humanity blinded, and all menaced by the triffids, the obligation upon the sighted to help their less fortunate fellows is obvious. Wyndham's hero Bill does not shirk the issue entirely, just as Defoe's Crusoe tries to make moral and religious sense of his experiences. At first, despite the uneasiness of his girlfriend Josella, he opts for survival of the fittest, because he feels that even if he were to help the blind, he would only be extending their misery and putting off their inevitable end: 'My dear . . . I don't like this any more than you do. I've put the alternatives baldly before you. Do we help those who have survived the catastrophe to rebuild some kind of life? – or do we make a moral gesture which, on the face of it, can scarcely be more than a gesture?' (p. 114).

With Josella, Bill now joins a group of people with a clear plan and means for survival. This group, organised by one Michael Beadley, has taken in a number of blinded but useful women, and one of its aims, from which Bill shrinks, is that the men, outnumbered by the women, should take on several wives; later, however, circumstances contrive that Bill should not have to obey this dictate. The group is soon attacked, its sighted members seized by a band of blinded people, and Bill and Josella, separated, are forced to help the very unfortunates from whom they had turned away: Bill is chained to a group of the blind and has to conduct their wanderings in search of food. Now he is being forced to do that which, undone, would have left him with a sense of guilt: if he had gone with the Beadley people, 'I would have been uneasy. I'd never be quite convinced that nothing could have been done for the sinking ship, never quite sure that I had not rationalised my own preference' (p. 147). Nevertheless, he holds by the line that it would be futile to help these people if there were no hope at all of rescue from outside – 'If, indeed, there was *no* possibility of organised rescue, then their [the Beadley group's] proposal to salvage what we could was the intelligent course' (ibid.). During his time in this situation the futility of Bill's task and his compassion in refusing, in the teeth of common sense, to desert his charges when he sees how he may, are stressed. But his involvement is never finally tested, because, in addition to the triffids, a mysterious sickness now preys on and decimates his group. Sure that there is now no hope of rescue, he decides to preserve himself, but a girl in the group turns his heart: however, immediately after, the remnants of the group conveniently having come to the belief that Bill (who has long since freed himself from the chain linking him to them) has abandoned them, leave the house where they have all been staying; and the girl, who is now herself sick, asks for and is given poison by Bill. Having served his time and placated his conscience, Bill is now free to revert, without hindrance, to his old instinct for self-preservation.

Wyndham has made an attempt to do justice to the moral issues; but, in a story where survival is the primary consideration, such standards have, in the end, to go to the wall. Wyndham's method here is, as we have said, different from Defoe's, in that he actually brings the status of moral issues into conscious question, where in Defoe's novels they are allowed to lapse, be islanded or quietly eroded – but the effect is the same: where practicality and survival are dominant concerns, ideas, morals and spiritual values must shrivel before facts. As Bill says to Josella when she has qualms about taking things from deserted shops, 'an obstinate refusal to face facts isn't going to bring anything back, or help us at all' (p. 90; cf. p. 102).

Other moral absolutes, seen close to, also become relative. Looting from shops is no longer a crime (one is reminded here of Moll Flanders's gradual acceptance of her career of theft, and her quotation '*Give me not Poverty lest I Steal*').[31] It is recommended as a positive virtue to take on several wives; and the Christian and humanitarian principles on which the colony run by Miss Durrant are founded kill them in the end (p. 285). The case is put by Dr Vorless of the original Beadley group: 'In the time now ahead of us a great many of these prejudices we have been taught will have to go, or be radically altered. We can accept and retain only one primary prejudice, and that is that *the race is worth preserving*' (p. 132; see also p. 134).[32] Similarly, when faced by the issue of his own preservation (and a certain amount of conscience), Defoe's Crusoe can hang back from doing anything about the cannibalistic feasts of the savages who visit his island, either on the grounds that in the sight of God such acts may not be the crimes they seem to European man (pp. 170–2), or (contradictorily) that God will himself punish them for their sins (pp. 232–3); in the end, however, he is sufficiently transported with rage at their doings to attack them. For Moll Flanders, even incest with her brother is not objectively a sin: 'there was no Crime in our Marriage on that score, neither of us knowing it' (p. 124). Crusoe tells us at one point that, though the weather was hot enough to make clothes unnecessary, 'yet I could not go quite naked; no, tho' I had been inclin'd to it, which I was not, nor could not abide the thoughts of it, tho' I was all alone'. We anticipate some moral absolute, some reluctance, say, to enjoy the nakedness that Adam forfeited; but what we are told is, 'The Reason why I could not go quite naked, was, I could not bear the heat of the Sun so well when quite naked, as with some Cloaths on' (p. 134).

The Day of the Triffids shows a truncation of human feeling similar to that in Defoe's novels,[33] though here perhaps it has gone rather further. When Josella, having met Bill, returns with him to her home and finds old Pearson the gardener, little Annie and her father killed by triffids, Josella's feelings are given only brief and conventional airing (pp. 82–3):

'Such a dear old man – I've known him all my life.'
'I'm sorry –' I began, wishing I could think of something more adequate, but she cut me short.

She has now seen Annie:

'Oh! – oh, it's Annie! Poor little Annie', she said.

I tried to console her a little.

'They can scarcely have known it, either of them', I told her. 'When it is strong enough to kill, it's mercifully quick.'

Again, when she finds her father, she is allowed a short lament before she takes control, and then a triffid interrupts further proceedings (pp. 83–4). The British stiff upper lip is doubtless here, but much more the sense, throughout the book, that in the circumstances there is no more than perfunctory time for such behaviour. 'Only those who can make their minds tough enough to stick it are going to get through' (p. 94).

As in Defoe's novels, reflective passages in *The Day of the Triffids* are intermittent, and it is difficult to trace a psychological continuum in the narrator Bill. On one occasion he finds the catastrophe invigorating (pp. 66–7); on another he informs us that he has got over this initial euphoria, and that he now feels the situation much more bleak (pp. 78–9). He tells us that he sees the catastrophe, but for a miracle, as world-wide (pp. 95–6), yet later that he helps the blind only on the basis of a hope that there may eventually be help from outside (p. 147): the two positions are reconcilable by him on the grounds that intelligence is often defied by hope, but they have been so islanded as to appear more contradictory than they are. The same effect is more largely seen in Bill's change from the motive of self-preservation to that of helping his fellows, and back again: human feelings and thoughts become an archipelago in an ocean of facts.

There are other incidental points of similarity between Defoe and Wyndham. As in Defoe's novels, there are no evil characters in those of Wyndham, only misguided or impractical ones. If moral values are emasculated, so too is the sense of evil. The lack of spiritual fixity in the novels of both writers can also express itself as a loss of personal identity. Moll Flanders (the name itself is fictitious) is so frequently disguised as a man that she partly becomes one. The condition is one of a need for constant adaptation, which is of course part of the ethic of constant change. Bill's associate Coker in *The Day of the Triffids* describes himself as 'a hybrid' and his career as orator as one of continual matching of himself to the needs of different groups and classes of people:

There's a whole lot of people don't seem to understand that you have to talk to a man in his own language before he'll take you seriously. If you talk tough and quote Shelley they think you're cute, like a performing monkey or something, but they don't pay any attention to what you say. You have to talk the kind of lingo they're accustomed to taking seriously. And it works the other way, too. Half the political intelligentsia who talk to a working audience don't get the value of their stuff across – not so much because they're over their audience's heads, as because most of the chaps are listening to the voice and not to the words, so they knock a big discount off what they do hear because it's all a bit fancy, and not like ordinary normal talk. So I reckoned the thing to do was to make myself bilingual, and use the right one in the right place – and occasionally the wrong one in the wrong place, unexpectedly. Surprising how that jolts 'em.   (pp. 179–80)

He describes himself very aptly as 'Wilfred Coker. Meetings addressed. Subject no object' (p. 180): the last phrase means to him that he does not have to believe what he says, that he can switch world-views at will; but it also means what it says – that Coker, as subject, is no object. Nor, one might add from this, is language. The language of both Defoe's and Wyndham's novels is singularly deracinated, filled with cliches, poor constructions and repetitions: it has at once the immediacy of being casual, and the dullness of a purely utilitarian object of communication.[34]

These similarities between Defoe and Wyndham can be seen in other works of science fiction, though Wyndham has perhaps brought them out rather more starkly. It needs only a glance at the work of Asimov, Aldiss, Wells or Frank Herbert to see most of the same features repeated. *Brave New World* and *Nineteen Eighty-Four* are specifically *about* the destruction of love, human feeling, personal identity, conservatism, contemplation and language.

The object here has been not to incorporate Defoe into the science fiction genre, but to show how, whenever the theme of survival is dominant in a work of literature, it produces the effects that we have seen in Defoe's novels. The question that remains is why this theme should so have dominated Defoe's imagination. On this we can only guess. It may be that, thrown as he was on his own resources for most of his life, the topic was a natural one; though this could be argued of many writers. What is peculiar to Defoe is a practical and reductive cast of mind, together with a Puritan individualist temper. What is peculiar to his age is, as we have seen with Donne, Milton and Dryden, the problem of a widening gap between the world of phenomena and the sense that can be made of them.

In almost every way Defoe is the summation of what Grub Street meant to the Scriblerians. He describes the various empirical world without selection, and with ultimately ineffectual attempts to make sense of it or to evaluate the behaviour of his characters. There is nothing of art in his novels, no structure, no enduring theme, no sense of language and, apart from *Robinson Crusoe*, no attempt at symbolism or allegory. The novels are aften episodic, and the transitions from one episode to another are handled with an abruptness which is in stark contrast to neo-classical insistence on grace and proportion. Defoe's novels have not only the roughness of disordered life but also the ambiguity, an ambiguity not comprehended, ironically or otherwise, by the author: the characters shift their motivation from romantic to coarsely practical, and their commentary from moral to worldly, as the mood takes them. What moral injunctions they offer are occasional and often vestigial; and their views are often inconsistent. Where Dryden and Pope write from within the fabric of society and civilisation, and from a hierarchic, Tory and 'polite' standpoint, Defoe describes those who, 'vulgar' by station or circumstance, live outside society and often have to prey on it to live; his novels generally have a lower or lower-middle class milieu and portray 'Whiggish' entrepreneurs. His characters are 'novel', not typical or 'what oft was thought': their existence and views are always implicitly, and occasionally overtly, a criticism of the accepted values of civilisation.[35] He is interested in the individual rather than the social;[36] and his individuals are, more or less unconsciously, driven by one value only, a value which has nothing to do with a civilised context of moral and political ideals, and indeed erodes them – the concern simply to survive. To this extent his work is taken up with practical details and the physical immediacies of life as Dryden's and Pope's poetry never is. So paramount is this interest in survival in Defoe's work that his characters often deliberately, and against all practical sense, put themselves in positions where it will be their only concern: where they are successful they often take risks, implicitly in order to court the disaster that follows. Indeed, the interest in survival itself is a function of an urge continually to be on the move, never to be settled and at rest, but always in a condition of becoming. This lust for constant mobility recalls that of earlier Puritan sensibilities – Bunyan and Milton; and it looks forward to Thomson, and even to Cowper. In contrast, almost the whole weight of 'Augustan' literature was on the side of the *status quo*. There is perhaps one partial exception, in Swift; and, indeed, not only in terms of actual literary indebtedness, but also in the empirical, even relativist, mode of his work, Swift is close to Defoe.[37]

8 Swift

Swift's satire is at once far more political and directly conceptual in emphasis than Pope's. Swift is much less concerned with attacking individuals or defending himself than with portraying general abuses and trying to produce change in the reader. Pope's satires are in a sense exhibitions; Swift's are intended to be acts. Swift is the reverse of Pope in that his only concern with his art is that it should become a part of life, affecting the reader as immediately as any other experience. To this end his satire is written to involve the reader, to make him take part, and then to betray him, so that he is the more forcibly propelled towards a reappraisal of his assumptions. Unlike Pope or Dryden, Swift does not, in his major satire, put forward norms of behaviour: his aim is so to push the reader back on his resources that he must rethink his values. Whatever we say about Swift as Tory, Anglican, Ancient or sceptic, he himself is not in his satires explicit on the subject. In fact, he refuses any kind of *a priori* valuation or point of view: like Kingsley's Mother Carey, he makes us make ourselves.

The skill of Swift's satire lies in his ability to transmit to us the energy to rebuild even as he demolishes. In the famous 'Digression on Madness' in his *A Tale of a Tub*, he offers us the mental categories of intellect, fancy and sense experience; encourages us to prefer one; exposes our preference; undercuts our switch of sympathy to another while reinstating the first; and so forces us to shift our preferences[1] that we soon begin to perceive that such a union of the three might soften the deficiencies of each, and actively attempt to work out such a *concordia discors* for ourselves. Swift does not allow any single view. For Pope and Dryden the world was absolutely divided into the realms of order and chaos, but Swift's satire portrays an analysed world of disjoined human faculties in which the only absolute is our final inability to give value to any single one of them. Taken literally, his satire is a picture of the world as he saw it – a Cartesian landscape, like the one portrayed a century earlier in Shakespeare's *Troilus and Cressida*, of conceptual warfare; taken from the point of view of what it says about this, Swift's satire is an attempt to remarry the opposites within the minds of his readers. What precise form that remarriage will take Swift is pragmatic enough to leave to the sense of the individual.

'AN ARGUMENT AGAINST ABOLISHING CHRISTIANITY' (1710)

> I am very sensible what a Weakness and Presumption it is, to reason against the general Humour and Disposition of the World. I remember it was with great Justice, and a due Regard both to the Freedom both of the Publick and the Press, forbidden upon several Penalties to write or discourse, or lay wagers against the *Union*, even before it was confirmed by Parliament: Because that was looked upon as a Design to oppose the Current of the People; which besides the Folly of it, is a manifest Breach of the Fundamental Law, that makes this Majority of Opinion the Voice of God. (p. 26)

Thus Swift begins, and thus he asks us where the majority of opinions is to be found. For, when he speaks of how with due regard to their freedom the public and the press both were muzzled, deprived of their freedom, he shows a breach between opinion and its expression which invites us to question whether the supposed representatives of the people in Parliament are truly representative; whether in fact they operate arbitrarily without reference to majority opinion, except to crush it where it might frustrate their ends, and, to keep the populace quiet, to proclaim it as the star by which they steer. The proposer thus becomes no mere eccentric and dangerous individualist, but a freeborn Englishman exercising the right of free speech against arbitrary sway. And that the sway is arbitrary is further suggested when he remarks of the mutability of 'opinion' how, far from being settled and of the people, it is in constant flux and is generated by those in power:

> I freely own, that all Appearances are against me. The system of the Gospel, after the Fate of other Systems is generally antiquated and exploded; and the Mass or Body of the common People, among whom it seems to have had its latest Credit, are now grown as much ashamed of it as their Betters: Opinions, like Fashions always descending from those of Quality to the middle Sort, and thence to the Vulgar, where at length they are dropt and vanish. (p. 27)

So much for the Voice of God. That 'Appearances' invites us to consider that such opinions are not 'realities'; and it sounds the note of that distinction between the nominal and the real which is to be the foundation of the proposal and the satire. In short, to a nominal disbelief in Christianity, a disbelief which has no foundation in truth or fact, and no final reality, the proposer is going to reply with an argument for nominal belief. And the arguments he uses will be just as shifting, just as contradictory, irrational and contemptible, as those used by the people he is attacking. It is going to be a case of a nail driven out by a nail; all of it done in a tone of such sweet humility and reason as to heighten the irrationality of the proposer's argument, and thereby that of his opponents.

The primary means by which this is done is through the proposer's acceptance of the terms on which the 'Majority of Opinion' is founded. Thus he argues that the postulated existence of a God, far from restricting liberty of conscience, gives an object on which blasphemy may be vented: 'Great Wits love to be free with the highest Objects; and if they cannot be allowed a *God* to revile or renounce; they will *speak Evil of Dignities*, abuse the Government, and reflect upon the Ministry; which I am sure, few will deny to be of much more pernicious Consequence; according to the Saying of *Tiberius*; *Deorum offensa Diis curae*' (p. 29). To the view that the expense to the kingdom of the revenues of a large body of clergy would be less wasteful if used for the maintenance of 'two Hundred young Gentlemen of Wit and Pleasure, and Free-thinking; Enemies to Priest-craft, narrow Principles, Pedantry, and Prejudices; who might be an Ornament to the Court and Town' (p. 30), the proposer replies, first, that in many parts of the country it is valuable to have, in a parson, '*one* Man at least, of Abilities to read and write'; second, that the figure of 200 gentlemen is rather in excess of the number that could be supported by the total monies of the Church; and, third, that the parsons, thanks to their enforced temperance and exercise, are breeders of good human stock, while the dissipations and corruptions of men of wit would, if allowed a monopoly of generation, reduce the nation quickly to 'one great Hospital' (p. 31).

Although the terms he is using here are marginally more respectable than those he attacks, they are nonetheless founded on worldliness and merely national goods: that is, they are not categorically different from those of his opponents. That the respectable and the less so are jostled together to produce the one conclusion can only destroy all value. It is argued by the 'world' that Sunday is a waste of one potentially profitable and pleasurable day in seven, and that the churches could be used, variously, as 'Theatres, Exchanges, Market-houses, common Dormitories, and other publick Edifices' (p. 31): very well, answers the proposer, is Sunday in fact treated as different from any other day, and do those who go to churches treat them in any other way than those the reformers recommend? As for the vulgar, who are generally 'as stanch Unbelievers, as any of the highest Rank', nominal Christianity may be of use as superstition. 'I conceive some scattered Notions about a superior Power to be of singular Use for the common People, as furnishing excellent Materials to keep Children quiet, when they grow peevish; and providing

Topicks of Amusement in a tedious Winter Night' (p. 34). The proposer frequently argues for nominal Christianity on the basis of its use in curbing enthusiasm (where Swift's view would be on this Augustan point is not immediately relevant). Thus he repeats the point made on the use of a God to divert blasphemy from the State when he argues that Christianity provides an umbrella under which the many and various sects endemic to every nation may practise their eccentricities: 'if Chrstianity did not lend its Name, to stand in the Gap, and to employ or divert these Humours, they must of Necessity be spent in Contraventions to the Laws of the Land, and Disturbance of the publick Peace' (p. 35). A variation on this type of argument is his suggestion that the populace needs a collection of people to attack on one day in seven what the world does on the other six, because without such denunciations and prohibitions there would be lost the pleasure of disobedience, and many would become afflicted by the spleen (pp. 32–3).

Clearly, then, the criteria used by the proposer are political expedience and freedom of self-expression; but the one does not march easily with the other (as is shown well-enough in the opening paragraph of the satire), and the proposer reconciles them by *confining* the freedom — giving it scope, satisfaction and purgation through the retention of nominal faith. Thus the political motive is dominant, and the freedom is as nominal as the religion on which it is to be a parasite. The issue of arbitrary power, of the country before the people, remains as background; and it is of course to be much more immediate in *A Modest Proposal*. But it raises one issue of central importance here. The proposer is continually putting the notion of the 'Country' against the concrete fact of its people: the latter are to be kept quiet that the former may continue safe and secure; and gradually we begin to ask what a country is without its people. This is not, however, simply a case of the madness of dualism portrayed in the digression in *A Tale of a Tub*, for the proposer is a thoroughgoing materialist. This fact is early brought home to us in the anti-climax where we realise that, in arguing against the abolition of Christianity, he is not arguing for the retention of a truly spiritual or metaphysical order of experience, but merely for a sham version of it, a nominal faith – nominalism of course being 'The view which regards universals or abstract concepts as mere names without any corresponding realities' (*Oxford English Dictionary*). And, throughout, his basing of his arguments on purely material criteria such as the maintenance of the racial stock or the avoidance of illiteracy furthers this picture of him as incapable of any but a physical or utilitarian notion of value. Where, then, patriotism? – and what *is* this patriotism? And where, then, since they depend on mind rather than body, the status of his arguments as arguments? If his aim is anti-metaphysical, what scope is left for discourse?

Swift pushes the last question further by making the proposer frequently contradict himself – by making him reveal himself incapable of consistency or systematic argument. One instance of this is the point where he is arguing for the keeping of nominal Christianity on the grounds that those who use up their blasphemous and mutinous instincts against a God will be tractable in civil employ: he acknowledges that this 'purgative' argument has been countered by one which claims that, if blasphemy against God is admitted, it will not exhaust but increase itself and spread:

> if . . . [it is] argued, as some have done, upon a mistaken Principle, that an Officer who is guilty of speaking Blasphemy, may, some Time or other, proceed so far as to raise a Mutiny; the Consequence is, by no Means, to be admitted: For, surely the Commander of an *English* Army is like to be but ill obeyed, whose Soldiers fear and reverence him as little as they do a Deity.   (p. 29)

But that last part of the sentence does indeed at face-value appear to admit the 'Consequence', for one is hardly prepared to suppose that those who blaspheme against God under the proposed system of nominal Christianity will in any way fear or reverence him. If the proposer is arguing, as to make his case he must be here, that blasphemy is truly performed, and its purgative benefits achieved, only when its object is one which awakens fear and reverence in the blasphemer, then he is arguing for a measure of real and not nominal faith. Here one touches on the central problem, and one he does not notice, of the proposer's case. He acknowledges that 'The System of the Gospel, after the Fate of other Systems is generally antiquated and exploded' (p. 27), and throughout his argument portrays all ranks of people, apart from the children of rustics, as quite free from all superstition and past all reverence for religion. In this case blasphemy cannot wholly be satisfied in venting itself on a God known not to exist. That the proposer equates such blasphemy with that against the body of the Church, which does exist, suggests further that he has been forced ignorantly into arguing for a measure of real, and not nominal, Christianity, if his point on mutiny is to hold.

Indeed, his position is a shaky one, and he can be drawn from it either way, into a measure of real faith or to a denial of the need for even a nominal Christianity. To the argument that 'the Gospel System . . . obliges Men to the Belief of Things too difficult for Free-Thinkers', he replies that nobody subscribes to such belief anyway, either in reality or even as a sham: 'Does any Man either believe, or say he believes, or desire to have it thought that he says he believes one Syllable of the Matter? And is any Man worse received upon that Score; or does he find his Want of *Nominal* Faith a Disadvantage to him, in the Pursuit of any Civil, or Military Employment?' (pp. 29–30). So much for nominal Christianity; so much too for any reverential citizens or soldiers using up their blasphemous urges on God. The pendulum goes the other way later, where the proposer argues that the abolition of Christianity would ensure the collapse of the established Church. While many of the points he uses against this are purely worldly, that which he emphasises most of all is the reverse – namely, that the removal of the episcopal Church would open the road either to the Presbyterians or the Roman Catholics. And he does this not on political grounds (say, that sectarianism would turn the State into a republic or plain anarchy), but because he *believes* the doctrines of these other churches to be false; and, that being the case, he is demonstrating that he really *believes* in the faith as put about by the Anglican Church. Thus of the sects: 'Their declared Opinion is for repealing the Sacramental Test; they are very indifferent with regard to Ceremonies; nor do they hold the *Jus Divinum* of Episcopacy' (pp. 36–7).

Perhaps the central self-contradiction of the proposer is that which he makes on the subject of names and things, words and realities. To the suggestion that, if Christianity were wholly abolished, all such invidious distinctions as those between 'High and Low Church, of *Whig* and *Tory*, *Presbyterian* and *Church-of-England*' (p. 31) would be removed, he replies that, though the names be removed, the substance of the opposition will merely take on new names (a notion used by Swift in relation to the Big- and Little-Endians in chapter 4 of the first book of *Gulliver's Travels*): 'Are Party and Faction rooted in Mens Hearts no deeper than Phrases borrowed from Religion; or founded upon no firmer Principles? . . . Because Religion was nearest at hand to furnish a few convenient Phrases; is our Invention so barren, we can find no others?' (p. 32). On the next page the proposer argues along precisely reverse lines, in opposing those who would abolish Christianity because this would abolish also 'those grievous Prejudices of Education; which, under the Names of Virtue, Conscience, Honour, Justice, and the like, are so apt to disturb the Peace of human Minds' (p. 33). He maintains 'how difficult it is to get rid of a Phrase, which the World is once grown fond of, although the Occasion that first produced it, be entirely taken away' (ibid.). Thus, where in his former argument content was substantial, and form accidental, here the opposite is the case. The particular applications of each argument may not be mutually inconsistent, but their statements as general truths are. The picture that emerges from all this is one of a man arguing for the form of Christianity rather than the content, who does not know the ontological status of either category. On one whose whole purpose is to remove the reality and leave only the outward form of Christianity this must cast further ironic light.

The proposer argues for no change: the existing state of affairs, with the Church reviled but still outwardly alive, is to continue. His argument is not for revolution, but for the *status quo*; his aim is not to effect, but to perpetuate, something. Roughly the same is true of the author of *A Modest Proposal*: while it was true that as yet Irish children were not being fed to be slaughtered for meat at one year of age, the physical conditions of the Irish were at least as bestial and degraded as such a plan, and the cold detachment and indifference of those who might have helped them but did not was no better than this scheme; the proposal was calculated not to disturb or divert present views and feelings. The conservatism of both arguments fits in with the political and patriotic objectives of each speaker – the maintenance of public quiet and the increase of national wealth; but it is also, of course, a peculiarly effective method of portraying the existing state of affairs through metaphor – that which is written as project is fact. This is one way of increasing the force of the satire. The other that Swift uses is that of giving us a double vision: we look not only at reality, but also at what the proposer makes of it. Disgusted at his portrayal of corrupt free-thinkers and blasphemers, or of a people reduced to the level of animals, and ready to grant his quietly certain manner an Olympian comprehensiveness, we lean to the projector to give us those civilised certainties we long for; only to find that he is a more subtle and vicious extension of the scene he describes – that his lack of value, his worldliness, his cunning and self-seeking are a sinister political version of his material. The very energy with which we recoil from the material and ask certainty in the proposer contributes to the force of our further recoil – and the depth in us to which the satire strikes and educates.

'A MODEST PROPOSAL' (1729)

This satire is rather more a test of the reader than is the *Argument Against Abolishing Christianity*. Given that the Irish are sunk in animal misery, and that they would welcome the scheme outlined (117–18), how many of us have a sneaking sympathy with a method that takes advantage of the prevailing state of affairs rather than tries to change it with an idealism that so far has proved ineffectual? We may think it stark against the basic principles of humanity to make children into cattle to be slaughtered for the profit of the parents, but, then, what finally is humanity? – for here in Ireland is a nation of beings who have been bestialised, and, if they are beasts, why not treat them as such?

Thus it is that we can find ourselves at least partially assenting to the proposer's arguments, even where we know the corrupt basis on which they are founded. When he argues against the use of children of between twelve and fourteen for the table, not only because their flesh is too tough (his first reason) but because such a practice would be cruel (p. 113), we do make a gesture towards the thought that, after all, children of one year old are not conscious of what is happening to them when slaughtered. Again, though we may reject the advantages he finds to the nation in his project – namely, the lessening of the number of Roman Catholics or the increase in national revenue – we are more tempted, however disgusting its basis, by the picture of the poor Irish tenants given a means of subsistence they are without (p. 112) or of the happier marriages and families that would result from his scheme. Such benefits are to be wished on the people; and that they are to be effected only by such hideous means – indeed, that they *can* be effected by such means – is part of the terrible force of the satire. Thus, drawn to the end and repelled by the means, the reader's sensibility is mangled.

The calculating style of the proposer, which at first repels, later attracts us. As he begins, walking through Ireland, finding a 'melancholly Object' in '*Beggars* of the Female Sex, followed by three, four, or six Children, *all in Rags*, and importuning every Passenger for an Alms', and considering only how these children may be made 'sound and useful Members of the Commonwealth', we are alienated, even while the easy flow of the style draws us in; and, as he proceeds to arithmetic, so do we further remove ourselves.

> The number of Souls in *Ireland* being usually reckoned one Million and a half; of these I calculate there may be about Two hundred Thousand Couple whose Wives are Breeders; from which Number I subtract thirty thousand Couples, who are able to maintain their own Children; although I apprehend there cannot be so many, under *the present Distresses of the Kingdom*; but this being granted, there will remain an Hundred and Seventy Thousand Breeders. I again Subtract Fifty Thousand, for those Women who miscarry, or whose Children die by Accident, or Disease, within the Year. There only remain an Hundred and Twenty Thousand Children of poor Parents, annually born: The Question therefore is, How this number shall be reared, and provided for? (p. 110)

But, as he proceeds to answer this question, and the full horror not only of his scheme, but also of the circumstances which make it practicable, become apparent, the reader begins to find the calculations a comfort, a systematising and distancing of a reality which would be unbearable to contemplate directly, a giving of order and control to obscene chaos. We are in short, brought halfway to *being* someone like Adolf Eichmann.

Twice the proposer destroys his own position. He argues that his scheme will have the advantage of preventing 'those *voluntary Abortions,* and that horrid Practice of *Women murdering their Bastard Children;* alas! too frequent among us; sacrificing the *poor innocent Babes,* I doubt, more to avoid the Expence than the Shame; which would move Tears and Pity in the most Savage and inhuman Breast' (ibid.). We are left to wonder what sort of a breast can outline a scheme for just such murder on a systematic and national scale. But then the answer is that of all exterminators: those they would do away with are not to them random and chaotic individuals, but a controlled mass of numbers. Again, at the end of his outlined scheme the proposer declares,

in the Sincerity of my Heart, that I have not the least personal Interest, in endeavouring to promote this necessary Work; having no other Motive than the *publick Good of my Country, by advancing our Trade, providing for Infants, relieving the Poor, and giving some Pleasure to the Rich.* I have no Children, by which I can propose to get a single Penny; the youngest being nine Years old, and my Wife past Child-bearing. (p. 118)

No children by *which* (!) he may gain; but equally none by which he may lose.

Yet, even while we are repelled by his arguments, we are fascinated; even when he is exposed, we still feel the force of his case. If we look for the human sympathy the proposer so clearly lacks, or for any alternative to his project, he is ready for us:

Therefore, let no man talk to me of other Expedients: *Of taxing our Absentees at five Shillings a Pound: Of using neither Cloaths, nor Houshold Furniture except what is of our own Growth and Manufacture: Of utterly rejecting the Materials and Instruments that promote foreign Luxury: Of curing the Expensiveness of Pride, Vanity, Idleness, and Gaming in our Women: Of introducing a Vein of Parsimony, Prudence and Temperance: Of learning to love our Country, wherein we differ even from* LAPLANDERS *and the inhabitants of* TOPINAMBOO: *Of quitting our Animosities, and Factions; nor act any longer like the Jews, who were murdering one another at the very Moment their City was taken: Of being a little cautious not to sell our Country and Consciences for nothing: Of teaching Landlords to have, at least, one Degree of Mercy towards their Tenants. Lastly, Of putting a Spirit of Honesty, Industry, and Skill into our Shop-keepers; who, if a Resolution could now be taken to buy only our native Goods, would immediately unite to cheat and exact upon us in the Price, the Measure, and the Goodness; nor could ever yet be brought to make one fair Proposal of just Dealing, though often and earnestly invited to it.*

THEREFORE, I repeat, let no Man talk to me of these and the like Expedients; till he hath, at least, a Glimpse of Hope, that there will ever be some hearty and sincere Attempt to put *them in Practice.* (pp. 116–17)

If the reader has been storing himself with such norms or expedients, the ground is quite removed from under him, and he is left only with an impracticable ideal. What each man may learn from Swift's satire, each man may learn: the object is to force him into questioning himself, not to present fixed values.

The question at the root of this satire is close to that of Book IV of *Gulliver's Travels*: what, finally, distinguishes man from the beasts? If we answer 'reason', then in the proposer of this satire we have a man whose reason is employed to bestial ends: he has no notion of the value of a single human life, no conception of man as finally distinct from the brutes, and no sympathy. And he is without all these things because, since nobody has shown human feeling to the Irish, there is no other attitude open but the one he gives (pp. 116–17). The Irish, we may say, are all body, wallowing in the dirt, animal and vicious; and he, surveying them thus coldly, is all mind. Doubtless a classic dualism or a case of dissociated sensibility on a national scale; but the proposer's mind, which can work only with physical data, which has a purely utilitarian idea of value, and which is left with no conception of any metaphysical or spiritual category, is this mind not finally as physical and bestial, as non-mental as the state it portrays? Thus, 'It is true a Child, *just dropt from its Dam*, may be supported by her Milk, for a Solar Year with little other Nourishment' (p. 110); 'there may be about Two hundred Thousand Couple whose Wives are Breeders' (ibid.); 'Twenty thousand [children] may be reserved for Breed; whereof only one Fourth Part to be Males; which is more than we allow to *Sheep, black Cattle,* or *Swine*' (p. 111); 'flay the Carcase; the Skin of which, artificially dressed, will make admirable *Gloves for Ladies,* and *Summer Boots for fine Gentlemen*' (p. 112); and 'Men would become as *fond* of their Wives, during the Time of their Pregnancy, as they are now of their *Mares* in Foal, their *Cows* in Calf, or *Sows* when they are ready to farrow; nor offer to beat or kick them, (as is too *frequent* a Practice) for fear of a Miscarriage' (p. 115). All of this is a picture of the animal level not only of the Irish people but also of the proposer's mind, and, through it, of the minds of those whose failures to help have made this project the only practical answer to the Irish condition.

Both *A Modest Proposal* and *An Argument Against Abolishing Christianity* portray a divorce between reason and passion. The proposers have no sentiments, only a utilitarian conception of value which, pushed to its extreme as here, is madness. At the same time, the vicious passions of men, their rapacity, lewdness, greed and complacency, have created a situation to which irrational reason is the only answer. In the fourth voyage of *Gulliver's Travels* we are presented with a dichotomous society of extreme animality in the humanoid form of the Yahoos, and of rationality in that animal shape which throughout the Renaissance had been the symbol of passion – the horse.[2] Swift would dare us to distinguish the Houyhnhnms, who propose the destruction of the Yahoos, from the modest proposer who plans the culling of the animal Irish: what Gulliver sees in Houyhnhnmland is the hypostasis of the divorce of reason and passion in mankind itself. Whether Swift really believed this does not matter; but it is at once the technique and the vision of his satire. As a vision, though, it involves a recognition of a split, between the ordering and energising forces in life, to which few other writers of the eighteenth century were prepared to admit, even while it crippled their work.

Unlike others of his age, Swift presents no norms, takes no partisan attitude to the world. He is comprehensive in his treatment of reality: like Marvell he sees both sides of an opposition, but unlike him he gives neither pole, as a pole, *any* value. He is one-sided, it is true, in the negative direction of his satire: he has little to say of man's better impulses of mind or heart. Yet it is not masochistic pleasure but unflinching spiritual rigour, together with humour at once mordant and zestful, that goes into the pictures he paints. His satiric journey is a kind of *via negativa* by which the way down feels, finally, like the way up. In his intensity, and perhaps in more, Swift anticipates Blake. Blake presents a poetic world in which opposites are married, not divorced: for him everything is of absolute value, for everything that lives is holy. Yet Swift's satire is of a potency to drive us to reconcile such opposites in our lives even where it exposes their disjunction; and, in the fusion of reason and energy in its procedure, enacts, on a literary level at least, something of the harmony it challenges us to find.

9 Thomson: *The Seasons* (1726–44)

Thomson's *The Seasons* owes much to Milton, but, where Milton set out to justify the ways of God to men, Thomson is more concerned so to justify the ways of nature, if within a context of cosmic optimism. *The Seasons*, like much eighteenth-century nature poetry, is indebted to Virgil's *Georgics* too, both for its form and subject matter, but Thomson's is the first major poem in English literature fully to explore the range and variety of nature's forms on earth and to try to make sense of them both morally and scientifically. Thomson is often considered an Augustan poet, and yet he is frequently quite at odds with the attitudes of Dryden or Pope. Where they are often sceptical in temper, he is far more curious. Where they abhor wildernesses, he is fascinated by them. Where their 'nature' and 'society' are strictly defined and limited, Thomson looks at every corner of society, from the shepherd to the king (as themselves, not as idealisations, or symbols of one another), and at every face of nature, from the Arctic to the tropics. He is perhaps the first poet to give stimulus to the idea that no generalisation is valid which has not come from as wide a survey of as many particulars as possible. The notion is a product of the extension of empiricism in eighteenth-century minds, and gives rise to an *a posteriori* mode of reasoning which is in direct contrast to the *a priori* method, which we saw in Milton, Dryden and Pope, of imposing value on material.

Nevertheless, there are many Augustan leanings in Thomson, as in his followers, and these are at odds with the 'empirical' approach. We might say that, where these two impulses were formerly seen to be divided between different writers, such as Pope and Defoe, now they are brought into conflict within one mind, because the subject-matter and orientation of poetry have been made a mixture of the two – of high and low, civilisation and wilderness, order and energy. The result is that Thomson's poem is full of inconsistencies of approach and argument, of which the basic opposition is that between his sense of the regularity of nature and his evident equal fascination with its irregularity.

The inconsistencies of the poem, as they illustrate Thomson's poetic character, will be our primary concern here.

In 'Spring' Thomson tells us that the mead, 'Full of fresh verdure and unnumbered flowers', shows 'The negligence of nature wide and wild' (504–5). Later he speaks of 'Nature's careless hand' (916), and throughout the poem he shows us examples of nature's prodigality. Yet all this he also sees as part of a plan, a scheme of divine economy whereby everything tends to use: thus, commenting on the young birds forsaking the nest and their parents, he declares 'Unlavish Wisdom never works in vain' ('Spring', 734; see also 'Summer', 733–40, 1660–63; and 'Autumn', 828–35). The problem is highlighted in such portraits as that of the vast unpopulated realms of nature in the equatorial regions ('Summer', 784 ff.). Thomson is filled with wonder at such rivers as the 'mighty Orellana' and the 'sea-like Plata' (840, 843); and with wonder also at the waste of their energies:

> With unabated force
> In silent dignity they sweep along,
> And traverse realms unknown, and blooming wilds,
> And fruitful deserts – worlds of solitude
> Where the sun smiles and seasons teem in vain,
> Unseen and unenjoyed.   (845–50)

(Not for nothing do these lines look forward to the sweetness wasted on the desert air in Gray's *Elegy*: Gray too, like many Augustans, is drawn to the notion of waste, even if not so admiringly.) Thomson goes on to follow the rivers to where, having forsaken the manless regions,

> O'er peopled plains they fair-diffusive flow
> And many a nation feed, and circle safe
> In their soft bosom many a happy isle,
> The seat of blameless Pan, yet undisturbed
> By Christian crimes and Europe's cruel sons.   (851–5)

Yet now he turns in revulsion against this idealising primitivism, and the disorder inherent in such plenitude, asking 'But what avails this wondrous waste of wealth, / This gay profusion of luxurious bliss, / This pomp of Nature?' (860–2). The 'whats' become more and more strident:

> what their balmy meads,
> Their powerful herbs, and Ceres void of pain?
> By vagrant birds dispersed and wafting winds,
> What their unplanted fruits? what the cool draughts,

> The ambrosial food, rich gums, and spicy health
> Their forests yield? their toiling insects what,
> Their silky pride and vegetable robes?
> Ah, what avail their fatal treasures, hid
> Deep in the bowels of the pitying earth . . .?   (862–70)

Thomson is implying that this plenitude will become useful only when
others more able and methodical than the natives subdue and harness it;
he is also now saying that none of this abundance has made the natives
advance one step from the level of brutish and inhuman savages (875–97).

> Ill-fated race! the softening arts of peace,
> Whate'er the humanizing muses teach,
> The godlike wisdom of the tempered breast,
> Progressive truth, the patient force of thought . . .
> Kind equal rule, the government of laws,
> And all-protecting freedom which alone
> Sustains the name and dignity of man –
> These are not theirs.   (875–8, 881–4)

Where now, we wonder, the 'happy isle[s]', each the 'seat of blameless
Pan'; and where the sense of the happy freedom of such peoples from
'Christian crimes and Europe's cruel sons'? Thomson has switched from
admiring the prodigality of nature, and the primitive simplicity of the
peoples it sustains, to repugnance at the waste, and a contradictory
condemnation of the natives as barbarous; it is as if he wrote first from
the stance of a wondering tourist, and then from that of a European
moralist.[1] And this dichotomy in Thomson's attitude between wonder
at plenitude and the demand for use is frequently evident in his poem.
    It is seen also in his different attitudes to trade and civilisation. On
one side he glorifies commerce, industry and civility, and on the other
the simple life of nature, free of what he then speaks of as the rapacity
of the 'developed' countries. The last hundred lines of 'Autumn' are an
attack on the evils of civilisation – on the tyranny of law, the intrigues of
courtiers and, particularly (the theme with which they start), the cruelties
of trade:

> Let others brave the flood in quest of gain,
> And beat for joyless months the gloomy wave . . .
> Let some, far distant from their native soil,
> Urged or by want or hardened avarice,
> Find other lands beneath another sun.   (1278–9, 1284–6)

Contrast these lines with the paean in 'Summer' to the storm-defying
adventurer:

> With such mad seas the daring Gama fought,
> For many a day and many a dreadful night
> Incessant labouring round the stormy Cape, –
> By bold ambition led and bolder thirst
> Of gold. For then from ancient gloom emerged
> The rising world of trade: the genius then
> Of navigation, that in hopeless sloth
> Had slumbered on the vast Atlantic deep
> For idle ages, starting, heard at last
> The Lusitanian Prince, who, heaven-inspired,
> To love of useful glory roused mankind,
> And in unbounded commerce mixed the world.   (1001–12)

(That phrase 'useful glory' is striking here.) Similar hymns to trade and civilisation are scattered through *The Seasons*: among them are the praise of London and of 'philosophy' as the informing force of industry ('Summer', 1457–78, 1758–81); the description of how industry raised man from his natural condition of penurious savagery and solitariness to the happiness of cultivated and social life ('Autumn', 43–150); and the account of the civilising energies of Peter the Great in waking his Russian people from their barbarous sloth ('Winter', 950–87). Yet this last is immediately preceded by a lengthy passage of admiration for the untutored Lapps, who 'ask no more than simple Nature gives' (845), and for whom Thomson performs his customary ritual of attacking the corruptions of civilisation: 'Thrice happy race! by poverty secured / From legal plunder and rapacious power, / In whom fell interest never yet has sown / The seeds of vice' (881–4). And elsewhere in the poem we find similar passages, like the praise of the 'ancient uncorrupted times, / When tyrant custom had not shackled man, / But free to follow nature was the mode', in which Palemon lived ('Autumn', 221–3); or the attack on cities in comparison to the simple joys of rural life ('Winter', 630–45).

Other inconsistencies parallel this. Often Thomson can praise man's powers of knowledge, his capacity to search out all secrets of the universe apart from God ('Summer', 1782–1805; 'Autumn', 1330–73); yet equally he can give vent to the same sceptical scorn that we find in Pope's *Essay on Man* ('Summer', 318–41). He can tell us that reason corrects ignorant superstitious fear at such prodigies as comets or meteors ('Summer', 1699–1729; 'Autumn', 1103–37); and yet leaves us in doubt as to whether Newton, in explaining the workings of the rainbow, is better off than the swain who wonders at it:

> Here, awful Newton, the dissolving clouds
> Form, fronting on the sun, thy showery prism;
> And to the sage-instructed eye unfold

The various twine of light, by thee disclosed
From the white mingling maze. Not so the swain;
He wondering views the bright enchantment bend
Delightful o'er the radiant fields, and runs
To catch the falling glory; but amazed
Beholds the amusive arch before him fly,
Then vanish quite away.   ('Spring', 208–17)

Then again, Thomson's attitude to art is ambiguous. He can tell us that in its primitive state 'lavish Nature the directing hand / Of Art demanded', and a little later that the child of nature Lavinia had a 'native grace' and that 'loveliness / Needs not the foreign aid of ornament, / But is when unadorned adorned the most' (Autumn', 75–6, 201, 204–6). Elsewhere he speaks of 'the negligence of nature wide and wild, / Where, undisguised by mimic art, she spreads / Unbounded beauty to the roving eye' ('Spring', 505–7); or of the equatorial regions where, 'retired / From little scenes of art, great Nature dwells / In awful solitude' ('Summer', 701–3); or of the natural virtue of a Stanley in whom 'moral wisdom mildly shone / Without the toil of art' ('Summer', 573–4). He declares that art is powerless to imitate nature:

Can imagination boast,
Amid its gay creation, hues like hers?
Or can it mix them with that matchless skill,
And lose them in each other, as appears
In every bud that blows?
('Spring', 469–73)

Yet he sees that nature is itself 'artful', as in the birds' construction of their nests ('Spring', 650–2), or in the stratagems they use to draw away intruders (687–701).

His view of nature's spiritual condition is also a double one. Having described the continual springtime of paradise, Thomson turns to complain that 'now those white unblemished minutes, whence / The fabling poets took their golden age, / Are found no more amid these iron times, / These dregs of life!'; and that 'The Seasons since have, with severer sway, / Oppressed a broken world' ('Spring', 272–5, 317–8). Yet soon the view is evolutionary, not devolutionary, in the picture of Britain in savage times:

Lost in eternal broil, ere yet she grew
To this deep-laid indissoluble state
Where wealth and commerce lift the golden head,
And o'er our labours liberty and law
Impartial watch, the wonder of a world!   (844–8)

The to-be-deplored seasons turn to 'the glories of the circling year' ('Summer', 14), which, round the 'beaming car' of nature 'lead, in sprightly dance / Harmonious knit, the rosy-fingered hours' (120–2). Later we hear that the pineapple is 'beyond whate'er / The poets imaged in the golden age', and see paradise, supposed lost, recovered in Abyssinia (686–7, 747–83). And of course we have, too, the 'Hymn to the Seasons' which rounds off the whole poem.

The poem shows a large uncertainty on the subject of suffering in nature: sometimes suffering is explained as part of a divine plan which we are too limited in vision to comprehend; sometimes Thomson turns from scenes of woe to blame'man for allowing them to happen; sometimes he simply presents the fact without comment. In his winter retreat, Thomson tells us, he would speculate on whether nature, destructive as he has seen her to be, 'Was called, late-rising, from the void of night, / Or sprung eternal from the Eternal Mind' ('Winter', 576–7); and would conclude with a 'moral world'

> Which, though to us it seems embroiled, moves on
> In higher order, fitted and impelled
> By wisdom's finest hand, and issuing all
> In general good.   (584–7)

This too is the answer with which 'Winter' ends, as Thomson looks towards apocalypse and the second birth, when all reasons for the apparently reasonless will be revealed, and when 'that your bounded view, which only saw / A little part, deemed evil is no more' (1066–7). Yet this answer is only occasionally touched on. Having shown the disasters caused to the peasant by the autumnal flood, Thomson turns to exclaim, 'Ye masters, then / Be mindful of the rough laborious hand / That sinks you soft in elegance and ease' ('Autumn', 350–2); and he similarly addresses the shepherds when he has portrayed the miseries of sheep in winter ('Winter', 261–8). The miseries themselves are not questioned: blame for their effect is placed on the negligence of man. The picture of the shepherd lost in the snow and of his bereaved family ('Winter', 276–321) shifts to a 'little think the gay licentious crowd' (322 ff.); thence to the speculation that, if they did so think, 'The social tear would rise, the social sigh; / And, into clear perfection, gradual bliss, / Refining still, the social passions work' (356–8); and, finally, directly after, to a consideration of the sins, rather than the mortal condition, of man (359–88). In other contexts Thomson can present suffering as at least partially deserved, as in the plague that strikes Cairo and 'Intemperate man' ('Summer', 1052–91); or, if apparently undeserved, as in the case of Celadon's beloved Amelia, struck down by lightning even as Celadon assured her that heaven protected its own ('Summer', 1169–1222), he admits the fact without comment, only to turn round a few lines later, when the storm he has described is over, to say,

> 'Tis beauty all, and grateful song around,
> Joined to the low of kine, and numerous bleat
> Of flocks thick-nibbling through the clovered vale.
> And shall the hymn be marred by thankless man,
> Most-favoured, who with voice articulate
> Should lead the chorus of this lower world?
> Shall he, so soon forgetful of the hand
> That hushed the thunder, and serenes the sky,
> Extinguished feel that spark the tempest waked,
> That sense of powers exceeding far his own,
> Ere yet his feeble heart has lost its fears?   (1233–43)

This is hardly the question which would occur to the reader, or man, since the God who stilled the storm also caused or allowed it to happen; what has Celadon to do but be other than thankless at the bitter irony that took his love from him even as he declared his trust in God? In a similar manner, Thomson can describe the ruin caused by winter ('Winter', 41–105), and then proclaim, 'Nature! great parent! whose unceasing hand / Rolls round the Seasons of the changeful year, / How mighty, how majestic are thy works!' (106–8); or speak of the season as 'A heavy gloom oppressive o'er the world, / Through Nature shedding influence malign' (58–9) and yet claim that winter is 'only to the thoughtless eye / In ruin seen' (705–6).

The inconsistencies of Thomson's poem are not all, of course, final ones. Some of the apparent contradictions on civilisation and primitive nature could be removed if distinction had been made between the good and bad aspects of both sides: if, say, Thomson had been more ready to show that primitive man is in one way happy, and in another benighted, or that civilisation increases both the capacity for virtue and that for vice. Such balance is not, however, evident, and we are left with a series of 'absolute' portrayals which can only stand in contradictory relation to those which give different views. Thomson illustrates that frequent Augustan inability to reconcile contrary views which underlies the habit of searching for 'general and transcendental truths, which will always be the same'; an inability which we shall trace further in Fielding, Johnson, Crabbe and Cowper. It has telling effect on what unity and consistency of vision his poem might have had.

However, this is far from the final truth about the poem. We have not yet shown exactly *why* Thomson's poem is so often so divided. If the various types of inconsistency are considered, it will be seen that nearly all of them may be classed as a division between 'planned' and 'unplanned'. Civilisation, art, society, knowledge, industry, God, providential suffering, all make sense of phenomena, give them a pattern and a meaning, even confine them and give them bounds, as their opposites do not. Thomson gives us the pictures of undeserved suffering: he does not shrink from them, as Cowper (whose *The Task* is not far from being *The Seasons* rewritten) is more inclined to do; but he tries to make sense of them. That the sense he does make is often so irrelevant to our experience of the pains described suggests that the division in Thomson's attitude to nature is at root one between admiration at nature's chaotic, profuse force and the desire to give it meaning, or, to put it another way, between wonder at the inscrutable fact of things and the need to make them more or less than fact. It is interesting here that, though 'Summer' and 'Winter' end on God as the author of all things, 'Autumn' can conclude with a hymn to 'Nature! all sufficient!' and the fervent prayer 'From thee begin, / Dwell all on thee, with thee conclude my song; / And let me never, never stray from thee!' (1352–3, 1371–3; cf. 'Winter, 106–17). To put it another way, 'order' and 'energy' tend to divorce in this poem. There seems no more telling index to this than the form of the whole, in which there is no central subject, no necessary order in the progressions, and a constant shifting from description to reflection; and at the same time a fairly constant attempt to impose meaning on the material. Here boldness and regularity seem at a real parting of the ways: the notion of *concordia discors*, the unifying principle of Renaissance art and literature, is breaking down.

It is, for example, typical of this poem that it should see even the action of frost, which freezes motion, in terms of energy. Thomson calls frost 'thou secret all-invading power' and asks, 'Is not thy potent energy, unseen, / Myriads of little salts, or hooked, or shaped / Like double wedges, and diffused immense / Through water, earth and ether?' ('Winter', 715, 717–20), as if ice were a species of the *élan vital*. The picture of its action continues this:

> all one cope
> Of starry glitter, glows from pole to pole.
> From pole to pole the rigid influence falls
> Through the still night incessant, heavy, strong,
> And seizes nature fast. It freezes on,
> Till morn, late-rising o'er the drooping world,
> Lifts her pale eye unjoyous. Then appears
> The various labour of the silent night –
> Prone from the dripping eave, and dumb cascade,
> Whose idle torrents only seem to roar,
> The pendent icicle; the frost-work fair,
> Where transient hues and fancied figures rise;

Wide-spouted o'er the hill the frozen brook,
A livid tract, cold-gleaming on the morn;
The forest bent beneath the plumy wave;
And by the frost refined the whiter snow
Incrusted hard, and sounding to the tread
Of early shepherd, as he pensive seeks
His pining flock, or from the mountain top,
Pleased with the slippery surface, swift descends.   (740–59)

We look out to the 'starry glitter' with the suggestion of heat in 'glows';
then, rebounding as it were from the repetition of 'from pole to pole',
immensity comes inwards in the 'fall' of the 'rigid influence' and its
seizure of nature, which is conceived as the grip of a predatory animal;
and the activity of this seizing is heightened by its contrast with the
'still night' in which it occurs and by the suspended syntax in line 743.
The force of the grip is then brought home by the picture of 'morn'
struggling and the mixture of words conveying rise and fall: morn is
'late-rising o'er a drooping world' and 'Lifts her pale eye unjoyous' –
the 'unjoyous' slumps back. 'The various labour' suggests sound and
conveys activity; 'the silent night' suggests the inactivity to which this
activity has reduced that on which it works. 'Prone' gives stasis, the
'dripping eave' flux; likewise, with the 'dumb cascade' and the 'idle tor-
rents'; and 'roar' inserts the energy denied it. The 'pendent icicle' made
by the frost goes down, while its other 'fancied figures rise'. (The use of
tensions between rising and falling, motion and stasis, freedom and re-
striction is frequent in Thomson's poetry). The 'wide-spouted' nature
of the frozen brook suggests the energy which has made it break its
bounds; and the 'livid tract' conveys the sense of bruised life. Continually the past-participle verbs, which give the sense of the frozen, are
thrown in conflict with suggestions of animation. The 'forest bent' puts
over the force of the frost, and the 'plumy wave' adds another element of
activity. To this point we have been surveying the scene: now we are
out with the shepherd experiencing it, feeling the hard ground answer
back to his tread. He himself draws energy from the environment, sliding
down the mountain; and his progress, to the top and then down, is seen
dynamically.

   Nature is conceived here, as often throughout the poem, in terms of
the impact of force on force – something close to a Hobbesian war of all
against all, but in a mood of admiration. Thus the accounts of the
oppressiveness of summer, the wonders of the 'torrid zone', the numer-
ous storms of 'Summer', 'Autumn' and 'Winter'. But nature is as often
seen as a creative force as a destructive one. Typical is this from the
account of the equatorial regions:

> Here lofty trees, to ancient song unknown,
> The noble sons of potent heat and floods
> Prone-rushing from the clouds, rear high to heaven
> Their thorny stems, and broad around them throw
> Meridian gloom.   ('Summer', 653–7)

Again the tension is between rising and falling: the trees are 'lofty', the 'prone-rushing' forces us heavily down (and has just enough ambiguity of reference to point momentarily to the trees), and then the 'rear high' throws us back up; the movement is balanced and completed in a horizontal direction.

The sense of nature's energy comes equally from such concepts as growth, plenitude, variety and the infusion of power. The last is particularly celebrated in 'Spring', in the accounts of instinct and love and of the way the elements transmit their potency to the earth in fruitful showers analogous to animal seed; but it is also found in 'Autumn', where Thomson asks the origin of natural springs (736–835). Plenitude and variety are in almost every description, even in those where Thomson turns aside to contemplation:

> He comes! he comes! in every breeze the Power
> Of Philosophic Melancholy comes!
> His near approach the sudden-starting tear,
> The glowing cheek, the mild dejected air,
> The softened feature, and the beating heart,
> Pierced deep with many a virtuous pang, declare.   ('Autumn', 1004–9)

The passage goes on to describe the variety of the faculties awakened, and the multitude of mental and moral effects they produce (1010–29). As for growth, it is present in every scene, because every scene describes development, whether the inception of a storm or the birth of a bird. The whole excited tone of the poem is a function of the energy it celebrates.

But for Thomson energy must be ordered; and yet much of the force in the poem escapes the patterns of meaning and civility which he would put on it, and to which he is as much committed. We are unlikely, for example, to make continuous reference to God as the source of all that Thomson describes, because, although he says that God, as energy, 'pervades, / Adjusts, sustains, and agitates the whole' ('Spring', 854–5; cf. 'Summer', 41–2), he does not present him as immanent in his creation; so that we are left more to wonder at the force and variety of nature than to feel awe at its stated origin.

Thomson is close to Blake in his sense that 'Without Contrarieties is no Progression', and in his love of energy. But he is close also, of course, to the one poem of Milton's which shows the same, and from which he drew much of his inspiration for *The Seasons*: *Paradise Lost*, and the picture of continuous process and prodigious energy and fecundity therein portrayed. As poets, Milton and Thomson are fairly exceptional in their times in using the freedom of blank verse. And there is, as we shall see, at least one more eighteenth-century poet who, like Thomson, drew much of his imaginative force from a fascination with 'process' and becoming: Cowper. All three poets, also, can slump back into utter stasis, like Samson shorn: [2] the stasis of *Paradise Regained*, where there is no dynamic of conflict; the only half-condemned lethargy of *The Castle of Indolence* (1748), which, if ironically seen, is known, and is temptation to Thomson; the constant shifts from the sofa to exercise, from activity to passivity which Cowper recommends. All three are drawn to energy which defies order, and are at once exhilarated and exhausted by it.

10 Fielding

With Fielding's novels, Augustanism moves away from the concentrated intensity of earlier satirists. Fielding's novels show little concern with final values or concepts: he is not interested in 'values' so much as in their expression in human behaviour; nor is any idea of social or political order more than implicit in his vision. To a large extent this is to be attributed to the fact that his disposition was that of a country gentleman, and he wrote from the standpoint of rural 'common sense': few of the characters or issues he presents have any immediate correlative in contemporary public figures or politics, because, like many writers of his time, he has moved in spirit away from the centre, the metropolis. Within the anonymity of the country, Fielding deals with the typical rather than the individual. His object is to fit in as much of what is representative of the world as he can, so that his vision will be more valid: like Johnson, he at least maintains that no picture of life is adequate unless it has been derived from as many particulars as possible.

Nevertheless, relaxation of stance, benevolence, suspension of prejudice and the desire to arrive at generalisations only after inspection of every datum or side of a case may go only so far. Such generosities, contained as they are with Fielding in a body of moral and social certainties, may have less freedom than confinement. Just how much, and just where, however unemphatically, the boundaries came for Fielding, is portrayed in *Shamela*. His *Tom Jones* offers a further consideration. We have seen, and shall further see, how, when the writers of this period try to assert just one truth, their work also reveals opposing views and tensions; we have yet to see what happens when one such writer tries to cater for both sides of the truth.

'SHAMELA' (1741)

Shamela, Fielding's parody of Richardson's *Pamela*, shows us the lineaments of his Augustanism within a framework of relaxed mockery.

Shamela is 'easy' ridicule: Fielding is not writing a *Dunciad* on Richardson; there is no apocalyptic sense that *Pamela* is the expression of a society in decadence. The values by which Fielding is judging Richardson's novel remain implicit: he can afford to react in purely personal and local terms, without drawing forth a philosophy. (In any case, he disliked metaphysics.[1]) Nevertheless, what Fielding reveals in *Shamela* is a very definite point of view which is set in opposition to a whole area of experience: his relaxation here is the expression not so much of generosity as of confidence.

Richardson's novel was written partly as a panegyric on that Puritan mode of conduct which, taking its light from the promptings of the individual soul, flies in the face of what is considered 'normal' or social behaviour. The code of Pamela's environment quite clearly finds it preposterous that she, a mere serving wench, should resist the assaults of her well-born master. The novel shows her not only resisting, but bending both him and his relatives, not to mention a whole social range of domestics, to her view of things. Private values, in short, overcome public codes. Indeed, the entire novel is about an assault on the individual integrity of a person (as is *Clarissa*). While Fielding might not have endorsed the aristocratic prerogative which *Pamela* attacks, what he shows himself to be uncompromisingly against in *Shamela* is this notion of privacy. And, clearly, behind him is the whole weight of Augustan suspicion of the individual setting himself against the social fabric, of the questioning of generally accepted values; and beyond that lies a moral fabric in which such activities are seen as leading to self-delusion and pride (Dryden, Pope, Swift). It seems clear that Fielding found such outraged cries of Pamela's as the millenarian

> Here's shamelessness for you! Sure the world must be near at an end; for all the gentlemen here are as bad as he, as far as I can hear! And see the fruits of such bad examples. . . .
> But, dear father and mother, what sort of creatures must the womenkind be, do you think, to give way to such wickedness? Why, this it is that makes every one to be thought of alike: and, a-lack-a-day! what a world we live in! for it is grown more a wonder that the men are *resisted*, than that the women *comply* . . .[2]

a mask of vanity, however humble Pamela may claim to be.

It is not that Fielding does not believe in disinterested virtue, but that he does not believe in disconnected virtue, one which presents itself without larger social authentication. Nor can he see Richardson's portrait of virtue rewarded in this world – the Puritan ethos of worldly success as a measure of spiritual growth – in any light but that of hypocrisy, of a virtue which exists in order to be rewarded. This virtue is a sham:

Pamela becomes Shamela* and virtue 'vartue'; and the *sententiae* in *Shamela* are reduced to the vulgar reflections of a cynical materialist. When she plays at resisting Booby, and he takes her at her word, Shamela reflects, '*O what a prodigious Vexation it is to a Woman to be made a Fool of*' (p. 329); during her mock-faint in bed when he tries to seduce her, '*Oh what a Difficulty it is to keep one's Countenance, when a violent Laugh desires to burst forth*' (p. 330). Charmed by Parson Williams she muses, '*Sure Women are great Fools, when they prefer a laced Coat to the Clergy, whom it is our Duty to honour and respect*' (p. 335), a consideration later amplified in the '*O Parson Williams, how little are all the Men in the World compared to thee*' (p. 341). On the word 'vartue', which she constantly brandishes at Booby, she rhapso-dises, '*O what a charming Word that is, rest his Soul who first invented it*' (p. 339). Behind these is Fielding's sense that moralising one's own experience is a disguised and therefore vicious and dangerous form of pride.

Other aspects of *Shamela* push the point further. Its sheer brevity compared to *Pamela* is clearly a comment by Fielding on the lack of wooing he feels to have been really required in Richardson's novel. He feels too that Pamela's virtue is given disproportionate significance: 'The Comprehensiveness of his Imagination must be truly prodigious! It has stretched out this diminutive mere Grain of Mustard-seed (a poor Girl's little, &c.) into a Resemblance of that Heaven, which the best of good Books has compared it to' (p. 322). Fielding senses that this interest in Pamela's virginity comes as much from prurience as from Puritanical fervour (p. 321). But what is at the root of his criticism is an Augustan dislike of words divorced from things, of theory from practice, of inner world from outer.

The critique extends to the style of *Shamela*:

The Squire, who had sat all this while speechless, and was almost really in that Condition, which I feigned, the moment he saw me give Symptoms of recovering my Senses, fell down on his Knees; and O Pamela, cryed he, can you forgive me, my injured Maid? by Heaven, I know not whether you are a Man or a Woman, unless by your swell-ing Breasts. Will you promise to forgive me: I forgive you! D—n you (says I) and d—n you, says he, if you come to that. I wish I had never seen your bold Face, saucy Sow, and so went out of the Room. (pp. 330–1)

The first part is written in what Fielding finds the prolix manner of Richardson, full of elaborate cliché; but the language eventually turns

---

* 'Pamela' is in Fielding's story the character's assumed and public name: she signs her letters to her mother by her true name, 'Shamela'.

into plain Punch-and-Judy (Fielding was particularly fond of puppet-shows) and the apparently settled protestations of Booby undergo an immediate *volte-face*. Much of *Shamela* is conducted as a series of insults used like cudgels – indeed the language, as is typical of Fielding, is itself a kind of action:

> Pamela, says he, what Book is that, I warrant you *Rochester's* poems. – No, forsooth, says I, as pertly as I could; why how now Saucy Chops, Boldface, says he – Mighty pretty Words, says I, pert again. – Yes (says he) you are a d—d, impudent, stinking, cursed, confounded Jade, and I have a great Mind to kick your A—. You, kiss – says I. A-gad, says he, and so I will. . . . Boldface, come hither – Yes, to be sure, says I; why don't you come, says he; what should I come for, says I; if you don't come to me I'll come to you, says he; I shan't come to you, I assure you, says I. Upon which. . . .   (pp. 328–9; cf. pp. 9, 13)

This is of course a *reductio ad absurdum* of the long assaults of Mr B. on Pamela: the object throughout *Shamela* is one of such cutting of cackle, stripping it to the bare facts of the sexual jungle warfare which Fielding believes it to be.

Fielding's dislike of the stress on privacy in *Pamela*, and his suspicion of the novel's prolixity as another form of divorce between the inner and outer worlds, is pushed further into prominence in the injunctions of his Parson Williams. Williams divides faith from works (to the neglect of the latter) in his sermon on the text 'Be not righteous overmuch',[3] which he translates as meaning that one should go to church and honour the clergy, but that one should not do good works; he concludes, 'That those People who talk of Vartue and Morality, are the wickedest of all Persons. That 'tis not what we do, but what we believe, that must save us' (p. 336). He is ignorantly right in the first statement, though by 'talk' he means 'think of them at all'. Later, when Shamela, now married, is out in a coach with Williams, he explains to her how she can have two husbands at once and commit no sin:

> [he] told me the Flesh and the Spirit were two distinct Matters, which had not the least relation to each other. That all immaterial Substances (those were his very Words) such as Love, Desire, and so forth, were guided by the Spirit: but fine Houses, large Estates, Coaches, and dainty Entertainments were the Product of the Flesh. Therefore, says he, my Dear, you have two Husbands, one the Object of your Love, and to satisfy your Desire; the other the Object of your Necessity, and to furnish you with those other Conveniences. . . . as then the Spirit is preferable to the Flesh, so am I preferable to your other Husband. . . .   (p. 351)

Thus Fielding pushes his attack on the implications of privacy and individual judgment to religious and metaphysical dimensions.

This theme is also clearly present in *Joseph Ándrews* and *Tom Jones*: in the first, clearly, in the attacks on hypocrisy, the gap between profession and practice, and perhaps less evidently in the way that Joseph's passive chastity is increasingly dropped for outgoing and active charity; in *Tom Jones* most centrally in the mask that is Blifil beside the plain and open Jones (though here Fielding tries to inculcate a morality of prudence, one which has the virtues but not the vices of caution). To the Man of the Hill – the nearest Fielding comes to giving privacy virtue, but still a man whose Olympian and misanthropic isolation from man has made him subtly but insanely proud (compare him with the astronomer in Johnson's *Rasselas*, chs 40–44) – is opposed Wilson of *Joseph Andrews*, the man who though in retirement from the vices of the city nonetheless goes out of himself with his family to do good for the country people about him. And Fielding is suspicious of people who pass most of their lives inside houses:[4] he has not much to say of many innkeepers, and the claustrophobic worlds of Ladies Booby and Bellaston are comically suspect or plain corrupt; he portrays Allworthy's Paradise-Hall from the outside (*Tom Jones*, Bk I, ch. 4); and it can be argued that the errors in the Booby household at the end of *Joseph Andrews* and those in the inn at Upton in *Tom Jones* are functions of a loss of relation between belief and fact which Fielding expresses more largely in the separation of the self from the world.

Throughout his work Fielding shows a distinct preference for action over contemplation: there are scarcely any scenes where characters are allowed, unhindered by irony, to engage in soliloquies or to draw philosophical and religious, rather than practical, conclusions from their experiences (the latter habit is specifically derided in Square and Thwackum of *Tom Jones*). *Shamela* thus uses Booby where Pamela appears more used by Mr B.; and is continually acting, where Pamela is often speculating. Fielding did not of course believe that Pamela was really passive and undesigning: he thought that image was a mask concealing self-interest, and he set out in *Shamela* to show the girl as he really believed her to be in Richardson's novel. This interpretation arose ultimately from his conviction that activity was more real than passivity: indeed, his belief that virtue and 'vartue' are alike essentially outgoing comes to a point where he takes an Aristotelian view of the self as realised only in act.[5] And hence we find such emphasis on sheer plot in his novels.

There is, however, a certain 'static' quality in Fielding's novels, stemming from his distrust of the notion in the sub-title of Richardson's novel – 'Virtue Rewarded'. For Fielding this is where 'virtue' and 'vartue' part company: vartue wants worldly benefits, but virtue, far more epicurean, seeks the spiritual pleasure of doing good to others; or, as Tom Jones puts it,

> I had rather enjoy my own Mind than the Fortune of another Man. What is the poor Pride arising from a magnificent House, a numerous Equipage, a splendid Table, and from all the other Advantages or Appearances of Fortune, compared to the warm, solid Content, the swelling Satisfaction, the thrilling Transports, and the exulting Triumphs, which a good Mind enjoys, in the Contemplation of a generous, virtuous, noble, benevolent Action? (*Tom Jones*, p. 659)[6]

This virtue of course, not seeking worldly reward, is unlikely to receive it, and indeed is often reviled or reduced to material wretchedness (ibid., pp. 783–4). Fielding does not fully face this view in his novels, where benefits of cash, rank and marriage are bestowed on the good at the end, and are dangled like carrots before the reader throughout. But, despite the overall forward movement resulting from this, his heroes always do good for its own sake. An instance is the period where Jones drops his own concerns to help Mrs Miller's daughter when she has been jilted by Nightingale. At the time this has nothing to do with the main design, from which it appears one more diversion; later, of course, Nightingale and the grateful Mrs Miller are to contribute to the approach of Jones's bliss because of it. *Pamela*, however, and therefore *Shamela*, was for Fielding simply evolutionary and dynamic in plot on the lines of Shakespeare's Richard II's 'they well deserve to have / That know the strong'st and surest way to get'; nevertheless, he cannot resist accomplishing Shamela's eventual exposure and ruin in the last sentence of the parody.

Fielding clearly also disliked the single point of view in *Pamela*. In that nov ˙ we are arguably given no other picture of, or attitude to, events than the ieroine's, and are allowed no form of ironic detachment from her judgments. Fielding did not believe in perfect characters, in life or literature (*Tom Jones*, Bk x, ch. 1): the very existence of *Shamela* poses the alternative view of Pamela's motivation which he believed Richardson's novel lacked. To work further against the single view, and to 'place' the story ironically, Fielding provides the framing devices of Conny Keyber's dedication and the letters of Parsons Tickletext and Oliver: we are thus given a picture of society reacting to Shamela, not a presentation of her mind in isolation.[7] Fielding shares with such other Augustans as Pope, Thomson and Johnson the desire for a universal or 'epic' view, for canvassing a whole range of experience, people and judgments to give a true, because full, picture of life – or, as he puts it in *Tom Jones*, 'Conversation in our Historian must be universal, that is, with all Ranks and Degrees of Men' (p. 494; see also p. 742).[8] He also had the conviction, prevalent in his time, that one learnt from experience by involving one-self in it, not by approaching it with self-begotten and 'novel' notions, or *a priori* principles, like Pamela; this is consistent both with his creation of good-natured, relatively unprincipled heroes, and with some of his difficulties in trying - to show them becoming morally disciplined and prudent.

Fielding's criticism of *Pamela* was also aimed at its democratic content and method. Central in this was for him the marriage of high- with low-born: Mr B. of *Pamela* becomes Mr Booby in *Shamela* partly because, except by fools, the lower orders are not to be brought to the same level as their betters.[9] Nor was Fielding happy with a female character as centrepiece: in *Tom Jones* he tells us how Mrs Miller 'shewed the highest Deference to the Understandings of Men; a Quality, absolutely essential to the making a good Wife' (p. 883). As a result Shamela becomes slightly 'butch' in her behaviour: it is of a piece with this that, at her manful resistance of him, Booby can only wonder, 'by Heaven, I know not whether you are a Man or a Woman, unless by your swelling Breasts' (p. 330); or to hear from Henrietta, Shamela's mother, in a brief letter, 'You will excuse the Shortness of this Scroll; for I have sprained my right Hand, with boxing three new made Officers. – Tho' to my Comfort, I beat them all' (p. 333).

Shamela's vulgarity is exposed not only in her behaviour but also in her language, and here not only in such crude early diction as 'desiring you to commodate me with a Ludgin' (p. 325), but also in the way these proletarian attempts to imitate one's betters, though they may develop, still finally show the mark of the beast. In the following, the syntax runs for a time polished and sophisticated, but soon tires:

I began now to grow uneasy, apprehending that I should have no more of Mr. *Williams's* Company that Evening, and not at all caring for my Husband, I advised him to sit down and drink for his Country with the rest of the Company. . . .

I don't know why I mention this Stuff to you; for I am sure I know nothing about *Pollitricks*, more than Parson *Williams* tells me, who says that the Court-side are on the Right on't, and that every Christian ought to be on the same with the Bishops.   (pp. 352–3)

We end with such gems as 'Parson *Williams* is, it seems, going thither too, to be *instuted*' (p. 353), and 'the first Syllabub hath too comical a Sound' (p. 354).

Fielding also satirises the lack of a sense of hierarchy in the feminine mind generally and in Pamela's in particular. Spiritual tribulation often in *Pamela* rubs shoulders with domestic detail: 'O dear heart! what a world do we live in! – I am now come to take up my pen again.'[10] Thus in

Shamela we find, 'And so we talked of honourable Designs till Supper-time. And Mrs *Jewkes* and I supped together upon a hot buttered Apple-Pie; and about ten o'Clock we went to Bed' (p. 340).[11] There is no sense of distinction in Shamela's books (p. 344): *The Whole Duty of Man* is jostled with *Venus in the Cloyster: Or, the Nun in her Smock* (we are reminded of the same mode of exposure in Pope's 'Puffs, Powders, Patches, Bibles, Billet-doux'). Similar point is behind the details Shamela gives us of what she ate for breakfast after her wedding-night with Mr Booby, and of what clothes they then put on (p. 347).

As for the form of *Pamela* generally, Fielding disliked the method of 'writing to the minute', of imitating 'the painful and voluminous Historian, who to preserve the Regularity of his Series, thinks himself obliged to fill up as much Paper with the Detail of Months and Years in which nothing remarkable happened, as he employs upon those notable Æras when the greatest Scenes have been transacted on the human Stage' (*Tom Jones*, p. 75; see also pp. 116–8). The slavery to time that he finds in *Pamela* is of course nowhere better parodied than in Shamela's account of herself about to be assaulted by Mr Booby: 'Mrs Jervis and I are just in Bed, and the Door unlocked; if my Master should come – Odsbobs! I hear him just coming in at the Door. You see I write in the present Tense, as Parson *Williams* says. Well, he is in Bed between us' (p. 330). What Fielding is also mocking here is the being too close, even too vulgarly proximate, to experience, which, like nature, should be distanced and refined by the civilised sensibility.

In his other writings Fielding is far less certain on the subject of rank, and shows his sympathies divided between the hierarchical view and the Christian principle that all men are equal.[12] *Tom Jones* is arguably broken-backed because of this: we are asked for most of the novel to consider true human value irrespective of birth,[13] in the dubious origins of the hero, and his demotic history; but at the end we are implicitly told that Jones's conduct was consistent only with his being the moneyed gentleman he then discovers himself to be. Within the briefer compass and the specifically parodic intent of *Shamela*, however, the view on rank can be single, if one-sided.

Shamela and *Pamela* may thus be contrasted as Tory versus Whig, Anglican versus Puritan, Augustan versus Grub Street, public versus private, social versus individual, male versus female, activity versus passivity, action versus contemplation, perhaps even Aristotelian versus Platonist. As we have observed, Fielding does not, as earlier Augustan writers tend to do, make any of these standpoints explicit or theoretic. For him, if not for Richardson with his more timeless zeal, the defensive need to insist on objective concepts of value had eased into the indirect portrayal of values generally accepted by like-minded men. Yet still the values are there, producing a one-sided approach to life. What happens when Fielding tries to be more various and generous morally and socially is portrayed in *Tom Jones*.

'TOM JONES' (1749)

That this is a comic novel, and that Fielding has a static and deterministic view of human character explain what happens at the end. Tom is said to have learned prudence, and we have been carried through a variety of experiences in which he is supposed to have done so. But we do not see prudence becoming part of his character, for Fielding finds it difficult to marry simple, unordered good nature with any sort of caution or watchfulness, however worthy.[14] He has Tom marry Sophia, whose name means 'wisdom', instead; and, while this tells us that Tom has become more careful, it does not show it. In short, Tom is left having learnt care as a lesson to which he gives allegiance, but not as one transformed by it; the transformation itself occurs beyond the story: 'He hath also, by Reflexion on his past Follies, acquired a Discretion and Prudence very uncommon in one of his lively Parts' (p. 981). And this is often a feature of comedy: in Shakespeare's *A Midsummer Night's Dream*, for example, the characters do not change, but are manipulated; do not develop, but learn: there is no psychic continuity between delusion and insight. Fielding is even a little nervous of specifying what it is that Tom learns, in as much as he commonly teaches prudence negatively, by examples of the forms it should not take, or of the imprudences to which one should not be subject;[15] and there is also the further question of how far, given Blifil's unfathomable evil intent and Allworthy's innocent gullibility, it was particularly his imprudence that caused Tom to be turned away in the first place. Nevertheless, this being comedy, and the characters being types, we are prepared on this level to take the will for the deed.

One is not so certain of the way the resolution of the plot is effected – even if we allow that once Tom may be supposed to have learned and once the moral conclusion has been reached, the action should resolve itself as a symbol of this. Square's repentance and his revealing letter to Allworthy on the subject of Tom's birth are a case in point. No reader could have anticipated it from the character of Square as presented earlier in the book: it is a total transformation. Some theoretic justification for it can be made out. Square's letter is written while he is on his deathbed (we recall Mrs Blifil, who also wrote a deathbed confession). Further, he is a philosopher now converted to Christianity, being in a position, therefore, for an increase of good heart to descend upon him (unlike his Christian rival, Thwackum). And perhaps we recall too that it was Square whom Jones caught with Molly Seagrim; and that, however shameful and ludicrous Square's plight in discovery, he had at least been at the kind of lively work of which, with reservations, Fielding might have approved (Thwackum gets his pleasure out of whacking people, and, one suspects, in more solitary contexts than his rival). Yet however much these reasons may explain how, theoretically, Square's change of heart could come to pass – and even though the change itself is a reported one – they do not fill in the chasm of different presentations. And this is because Square, like all of Fielding's characters, is presented as a 'humour' or 'type' figure, whose earlier beastliness was portrayed as steady and unmitigated. The problem here of the level of probability in character was one of which Fielding was well aware, and claimed he would avoid:

> It is admirably remarked by a most excellent Writer, that Zeal can no more hurry a Man to act in direct Opposition to itself, than a rapid Stream can carry a Boat against its own Current. I will venture to say, that for a Man to act in direct Contradiction to the Dictates of his Nature, is, if not impossible, as improbable and as miraculous as any Thing which can well be conceived. . . .
>
> Our modern Authors of Comedy have fallen almost universally into the Error here hinted at: Their Heroes generally are notorious Rogues, and their Heroines abandoned Jades, during the first four Acts; but in the fifth, the former become very worthy Gentlemen, and the latter, Women of Virtue and Discretion: Nor is the Writer often so kind as to give himself the least Trouble to reconcile or account for this monstrous Change and Incongruity. There is, indeed, no other Reason to be assigned for it, than because the Play is drawing to a Conclusion. (pp. 405–6)

Similar is his later protestation that he will not employ supernatural means to rescue Jones from the gallows (pp. 875–6). But the question remains as to how far the will shows itself in the deed, or can even be taken for it.

A related issue here is the attitude to Squire Western and his values at the end. For most of the novel we have been asked to accept that Western's refusal of Jones as a husband for Sophia, on the grounds of his meanness and poverty, is reprehensible; but at the end Tom is made to be of good birth and money, and receives the squire's blessing. Thus Tom has had to come up to the corrupt demands of Sophia's father, rather than Western learn humility and generosity. Further, the novel endorses Western at the end as an endearing character. There may be a condemnatory edge in the portrayal of his first reaction to the news of Tom's changed status:

> Men over-violent in their Dispositions, are, for the most Part, as changeable in them. No sooner then was *Western* informed of Mr.

Allworthy's Intention to make *Jones* his Heir, than he joined heartily with the Uncle in every Commendation of the Nephew, and became as eager for her Marriage with *Jones*, as he had before been to couple her to *Blifil*.   (pp. 957–8)

Yet after this he returns to his position of lovable blustery eccentric, bursting in on Tom and Sophia with a 'To her, Boy, to her, go to her. – That's it, little Honeys, O that's it' (p. 974).[16] Clearly, our moral distrust of Western is lost in this sense of his exuberance; and this is not the only instance in the novel where energy of nature tends to eclipse moral defects; or, to put it another way, where the single view strangles the possibility of a duality.

The same difficulty is present in the wider characterisation of the novel. Fielding often protests that his characters are subtly individuated, and particularly that they are often a moral mixture: he tells us

> not [to] find out too near a Resemblance between certain Characters here introduced; as for Instance, between the Landlady who appears in the Seventh Book, and her in the Ninth. Thou art to know, Friend, that there are certain Characteristics in which most Individuals of every Profession and Occupation agree. To be able to preserve these Characteristics, and at the same Time to diversify their Operations, is one Talent of a good Writer. Again, to mark the nice Distinction between two Persons actuated by the same Vice or Folly is another. . . .
> . . . [do] not . . . condemn a Character as a bad one, because it is not perfectly a good one. . . .
> The Foibles and Vices of Men in whom there is great mixture of Good, become more glaring Objects, from the Virtues which contrast them, and show their Deformity. . . . (pp. 525–7; cf. pp. 96–7, 328–9)

Yet one wonders whether his landladies, to take Fielding's example, are sufficiently differentiated. All operate by the rule of deference to gentility and money, and by that of rapacious cruelty to those without it; and at one point Fielding lists the rules of inhospitability by which all publicans act (p. 429). There is little differentiation among them, because all are consumed by precisely the same motives in relation to their guests, and we see them in little other light. Marital relationships are described, but, although these are various from one pair to another, that variety is never at the forefront of our notice. Thus in one case the landlady masters her husband (pp. 428–9) and in another *vice versa* (pp. 576–8, 611), but the difference is neither important nor striking.

This inevitable simplification of character is also evident in the moral portrayals. We may allow for a moment that Black George loves Tom, but his stealing of his pocket-book, his hypocrisy in pretending to help

Tom find it, and his readiness to refuse to give him charity must make that love for the time non-existent. Fielding declares, 'I believe there are few Favours which he would not gladly have conferred on Mr. *Jones*; for he bore as much Gratitude towards him as he could, and was as honest as Men who love Money better than any other Thing in the Universe generally are' (p. 314). This may be intended to show Black George morally mixed; but it surely fails, because there really is no way of harnessing the two extremes of love for Tom and absolute failure of love; and, further, we are asked to attend to one side at a time only, rather than to see both operative at once. Nor is this the first time that George has been less than loving to Tom (pp. 120–3, 132–3). If Fielding is so much of a Cressida as to believe that one can love even where one betrays that love, then one feels that such generosity may, by its excess, court a lurch into cynical despair. It may be, perhaps, that this is what has happened in other parts of the novel.[17] Many of the minor characters are presented as people of complete if not vicious depravity:

> In these Censures, my Landlady did Mr. *Fitzpatrick* great Injustice; for he was really born a Gentleman, though not worth a Groat; and tho', perhaps, he had some few Blemishes in his Heart as well as in his Head, yet being a sneaking, or a niggardly Fellow, was not one of them. In reality, he was so generous a Man, that whereas he had received a very handsome Fortune with his Wife, he had now spent every Penny of it, except some little Pittance which was settled upon her; and in order to possess himself of this, he had used her with such Cruelty, that together with his Jealousy, which was of the bitterest Kind, it had forced the poor Woman to run away from him.   (pp. 534–5)

The possibility of generosity, of but a few blemishes, is raised so that its removal may the more surely damn. Similar are the portraits of great men's servants (pp. 643–4) or of people's attitude to charity (p. 722).

One way of avoiding this situation might have been the technique of 'double irony', of which so much has been made in recent criticism. By this method the reader both judges and is judged at the same time, so that the problem of only subsequently correcting valuations made by him does not arise. Thus, when Jones is caught with Mrs Waters in her bedroom, and she pretends that he had come to her rescue on hearing her door being broken in, we are told,

> And hence, I think, we may very fairly draw an Argument, to prove how extremely natural Virtue is to the Fair Sex: For tho' there is not, perhaps, one in ten thousand who is capable of making a good Actress; and even among these we rarely see two who are equally able to personate the same Character; yet this of Virtue they can all admir-

ably well put on; and as well those Individuals who have it not, as those who possess it, can all act it to the utmost Degree of Perfection.   (p. 532)

The first sentence surprises us, because it is not the sort of conclusion that we have come to about the behaviour of Mrs Waters; and when Fielding goes on to talk about women as actresses we are happy to interpret it as having been an ironic way of saying that she is a consummate fake. But the last statement cannot simply be read in terms of the False Florimell beside the True: that women without virtue can act it as well as those with it is a real compliment to femininity. We are forced to see the limitations of the judgment we make.

This technique is, however, much more rarely used by Fielding than its votaries allow: there are only a few examples in *Tom Jones* – more, proportionately, in Fielding's journalistic writings. What happens far more often is that Fielding judges moral behaviour, while elsewhere protesting that nobody has the right to do so (for example, in *Tom Jones*, contrast pp. 159 and 258 with pp. 284 and 345–6). This is precisely the difference (and one we saw in Dryden also) between the Horatian insistence on good manners and doing to others as you would have them do to you, in the 'Essay on Conversation', and the Juvenalian exposure of vice in the 'Essay on the Knowledge of the Characters of Men'; or the contradiction that exists between the claim in the preface to *Joseph Andrews* that human follies will be the primary object of ridicule, and the fact that much of the book is concerned with lashing vice.[18] And Fielding was also, of course, both a Christian believer in the injunction 'Judge not . . .', and a justice of the Bench. The clash of these two sides is evident throughout *Tom Jones*: it is particularly salient in Fielding's attempting to justify Allworthy's open-hearted trust of Thwackum and Blifil, while at the same time showing the reader, in the hidden depravity of the beneficiaries of this Horatian Christianity, that it is based on total ignorance of their true natures.

What we see in *Tom Jones* is in part the penalty of 'type' characterisation in a novel of real life, and Fielding's declaration 'once for all, I describe not Men, but Manners; not an Individual, but a Species' (*Joseph Andrews*, p. 168) come home to roost. But in the fullest terms it is the product of a one-sidedness in Fielding, an inability to yoke, in any but an additive, and often mutually contradictory, relation, opposed modes of seeing.[19] Unlike Dryden or Pope, he can at least entertain different attitudes to an issue, but he oscillates between support for one side and for the other, without more than occasionally attempting to reconcile them.

11 Gray: *Elegy Written in a Country Churchyard* (1751)

Augustan pastoral had usually idealised and 'neo-classicised' the country: the actual condition of rustics had been ignored for an Arcadian idyll in which nature was 'wrought up to an higher pitch' (Dryden). Gray, it must be said, was not the first to describe some of the realities of rustic life in poetry, but he was one of the first 'civilised' poets to do so, and certainly the first to put them at the centre of a major poem. With Gray we see also how, as in Thomson and Fielding, the urge to impose one's vision upon external reality in an *a priori* manner is shifting to a more empirical approach whereby that reality is seen for what it is before the attempt is made to make sense of it. Gray's poem had a special meaning for Johnson, who asked that 'the occasion which is supposed to produce [pastoral] be at least not inconsistent with a country life'. If Johnson's remarks are compared with those of Pope in his 'A Discourse on Pastoral Poetry' (1704), it can be seen how the standard has moved from decorum according to genre and intention, to decorum according to subject and nature: for Pope, pastoral well-written is a pleasure to the cultured and a delight to the well-mannered; for Johnson pastoral should not be 'less likely to interest those who have retired into places of solitude and quiet than the more busy part of mankind' (*Rambler*, no. 37).

In the latter part of the eighteenth century the Arcadian impulse of pastoral poetry is steadily eroded. In Gray we shall see the mingling of a desire for rustic values and retirement with an awareness that the rustics themselves would seek to leave those supposed delights, or else only partially accept them. In *Rasselas* Johnson explodes Nekayah's dream of pastoral innocence with coarse reality. In *The Deserted Village*, a more Augustan pastoral, Goldsmith shows us the rustics leaving the Arcadian dream – if here not because it is false, but because it is both true and lost for ever. Crabbe's *The Village* shows the hatred of the rustics at having to remain fixed in what is for them a wretched life. Even where primitivism might have taken the place of the more civilised and artificial Arcadias, as in Thomson and Cowper, we find both poets torn between this romantic urge and that progressivism which sees the life of the savage as brutal and stagnant. (So too would Pope have found the savage; but, where he would have refined him, Thomson and Cowper place a stronger value on empirical fact, and therefore involve themselves in self-division.)

Gray is the first English poet to give extended treatment to the theme of frustrated rustic worth.[1] Where this theme appeared at all in earlier literature, the limitations on talent were usually seen, as Gray himself at first tries to see them, to be resolved in the general levelling of death: examples are Parnell's 'Night-Piece on Death' and Young's *Night Thoughts* (I, 123 ff., which sees life as an embryo state). Gray's poem, however, is concerned with life as an embryo state *within* life, not in relation to death – as an aborted birth. Pastoral elegy had previously dealt with the theme of blighted hopes and talents, but only in relation to civilised men in rustic guise. A Christian pastoral such as 'Lycidas' shows how the fact that all manner of talents may be cut off in a civilised man before their full expression within life does not finally matter, since the temporal loss is resolved in eternal gain; but this Christian certainty is not part of Gray's *Elegy*.

One condition for Gray's novel subject was the simple fact that empiricism led to a direct increase in the range and number of subjects and themes available for treatment in poetry. Other factors make it unsurprising that this theme had not been largely treated before. It was hardly one likely to appeal to the Augustans, not only because it dealt with actual rustics and with what oft was *not* thought, but because the notion of a failure of self-realisation within the scale of cosmic plenitude would have appeared a criticism of divine providence.[2] Besides, the theme involves consideration of the hidden and the private, and of one 'unrepresentative' area of life. Nevertheless, it is strange to find such novelty in a poem the lines of which are so often modified thefts from earlier poets.

Gray's reasons for his choice of theme probably cannot finally be plumbed. We may note, however, that as a scholar he was interested in hidden or buried knowledge all his life, whether in exploring the minute in the form of insects or the mechanisms of plants, or in his researches into the habits and customs of ancient cultures.[3] And as an English poet he was – in common with Collins – determined to revive the lost Celtic culture of Britain: the Celts can be paralleled to the rustics of the *Elegy*, driven to frustrated obscurity by the Normans as the peasants are by the great and the 'civilised'. Certainly the attempt to reanimate folk culture involves an increased interest in the 'folk'. But there was a possible personal reason too for Gray's choice of theme in the *Elegy*. Several of his poems – the *Eton Ode*, the sonnet to West and the bardic odes –

deal with the theme of blighted hopes: 'My lonely anguish melts no heart but mine; / And in my breast the imperfect joys expire.' In his bio-logical studies Gray shows a recurrent fascination for freaks of nature, prodigies which have veered from the path of nature's uniformity:[4] here again the interest is in a promise which has not been realised. It is quite possible that this interest arises from a sense in Gray that he him-self had not realised his own potential to the full, that he was frittering away his lifetime's energies: certainly not one of his scholarly projects ever came to completion. Nevertheless, we can only infer this, for Gray never admitted to it. So too with another possible speculation – that the rustics are a type of his dead friend West, while the great are analogues of Walpole, and that Gray is choosing between the kind of emotionally involved relationship he had with the former and the more urbane companionship of the latter.[5]

The first stanza of the *Elegy* sets the tone of solemnity of the poem:

> The curfew tolls the knell of parting day,
> The lowing herd wind slowly o'er the lea,
> The ploughman homeward plods his weary way,
> And leaves the world to darkness and to me.

Each line, containing a unit of sense, suggests the steady tolling of a bell for the death of day. But Gray describes the scene as one in which the darkness and silence are slightly interrupted:

> all the air a solemn stillness holds,
> Save where the beetle wheels his droning flight,
> And drowsy tinklings lull the distant folds;

> Save that from yonder ivy-mantled tower
> The moping owl does to the moon complain
> Of such as, wandering near her secret bower,
> Molest her ancient solitary reign.

The will to silence is not complete, and the owl is not undisturbed.
    The next stanza begins to explain this: we move from the landscape and the animal creation to man:

> Beneath those rugged elms, that yew-tree's shade,
> Where heaves the turf in many a mouldering heap,
> Each in his narrow cell for ever laid,
> The rude forefathers of the hamlet sleep.

The turf 'heaves'; each is laid (perhaps like an egg) in a restrictive cell; all sleep. The suggestion is one of refusal to enter the nonentity of death, of stubborn defiance of equally stubborn or 'rugged' fact. But that the latter must always finally win is also suggested by the way we come upon the dead in the midst of natural phenomena, hemmed in by trees, shut in by the ground in 'many a mouldering heap': identity is being lost even as it is asserted. The interruptions of the darkness are a pre-figuring of what is portrayed here. And the way that in the first three stanzas the poet is *waiting* for the right 'atmosphere' heralds other ex-pectations that are to be spoken about later in the poem.

The next three stanzas describe the former relations between the dead peasants and their environment. In stanzas 5 and 6 these relations are hierarchically portrayed:

> The breezy call of incense-breathing morn,
> The swallow twittering from the straw-built shed,
> The cock's shrill clarion or the echoing horn,
> No more shall rouse them from their lowly bed.

We move from the inanimate (though seen through the spectacles of pathetic fallacy) to the animate, and last to the human; the cock's clarion is a natural phenomenon used by man, and the echoing horn of course needs human agency to make it sound. But none of the creatures or items in this list does what it does for the specific purpose of wak-ing man from his sleep. This voluntary level of relationship between man and his environment is portrayed in the next stanza:

> For them no more the blazing hearth shall burn,
> Or busy housewife ply her evening care:
> No children run to lisp their sire's return,
> Or climb his knees the envied kiss to share.

Here the fire is made to warm the peasant: where the occurrences in the list in the previous stanza were organised by him or by others for their use, those here deliberately minister to him. In this stanza there is again a progression. The fire implies a human hand behind it but one not seen. The welcome of his wife is nearer to the peasant, in that the thing being done and the person doing it can both be seen, but, as work, her welcome is still at one remove. Finally, after these variously in-direct welcomes, it is the children who greet him directly, and then even more closely by climbing all over him.

This notion of physical impact is continued in the next stanza. We have seen what came to him and ministered to him from his surroundings;

now we see him going out to those surroundings and impinging upon them:

> Oft did the harvest to their sickle yield,
> Their furrow oft the stubborn glebe has broke;
> How jocund did they drive their team afield!
> How bowed the woods beneath their sturdy stroke!

Each line is like a blow on the soil, if the whole is mournfully ironic in that the peasants have now yielded, the stubborn glebe has broken them, and they now bow beneath the woods. This and the preceding two stanzas have vital movement, in contrast to the initial solemn rhythms of the poem (and the morn is at once both hearty and gentle, 'breezy' and 'incense-breathing'); but the tolling 'no more' cuts under these, suggesting an almost universal finality – not only that the fire will no longer burn or the children run, but that the morn will no longer call or the swallow twitter for anyone, because the centre of all in the peasant has gone.

At this point the poem apparently changes its subject.

> Let not Ambition mock their useful toil,
> Their homely joys and destiny obscure;
> Nor Grandeur hear, with a disdainful smile,
> The short and simple annals of the poor.

We have been hearing about the nature and implications of peasant death, but, without being Augustans, we have not thought of these deaths as unworthy of record. Yet this seeming self-conscious lurch is in fact one of the ways in which Gray makes his poem more universal.

It might be supposed too that the above stanza would be followed by some account of the worth of peasant life compared to that of the great, but, though the first two of the next lines suggest this, the notion is not continued:

> The boast of heraldry, the pomp of power,
> And all that beauty, all that wealth e'er gave,
> Awaits alike the inevitable hour.
> The paths of glory lead but to the grave.

We have returned to the theme of mortality, and with a 'death levels all' topic which is insufficient answer to the issues raised. Is obscurity a good thing? Are short and simple annals best? In death all may be equal, but what of life? The speaker goes back, in what might appear the gesture of an irritated sensibility, to the theme of peasant poverty, raised in the eighth stanza:

> Nor you, ye Proud, impute to these the fault,
> If Memory o'er their tomb no trophies raise,
> Where through the long-drawn aisle and fretted vault
> The pealing anthem swells the note of praise.

He then proceeds, in the next stanza, to ask whether any monument, however rich and ornate, can do the dead any good (this is a continuation of the 'breaking-of-links' motif in stanzas 5–7): 'Can storied urn or animated bust / Back to its mansion call the fleeting breath?' Yet in the context of the poem as a whole Gray does not see death in such final terms; he sees that all men call for remembrance in the breasts of the living, and that memorials have a part to play.

Just as he does not fully accept simple memorials, so Gray is not satisfied with the simplicity of peasant life which he has just eulogised. He now turns, therefore, to show how the peasants had the potential for the virtues of the great, which, had it not been that 'their lot forbade', they could have exercised, and been equal with those who despise them. This section of the poem, from stanzas 12 to 19, is about the value of peasant life, not about their state in death, a state to which the speaker returns only at stanza 20.

This interweaving of the deaths and lives of the peasants can be viewed as showing that the one is in a sense like the other. The basic subject of this poem seems to be the propitiation of the vexed soul: of the dead, in whose ashes 'live their wonted fires' (stanza 23); of the living peasants who have to resign themselves to the gravelike circumscription of their virtues and talents; and of the speaker himself, who has to find some way of silencing his own doubts as to the worth of simplicity. That propitiation is given both by the poem as commemoration, and by its speaker, who, with all his talents and the capacity to exercise them, offers himself to the rustic community, lets himself be lost in the later ignorant vision of him uttered by the 'hoary-headed swain'. The apparent jerks of context in the poem may thus be meant to force our awareness of the interrelation of its themes, and the hesitations and uncertainties of the argument the movement of a sensibility towards resigned self-immolation. The dead and the living, the poor and the great, and the poet moving between the two poles are mutually and mutely metaphoric.[6]

Whether Gray himself was clear on this point is another matter. It would seem from such sketchy critical views as he has left to posterity that he had scant respect for the 'Rules', and that he expected poetry to work imaginatively and emotionally; but it is equally clear that he insisted upon careful organisation in art.[7] Knowing how frequently and carefully he revised the poem, we will be inclined to feel that its apparent lack of organisation might be deliberate poetic strategy; yet knowing also that Gray's primary attention in these revisions (apart from the well-known change from the Eton MS.) was to versification and the meanings and overtones of individual phrases, it is possible that the vast was missed for the minute; and again, from what we know of Augustan uncertainties at conscious levels of organisation, it is more than likely that, as in several such poems, the unity of Gray's is created unconsciously.

In stanza 10 the funerals of the rich have adjectives, while the 'tomb' of the peasant has none. Yet 'the long-drawn aisle' suggests tedium, 'the fretted vault' irritated sleep, and 'the pealing anthem swells the note of praise' unnecessary accompaniment. This stanza tells the rich not to condemn the poor for lack of monuments on their graves: stanza 11 continues, in explanation of this,

> Can storied urn or animated bust
> Back to its mansion call the fleeting breath?
> Can Honour's voice provoke the silent dust,
> Or Flattery soothe the dull cold ear of Death?

But in stanza 10 the point was not one of the efficacy of these monuments in recalling the dead to life, but their implicit value as commemoration of renown. And, as far as renown goes, elaborate tombs and funerals can do more than humble stones. The speaker is not happy with the 'neglected spot' (stanza 12) or the 'frail memorial' of the peasant (stanza 21): indeed, he has written his poem as a further epitaph (the title he first gave it) and disseminator of fame (stanza 24). Here again he shows himself divided between humble simplicity and the rise of talent, between obscure privacy and self-expressive publicity. And the subject has quietly changed: in stanza 9, pomp and wealth could not delay death; now they are shown as unable to reverse it. But both point to the gulf between life and death, the impossibility of a link; and this takes us back further to the breaking of the links between the peasant and his environment in death. The poem is so written that, as we come upon these apparent shifts of subject, we are forced into making the thematic connections for ourselves (and perhaps in reconciling the gulfs of sense, thus enacting or bringing to be a web of interrelation which is in one (poetic) way an answer to the disjoined contexts of life and death).

Stanza 12 continues the seeming reversals:

> Perhaps in this neglected spot is laid
> Some heart once pregnant with celestial fire;
> Hands that the rod of empire might have swayed,
> Or waked to ecstasy the living lyre.

If we set this beside stanza 8, which bade Ambition not to 'mock their useful toil', it would seem that this stanza is allowing for its being so mocked. The speaker is now justifying the peasant not as simple man, but as great man circumscribed, or, as he puts it in stanza 13, 'Chill Penury repressed their noble rage, / And froze the genial current of the soul.' The tension in the speaker between his desire to accept the peasants for what they were and his equal need to justify them in terms of what they might have become – itself a mirror of the half-resignation of the peasant both in life and in death – is now fully articulated. And, to push the reader into making these connections, the speaker not only contradicts himself, but keeps changing subject, as here, where we are turned from the state of death to consider the lives of the rustics.

The last two lines of this stanza are arranged, like those of stanzas 5–7, to suggest the gap between potential and act. The 'rod of empire' that the hands might have swayed is symbolic: the hands hold the rod, not the empire itself – the whole man does that – and there is just a tincture of suggestion that the empire might so have been held in name rather than in fact. But the hands that woke the lyre to ecstasy are immediately involved in the whole action. The one is thus a symbolic, the other a concrete, activity.

But the hands could not perform either activity, because, as stanza 13 tells us,

> Knowledge to their eyes her ample page
> Rich with the spoils of time did ne'er unroll;
> Chill Penury repressed their noble rage,
> And froze the genial current of the soul.

This is saying both that they had no opportunities, and that they 'dried up' (or, in the poem's terms, that the 'heart once pregnant with celestial fire' was frozen). Knowledge here, in the word 'spoils', is conceived as a plunderer sharing loot – another instance of the attempt to come to terms with the peasant lot. The speaker is at this point portraying the urges of the peasants to better things as urges that were silenced by and during their penurious lives. Already we have wondered whether the celestial fire that once warmed the peasant heart was there all his life or was stopped during it: the speaker of the poem himself shifts the emphasis in the next stanza.

Thus, in stanza 14 we are told, in that celebrated and much-debated imagery,

> Full many a gem of purest ray serene
> The dark unfathomed caves of ocean bear:
> Full many a flower is born to blush unseen
> And waste its sweetness on the desert air.

Here the potential of the peasant has become actualised, if only where it can have no effect on the wider world. The gem and the flower express peasants with knowledge and with freedom for their celestial fire: what they now lack is someone to notice them. Now too we are told that they are 'serene', which in no way agrees with the 'celestial fire' or 'noble rage' that we have heard about before. Now too the rustic life of the peasant so lovingly portrayed in earlier stanzas has become 'the dark un-fathom'd caves of ocean' and the 'desert air'; and their 'useful toil' (set against the uselessness of Grandeur in stanzas 9 and 11) is seen as 'waste'. There is no need to peel off the counterlogical elements of the image, for counterlogic is the way by which this poem works – here, particularly in portraying the uncertainties of the speaker. The double sense of the image must be retained: one must keep both the sense that the state of affairs is a natural one (many gems have to be obscure, and many flowers have to spend their beauties in vain), and at the same time that in such lack of provision nature is to be deplored. It really will not do to argue, as William Empson does, that flowers prefer not to be picked[8] – and in any case, the poem talks only of their being *seen*, not of their being gathered.

In the next stanza the notion of peasant waste is variously modified:

> Some village-Hampden that with dauntless breast
> The little tyrant of his fields withstood;
> Some mute inglorious Milton here may rest,
> Some Cromwell guiltless of his country's blood.

The village-Hampden does exercise his virtue on some society, however small; all is not quite desert, although it has been reduced to the minia-ture, even the toy-like. However, the Milton, it would seem, is quite mute; he has never expressed himself. The Cromwell in a sense comes to be by never being; it is better that he is circumscribed, because his vices will never be exercised. The very mention of names from history suggests that the escape of the rustics from their lot would not have been into self-expression or originality, but into the typical (though here Gray's Augustanism may be responsible). What is further significant is the choice of names: all are rebels and Nonconformists. Doubtless the Gray of Pindaric odes would have sympathy with the 'celestial fire' and the 'ecstasy' of stanza 12, or the 'noble rage' and the 'genial current of stanza 13, but there is also the Augustan Gray, who first finished this poem with an injunction to the peasants not to repine, and who is probably at this point more on that side of the narrator which tries to accept the existing state of things.

Stanzas 16 to 18 are balanced in the contemplation not only of the virtues that the peasants could not exercise in the wider world, but also (continuing the notion begun in the mention of Cromwell) on the vices which had no wider scope; they describe not only the fame they might have earned, but also the infamy. Stanza 16 is full of tensions:

> The applause of listening senates to command,
> The threats of pain and ruin to despise,
> To scatter plenty o'er a smiling land,
> And read their history in a nation's eyes. . . .

The unfinished syntax makes a list of dangled possibilities. The 'command' of the first line has overtones of enforced ovation, and the notion of the great being above humanity is continued in the picture of them despising the threats of pain and ruin. Johnson at least would have disagreed with this picture of immunity to fate, and one wonders whether the line is there not for its truth, but to emphasise the dubious nature of being above the common lot. Scattering plenty over a smiling land is of course unmixed value: yet we are reminded that it was just such plenty that the peasant scattered in his labours in the fields (stanza 7). With these reticences, the last line, with its nakedly quantitative order of evaluation, seems a shade vulgar. The speaker is trying to be true to the facts and yet make the fact of peasant confinement acceptable.

In stanza 17 we are told, 'nor circumscribed alone / Their growing virtues, but their crimes confined'. This returns us to the issue of whether the urges of the peasants were frozen by, or exercised within, their lot. Stanza 19 raises again the related question of peasant contentment:

> Far from the madding crowd's ignoble strife
> Their sober wishes never learned to stray;
> Along the cool sequestered vale of life
> They kept the noiseless tenor of their way.

This is partly a picture of the rustic calmly choosing his humble lot in knowledge of what he would suffer in the wider world; Gray originally wrote 'knew' instead of 'learned'. Cleanth Brooks has pointed out the irony of learning to stray from a path (one thinks of straying as done normally in ignorance):[9] the speaker is attempting to equate knowledge with deviation – even with the deeper form of ignorance. All of this is in stark contrast to what we have at one point earlier been told: that 'Chill Penury repressed their noble rage', and that, rather than their refusing it, knowledge refused them, did not unroll its ample page to them. Further, to make the point here, the speaker has turned from the value he admitted in eminence before: all greatness is now the 'madding crowd', all power 'ignoble strife', all ambition drunkenness.

In stanza 20 the speaker apparently turns from the theme of hidden powers to contemplate once more the frail memorial to the rustic dead 'with uncouth rhymes and shapeless sculpture decked'. But the change of subject is in fact a formal one, forcing us into realisation of a deeper continuation of the theme. The tomb also is confinement, as we are to hear:

> Ev'n from the tomb the voice of nature cries,
> Ev'n in our ashes live their wonted fires.

And tombs so crude are another form of circumscription: without proper epitaph the dead are repressed, refused the expression of their proper nature and worth – unless, that is, someone of the sensibility of the speaker should pass, and be moved by the very inadequacy of the memorial, which 'Implores the passing tribute of a sigh', to do more justice to the memory of those beneath it. The rustic tomb is Augustan, only one side of the truth that this poem has admitted: it demands resignation –

> Their name, their years, spelt by the unlettered Muse,
> The place of fame and elegy supply:
> And many a holy text around she strews,
> That teach the rustic moralist to die.

The 'name', even allowing for the generalising form of the verse, still suggests that all have been reduced to one name, that their separate identities have been ignored and lost in this epitaph. The last line implies that only rustic moralists could be taught to die: in a sense they do not have to be taught, because they already think in this way. Others, one is to feel, would not so readily submit.[10] And in the next two stanzas the speaker goes on to portray such refusal of the dying to break links with the living:

> For who to dumb Forgetfulness a prey,
> This pleasing anxious being e'er resigned,
> Left the warm precincts of the cheerful day,
> Nor cast one longing lingering look behind?

To the complexities the poem has admitted there is no facile answer. What is needed is sympathy, and more sympathy. The speaker now turns, having given a poem which is more true to the 'unhonoured dead' than the rustic epitaph, to give himself to their condition. But the sympathy is one in which he gains as well as loses: he breaks free of his own self-division between rest and restlessness, acceptance and struggling potential, while he immolates himself in rustic life and death. As happens in 'Lycidas', the loss of the speaker is subsumed and calmed in a uni-

versal condition (indeed, the echoes of that poem in the lines that follow
are quite frequent, for example in stanzas 24, 25, 28). Beginning the self-
immolation, he turns first to address himself:

> For thee who, mindful of the unhonoured dead,
> Dost in these lines their artless tale relate;
> If chance, by lonely Contemplation led,
> Some kindred spirit shall inquire thy fate. . . .

The 'thee' here is not only the speaker, but all men of his character, perhaps even the reader of his poem. The speaker is already fading into the
landscape; he now sets himself in nature, at the foot of a beech, by a
brook, a wood, a hill or a lawn; in death he rests his head upon 'the lap
of earth' (stanza 30). The further stage of dying and of self-denial is to
let himself be viewed in life through the more distant and ignorant eyes
of the 'hoary-headed swain', who will tell the passing inquirer of how the
speaker wandered about the countryside and of how he would 'mutter'
what seemed to the swain his 'wayward fancies', 'Now drooping, woeful
wan, like one forlorn, / Or crazed with care, or crossed in hopeless love'
(stanza 27). This illiterate swain will be unable to read the speaker's
epitaph, but it is to be hoped the inquirer will (and perhaps the idea here
is that he will himself be stimulated to continue the chain of sympathy –
thus establishing a linking round of love which will heal the broken links
of potential and act, life and death, that are the untreated condition of
life).

The epitaph which the inquirer will be directed to read will recount
first that the dead man was like and unlike the peasants – so the poem
itself has veered in its identification with them. He was like some of them
in that 'Fair Science frowned not on his humble birth' and in that he
was 'to fortune and to fame unknown'; but unlike them in that this
oblivion was brought about by 'Melancholy', a personal trait, not a general
factor like the limitations of the rustic lot. What repressed the dead
poet's noble rage was thus idiosyncratic and atypical. But this atypical-
ity, this personal melancholy, is validated by being itself set in a more
general groan: gains certainty in an objective correlative, while giving itself
in charity. The notion of giving and gaining comes out clearly in the
second stanza of the epitaph:

> Large was his bounty and his soul sincere,
> Heaven did a recompense as largely send:
> He gave to Misery all he had, a tear,
> He gained from Heaven ('twas all he wished) a friend.

The third line, with its overtones of the widow's mite, and the largeness
of the love behind that, is humble commentary on what propitiation of

the vexed soul all he had could achieve. The emphasis of this and the next line is on sympathy and love, which exist as much in the one as in the all, and flourish in small compass, like the peasant lot, as readily as in the great.

The note has become both a private one, and one that points, in the 'all he had', 'all he wished', to the frailty of human things. The last stanza continues this:

> No farther seek his merits to disclose,
> Or draw his failties from their dread abode,
> (There they alike in trembling hope repose)
> The bosom of his Father and his God.

The speaker draws a limit to personal commemoration: his epitaph strikes a balance between the shapeless anonymity of the rustic memorials with their facile 'public' didacticism, and over-indulgent biography. He claims his right as an individual only so far: the rest is with the dead and with God. The epitaph is his propitiation: having uttered it he cuts his links with the living; there are to be no wonted fires in these ashes. It has at this point become as vulgar for the living to wish to make the dead live further as for the dead to wish to. The 'trembling hope' with which the poem ends has now moved from the frustrations of life to the better mercies of eternity.

The shifts of subject and the inconsistencies and contradictions of this poem are thus (known or unknown to Gray) functions of a larger imaginative unity. They are a method, first, of forcing the reader to compare the frustrated life of the peasant, his unquenched death, the tension in the speaker between resignation and rebellion, and even the existence of the poem itself. Second, they show the impossibility of a rational or moral answer to issues the complexity of which is so fully portrayed, and they drive us to understand how the charity of the speaker can be the only acceptable form of consolation. Finally, the continual changes of subject may also be seen as an imitation of the broken potential and the frustrations that the poem describes.

In Gray's poem rustic life (or death) is no longer, as in a Renaissance pastoral such as 'Lycidas', a metaphor for all life, a guise under which to speak of that condition of mortality in which we are all set: the rustics here are in this no more than rustics, and are contrasted with another order of human life – that in which self-expression is achieved. Nature no longer has a metaphysical role which covers every sphere, but is seen as the natural, the uncultivated, and is set against civilisation. The purview is less universal, much more specifically social, even if, as in 'Lycidas', the speaker subsumes himself in the plight of his swains. Nor is there any universally valid remedy, as in 'Lycidas', to the problem of frustrated powers: in that poem the movement is towards an answer to man's suffering and loss, where in Gray's it is towards the silencing of the troubled spirit; there is no final solution.

Though the subject of the *Elegy* is non-fulfilment, its object is plangency – especially after Gray had removed the Augustan counsel of submission in the first draft. He wrote of elegy, 'Nature and sorrow, and tenderness, are the true genius of such things. . . . poetical ornaments are foreign to the purpose; for they only show a man is not sorry; – and devotion worse; for it teaches him, that he ought not to be sorry, which is all the pleasure of the thing.'[11] The poem is not a social protest: it does not ask for any reforms by which the rustics might better realise their potential. Much the same resignation is to be found in poetry for the rest of the century: what is portrayed is a fixed condition which is not subject to alteration, and the primary orientation is towards the awakening of sentiment.

At first sight, Gray's poem appears to contain features common in eighteenth-century poetry. It seems fragmentary and rambling in character, deficient in such 'rational' elements as sequence, consistency and logical relation. It appears, too, to be divided in its sympathies, veering between one attitude and another, just as other poets are divided between such opposites as sympathy and detachment, reason and feeling, town and country, facts and significance. Gray, however, can be seen as having made his very inconsistencies and uncertainties part of his subject, so that they are comprehended and transcended. Whether or not he was consciously aware of this reconciliation of opposites in a higher third, it makes him one of the most imaginative poets of his period.

12 Johnson

We speak of Johnson as an Augustan, yet in both *The Vanity of Human Wishes* and *Rasselas* he is concerned not to condemn the nonconformist characters who make the central interest, but to portray the inevitability and the poignancy of their urge to move beyond their lots, to become, rather than simply to be. His subject is, like Gray's, frustration, though here a frustration which is a feature of all life, not of only one section of it, and which is present even at the moment of self-fulfilment. Johnson laments the circumscription of life: his search for observation with extensive view is in part the expression of his urge to break down the walls of the world and fly beyond.

Johnson is not, like earlier writers, trying to make the world conform to one truth. He at least maintains that general truths concerning the human condition are not properly to be imposed on that condition *a priori*, but are found only after as full an experience of the varieties of life as possible, *a posteriori*. He is still looking for general laws, but, by the time he writes, empiricism has made sufficient impact on English culture for it to behove him to try to start from experience, not first principles. There remains, of course, the subjective vision which colours all experience, however impartial one would be; and to this extent the general truths Johnson reveals are truths he set out to find.

'THE VANITY OF HUMAN WISHES' (1749)

In the first lines of *The Vanity of Human Wishes* Johnson proposes a settled and Olympian view of all human desire,

> Let Observation with extensive View,
> Survey Mankind from *China* to *Peru*

which is far from realised within the poem. Where his source Juvenal is derisive of human folly and vice, Johnson is often sympathetically involved.[1] Throughout his imitation he stresses the pitiable helplessness of man, whereby

> Fate wings with ev'ry Wish th' afflictive Dart,
> Each Gift of Nature, and each Grace of Art,
> With fatal Heat impetuous Courage glows,
> With fatal Sweetness Elocution flows   (15–18)

until by the end he has reached the point where he has to ask, 'Must helpless Man, in Ignorance sedate, / Roll darkling down the Torrent of his Fate?' (345–6). Throughout, too, the imagery of the poem insists that man's fate preys on him, fires and later burns him, wars against him, diseases and crowds him; and the imagery of rising and falling, and of the inevitable transience of flowers[2] adds further the sense of man as tragic victim, an object of pity rather than detached Boethian inquiry.[3]

The problem of stance is exacerbated by the subject-matter of the poem. Johnson gives an encyclopaedic picture of vanity, describing both those wishes which could be seen as vain in the sense of sinfully proud, going beyond one's station and Augustan bounds, and those more natural human desires which are 'in vain' – that is, frustrated. We may think that the first type of vanity is exhibited in the portraits of the megalomaniacs Charles XII, Xerxes, Charles of Bavaria or even Wolsey, and the second by a picture like that of the virtuous and healthy old man who, while he passes towards death 'with unperceiv'd Decay, / And glides in modest Innocence away' (293–4), is nonetheless subject to the miseries of the deaths of relatives or friends and to the sad knowledge of his own increasing irrelevance in the world (299–310). The stress on fate and human helplessness throughout the poem, however, the sense that the ambitious are largely driven by rather than driving their desires (for example, in Charles XII's Pavlovian responses: 'War sounds the Trump, he rushes to the Field' – 198), makes such a distinction finally frail. There is no ultimate difference on this level between Xerxes, who is derided, and Wolsey, who is not: both are fired by lust of power, both are 'wav'ring Man, betray'd by vent'rous Pride' (7); and the law by which fate marks out some men for distinction and ruin (15–18), letting others remain untouched by ambition, leaves small room for a more mocking treatment of Wolsey than of the good old man. Fatalism leads to antinomianism: thus, while Johnson tries to express a sense of moral difference among the character-portraits by being now more mocking, now less, sympathy for the common plight undermines this. The net result is uncertainty both of attitude and of tone.

It may be that it is partly from his method of observation with extensive view that Johnson's sense of man's helplessness and, hence, Johnson being Johnson, his sympathy arise, or that in moving away he comes nearer. Certainly the invocation of Democritus to return and mock these scenes of human woe (49–68) is only too clearly an attempt to arrive at total detachment from a scene which he finds often deeply painful. In a sense – and it must be unconsciously – Johnson's wish for detachment is the same kind of aspiration as drives Charles XII or the scholar to try to put themselves above the human wishes he portrays; in the constant shifts from judicious detachment to involved pity he illustrates his own curve for the lives of ambitious men: 'They mount, they shine, evaporate, and fall' (76).

Johnson's attitude to the great is confused not only by the uncertain mixture of pity and mockery, but also by the admiration he feels for them. Larger of soul than other men, they live out their destined monomanias to the full. They push the limits of human experience further: they have individual names and histories, where the others are typical of recurrent circumstance; they offer, too, an element of novelty within the pattern, which was what Johnson saw as the essence of wit (and this may explain why he gives not one but three portraits of the military great). Johnson's admiration for their 'involvement' is particularly evident from his contemptuous treatment of meaner minds. Those who can stand back and put safety before achievement are scorned. Avoidance of Wolsey's fate by living 'with safer Pride content, / The wisest Justice on the Banks of *Trent*' (123–4), is no real alternative: Johnson's disdain for the big fish in the little pond is clear.[4] Similar is his view of the 'Low . . . Hind' who, while the land is in anarchy, 'sculks . . . beneath the Rage of Pow'r' (33), or the 'meaner Minds' who escape Laud's fate (169). Johnson has nothing but contempt for the toadies of powerful men, who shift their allegiance at the first hint of decline (109–12), and for the 'supple Tribes' of the contemporary English populace, who, rather than see justice done to the great, 'ask no Questions but the Price of Votes' (95–6).[5]

Throughout the poem Johnson undermines positions of detachment, not simply because it is his aim to show no one exempt from vain human wishes, but also because he is drawn by the idea of involvement in life and its vicissitudes. Even when he turns to contemplate 'The needy Traveller, serene and gay / [Who] Walks the wild Heath, and sings his Toil away' (37–8), the idyll cannot last:

> Does Envy seize thee? crush th'upbraiding Joy,
> Encrease his Riches and his Peace destroy,
> Now Fears in dire Vicissitude invade,
> The rustling Brake alarms, and quiv'ring Shade,
> Nor Light nor Darkness bring his Pain Relief,
> One shewes the Plunder, and one hides the Thief.   (39–44)

The description makes it sound as though the deed is actually done, as though, like fate, we watch this serene character, envy him, and leap on him – as though, in short, such serenity is exceedingly frail.[6] Similar, of course, is the picture of the old man who seems to be dying gracefully and at peace, but of whom it is then pointed out how 'ev'n on this her Load Misfortune flings' (299). What Johnson seems to give with one hand he immediately removes with the other.

For these reasons the religious detachment that he proposes at the end of his poem as a way out is belied by what has gone before. It can only be a prayer:

> Implore his Aid, in his Decisions rest,
> Secure whate'er he gives, he gives the best.   (355–6)

It is the same Christian stoicism that we find in Pope's *Essay on Man*, and here, because the poem has shown that things are quite other than consistent with the best of all possible worlds, it is far less convincing. And, like Fielding, Johnson was suspicious alike of Roman stoicism and medieval *contemptus mundi* even while they presented themselves as the sole answer to his dilemma. To suggest to the suppliant,

> Pour fourth thy Fervours for a healthful Mind,
> Obedient Passions, and a Will resign'd;
> For Love, which scarce collective Man can fill;
> For Patience sov'reign o'er transmuted Ill   (359–62)

is to recommend an Olympian stance towards suffering which, with its emphasis on the inevitability of pain and one's immersion in it, the poem has denied. Johnson is desperately anxious to wring some certainty from the constant flux he has portrayed (thus the sense of piles being driven in the closed couplets at 349–56), but to do so he has to go against his own vision. And, of course, the prayer is frail. The poem has yielded no moral prescription by which man may help himself: like Pope's poetry and that of many Augustans, it gives a deterministic picture of human life; the answer to man's helplessness is not soluble by man, and only with luck by God – 'Petitions yet remain . . .' (349). The pain of seeking and not finding here, and of therefore having to seek and try to find solely elsewhere, is part of what gives Johnson's art its melancholy force.

In *The Vanity of Human Wishes* Johnson is thus torn between the desire for a detached view of human life and involved, committed experience of it. The same dichotomy is behind *Rasselas*, though there it is contained not within a search for right action, but within the issue of truth-perception.

'RASSELAS' (1759)

Why does Rasselas want to escape from the happy valley? We are told of those who live there that 'Such was the appearance of security and delight which this retirement afforded, that they to whom it was new always desired that it might be perpetual; and as those, on whom the iron gate had once closed, were never suffered to return, the effect of longer experience could not be known' (p. 3). The last phrase has ominous suggestions, but these are later denied, for we are informed that the methods used to keep the princes and princesses of the house of Abyssinia happy there were 'generally successful' (p. 5), and that most passed their lives there 'in full conviction that they had all within their reach that art or nature could bestow, and pitied those whom fate had general rule. Further, considerable doubt is quickly thrown in *Rasselas* that he is 'the first who has complained of misery in the *happy valley*' (p. 8). Later still, however, Imlac maintains that the attendants, who, unlike the royal children, have been brought in from the world outside, are as one in lamenting the day when they were shut in the happy valley, and that they are 'either corroded by malignant passions, or sit stupid in the gloom of perpetual vacancy' (p. 36). Whatever the case, it is clear that, as far as the condition of the princes goes, Rasselas is the first to object to it, and that his objection, though it may be what men ought to make, is what very few feel the need to make. Most men, if bred to it, the story seems to say, do not question their situation; and those who do are not representatives of the highest in man, but exceptions to the general rule. Further, considerable doubt is quickly thrown in *Rasselas* on the notion that such rebellion is aspiration 'Above the vulgar flight of low desire' rather than, as Imlac puts it, the case of one 'whose real wants are supplied [and who] must admit those of fancy' (p. 21): that is, the Prince is seen rather more as dilettante than as pioneer. It follows then that the questions Rasselas asks not only of the happy valley but of the world outside lose substance and generality in relation to his not being as most men would be in his situation; and, secondly, that they are mocked as in some way lightweight.

This lightweight quality is seen in every motive Rasselas has for escape. First the Prince feels a vague discontent, which leads him into solitary broodings: with his every apparent want satisfied, he still feels want; and, knowing nothing but the happy valley, he cannot give this foreign want a name or an object (p. 8). But the want is always only for increase of pleasure, or the removal of satiety: Rasselas's cast of mind is neatly caught in the comment after his lament on the peculiar pains to which man is subject: 'With observations like these the Prince amused himself as he returned, uttering them with a plaintive voice, yet with a look that discovered him to feel some complacence in his own perspicacity, and to receive some solace of the miseries of life, from consciousness of the delicacy with which he felt, and the eloquence with which he bewailed them' (p. 7). The sage tells Rasselas that 'if you had seen the miseries of the world, you would know how to value your present state', and the Prince, seizing on this, replies, 'I shall long to see the miseries of the world, since the sight of them is necessary to happiness' (p. 9) – that is, he will see the miseries not to do anything for those miserable, but simply to give renewed flavour to happiness. Similar is the description of how he then passes 'twenty months' in making himself happy in imaginary schemes of benevolence for the relief of mankind (p. 10); there follows, in the form of Rasselas's pursuit of an imaginary thief (10–11), a mocking picture of the result of such fancies being taken as realities.

Aside from the problem of why Rasselas should be the first to rebel against the happy valley, Johnson's portrayal of the development of the Prince's motivation is very fine. First, as we have seen, he has a desire for he knows not what. Then the sage unwittingly gives him the object of seeking out the miseries of the world in order to value his happiness by contrast. Next, we see Rasselas enjoying the thought of gaining pleasure from relieving the distressed; by now he is no longer thinking in terms of returning to the happy valley with renewed appetite, but of finding his pleasure in the world outside. Finally, the motivation directs itself much more to the outside world in the form of the 'choice of life' (p. 33);[7] this, which becomes the governing motive of the rest of the book, is the search for one sphere of happiness which offers more than that of the happy valley. One can really believe that this is how someone in Rasselas's position would switch in resolve.

But it is all hedonistic and dilettante, even if Rasselas cannot help its being so. 'Very few', says Imlac, 'live by choice'; and the Prince replies, 'I am pleased to think . . . that my birth has given me at least one advantage over others, by enabling me to determine for myself' (p. 47). His situation is thus more that of the luxury article than of the spirited representative of all mankind. The account of his life in the outside world becomes one of dipping his finger in one sphere of life after another, and of always finding some deficiency which makes him refuse to commit himself. This of course is partly to be expected of one whose primary initial drive is escape, and whose detestation is for the single or uniform situation; even though, had any one sphere of life managed to contain Imlac's ideal for art, variety with uniformity (pp. 27–9), he might conceivably have chosen it. At the last, he fixes on a choice which in a sense is no choice, since he is forever trying to break its bounds: 'The Prince desired a little kingdom, in which he might administer justice in his own person, and see all the parts of government with his own eyes; but he could never fix the limits of his dominion, and was always adding to the number of his subjects' (p. 133). And in the very end, realising that none of their wishes can be realised, all resolve to return to Abyssinia (p. 134). Like the remainder of humanity, they too are finally driven to accept their lot.

Rasselas is thus not a representative, but an observer throughout the story, and a very particular observer at that. He is the exception in being free to choose his way of life, and yet his experience of all the varieties of life makes him unable to exercise his choice. The book is therefore not about choosing, or the choice of life, but about what is chosen or, rather, what is determined; it becomes, in short, a picture of the vanity of human wishes rather than the vanity of human choice. Rasselas and his sister Nekayah (who leaves with him) are there to mediate this vision and to provide an ironic centre for the story.

Whether the vision can thus be successfully mediated is another matter. The vision is, as Imlac puts it, 'Human life is every where a state in which much is to be endured, and little to be enjoyed' (p. 33). Yet the following picture of Rasselas, whether or not at this stage intentionally, is inevitably ironic (he is speaking to the animals of the happy valley):

> 'Ye', said he 'are happy, and need not envy me that walk thus among you, burthened with myself; nor do I, ye gentle beings, envy your felicity; for it is not the felicity of man. I have many distresses from which ye are free; I fear pain when I do not feel it; I sometimes shrink at evils recollected, and sometimes start at evils anticipated: surely the equity of providence has ballanced peculiar sufferings with peculiar enjoyments.' (pp. 6–7)

Rasselas poses the greater happiness of man only to insist on his larger pains: points to the equity of providence while weighing only the sufferings and not the enjoyment. The irony continues strongly in the next comment: 'With observations like those the Prince amused himself.' What, then, are we to make of observations like these when they are made by the author to be what is for him a true picture of the miseries of the world throughout the book?

Throughout *Rasselas* the single view is attacked, whether in the observers or the observed. When Rasselas tries the delights of the youthful hedonists, but, growing unhappy and ashamed, counsels them against their levity, he is derided and rejected (pp. 47–9). We feel that the hedonists may be wrong in their course, but that Rasselas is both naïf and a little priggish to tell them so. The happy stoic who lives by the rule of reason, and whom one day Rasselas finds passionately lamenting the loss of a child, is another example of the unbalanced single view being self-destructive (pp. 49–51). The hermit, who fled in disgust from the world to the simplified retreat of the ascetic life, now hates his solitary life and wishes to return to the city from which he fled (pp. 55–7). The man who recommends a life lived according to nature has become thoroughly removed from it: when Rasselas asks him to explain his secret, the Shaftesburian language of his answer reveals a man in whom what should be the concrete has become the abstract, what simple, complex, and what natural, unnatural: 'To live according to nature, is to act always with due regard to the fitness arising from the relations and qualities of causes and effects; to concur with the great and unchangeable scheme of universal felicity; to co-operate with the general disposition and tendency of the present system of things' (p. 60). This shows what happens when generality is used at the expense of particularity, the two criteria which for Imlac are to be interwoven in art.)

The theme of the dangers of the single view is frequently related to an attack on delusive fancy (pp. 1, 10–11, 17–18, 21, 85, 92–3), whereby, without the moderating influence of judgment or a sense of proportion, a conviction may move through obsession to madness. Such is the portrait of the astronomer, who, confessing, 'I have passed my time in study without experience' (p. 122), has come to believe that the weather and the seasons are under his control and is in despair at what the consequences of his death will be for the world (pp. 109–12). Behind this mania, however humbly put, is pride. It is a pride that relates to Rasselas, Nekayah and Pekuah her waiting-maid too, for they have all had their own obsessions which have conflicted with reality: Rasselas his ideal of good government, Nekayah hers of pastoral innocence, and Pekuah hers of becoming the Queen of Abyssinia. All now disown these obsessions, but by the end of the story they are shown ironically either to have resumed them, or to have taken up others (pp. 133–4). If all these forms of absolutism are attacked, what can the reader do with the absolutism that the story asks us to accept – namely, that all life is wretched or worthless, look where we may?

The central episode in this consideration, and the one that raises a number of other problems, is the debate of Rasselas and Nekayah on marriage. The Prince, having found little of what he had hoped from the sphere of public and political life which he has been exploring, is not backward in condemning the pessimism of Nekayah concerning private life. The Princess portrays the discords she found in families, between husbands and wives, parents and children, the suspicious caution of age and the contemptuous temerity of youth, and, when Rasselas challenges her survey as having been too limited, describes how domestic discord 'is not inevitably and fatally necessary; but yet is not easily avoided. We seldom see that a whole family is virtuous: the good and evil cannot well agree; and the evil can yet less agree with one another: even the virtuous fall sometimes to variance, when their virtues are of different kinds, and tending to extremes' (p. 68). She concludes, 'as it is always more easy to do evil than good, though the wisdom or virtue of one can very rarely make many happy, the folly or vice of one may often make many miserable' (p. 69).

When the Prince says that, if this is the truth, he will avoid marriage, Nekayah replies with a grim portrayal of the miseries of celibacy, ending, 'Marriage has many pains, but celibacy has no pleasures' (ibid.). Again the Prince accuses her of pessimism, but then proceeds to undermine his case in his own picture of the pains he found in public life and in his admitted hope that Nekayah's area of survey would yield him consolation (pp. 70–1). He argues that, since marriage is the dictate of nature and men and women were meant to be companions, it must therefore be 'one of the means of happiness' (p. 73), to which the Princess replies with so devastating a portrayal of the miseries of the marital state as to conclude that 'marriage is rather permitted than approved, and . . . none, but by the instigation of a passion too much indulged, entangle themselves with indissoluble compacts' (pp. 73–4). Rasselas's retort to this is that she has therefore contradicted her previous assertion that celibacy is worse than marriage. Now the Princess answers in one of the most revealing passages of the book,

> I did not expect . . . to hear that imputed to falshood which is the consequence only of frailty. To the mind, as to the eye, it is difficult to compare with exactness objects vast in their extent, and various in their parts. Where we see or conceive the whole at once we readily note the discriminations and decide the preference: but of two systems, of which neither can be surveyed by any human being in its full compass of magnitude and multiplicity of complication, where is the wonder, that judging of the whole by parts, I am alternately affected by one and the other as either presses on my memory or fancy? We differ from ourselves just as we differ from each other, when we see only part of the question, as in the multifarious relations of politicks and morality: but when we perceive the whole at once, as in numerical computations, all agree in one judgment, and none ever varies his opinion.   (p. 74)

This admits the weakness in her case: not seeing all, she is bound with limited materials to judge subjectively – 'all Opinion's colours cast on life' (Pope). But the implications concerning the Johnsonian method as seen in *The Vanity of Human Wishes* and Imlac's portrayal of the poet (ch. 10) are clear: if no human being can ever fully survey the parts of marriage or celibacy, or of politics and morality, when then becomes of the validity, when based on a limited purview and therefore on the subjectivity of the human observer, of 'general and transcendental truths, which will always be the same' (p. 29) – or, for that matter, of 'Observation, with extensive View'? How are universal truths ever to be discovered when the facts from which they are drawn must be less than the whole picture? We may argue that we are meant to feel that Nekayah is wrong, that she could have drawn a more adequate universal truth by concluding that marriage shows a peculiar mixture of pleasure and pain rather than nothing but the latter; but it is not in her creator's nature to admit such diversity, for in his own art he always emphasises the misery of the human lot.

The generalising habit receives another, and, again it would seem, unintentional, blow when Rasselas returns to his argument that 'The good of the whole . . . is the same with the good of all its parts. If marriage be best for mankind it must evidently be best for individuals' (p. 75). He is arguing both that no amount of misery in the wedded state can devalue the institution, because it is our appointed lot; and that, because marriage in itself is a good, it cannot be a misery for most people who enter into it. The first point values the general at the expense of the particular, and the second argues that the general or abstract may determine the individual and concrete situation: either way the universal is put before the particular. In the same way we have seen the Princess move from what must be a limited number of examples to a general conclusion. Both do this, because, whether as optimist or pessimist, both are absolutists. Together, in short, they unwittingly expose both the *a priori* and the *a posteriori* method of arguing, and thereby the whole process of generalisation. At the same time, the playing of the Prince's absolute optimism against the pessimism of the Princess suggests that neither is right. The whole mode of presentation directs us towards the individual case and the middle way, and yet the official and objective tendency of the book is to universalise and to simplify into a pessimistic view of humanity. One can only suppose that in *Rasselas* a sense of the variety of the singular in the ironically-viewed centres of consciousness is undermining the overt Johnsonian intention – or that the 'Romantic' is weakening the would-be Augustan.

The 'marriage' debate is not yet over. The Princess describes how those who marry late are generally so set in their ways as to make agreement impossible; and how, though they may enjoy their children without the jealousies to which couples nearer in age to their offspring are subject, they nonetheless may die early and have to leave their children to a guardian, and certainly have to leave the world 'before they see those whom they love best either wise or great' (p. 78). Conversely, those who marry young will adapt to one another and grow in love, but will suffer the rivalries of their children. She concludes her account, which as usual has stressed the defects of either situation, thus, surprisingly: 'I believe it will be found that those who marry late are best pleased with their children, and those who marry early with their partners' (ibid.). The Prince therefore suggests that the two happinesses might be united in a marriage made by partners neither too young or too old. Nekayah answers that there is no such middle ground, and quotes Imlac: 'nature sets her gifts on the right hand and on the left'.

Those conditions, which flatter hope and attract desire, are so constituted, that, as we approach one, we recede from another. There are goods so opposed that we cannot seize both, but, by too much prudence, may pass between them at too great a distance to reach either. This is often the fate of long consideration; he does nothing who endeavours to do more than is allowed to humanity. Flatter not yourself with contrarieties of pleasure. Of the blessings set before you make your choice, and be content. No man can taste the fruits of autumn while he is delighting his scent with the flowers of the spring: no man can, at the same time, fill his cup from the source and from the mouth of the Nile. (pp. 78–9)

This exposes the idealism and utopianism of Rasselas in hoping that the two *extremes* might be united, but equally it exposes Nekayah's pessimism, for it is possible that, while the limits of both happinesses might not be enjoyed, some lesser compromise might be reached. It is interesting that the Princess is now discussing the benefits of different types of marriage where previously she emphasised the pains: the argument has almost become argument for its own sake, and we rebel at the neat categorisations of life that are being so confidently offered, particularly here in the way a well-turned formula is used to encapsulate the very untidiness and imperfection of human relationships. Perhaps Johnson senses this in that he has Imlac end the discussion with, 'It seems to me . . . that while you are making the choice of life, you neglect to live' (p. 79). Yet Nekayah is given the last word here against Rasselas; and one cannot overlook the fact that Johnson himself avoided most of the (short) marital life he might have had with his wife Tetty, and had no children.

That aphorism, 'Of the blessings set before you make your choice, and be content', remains. Rasselas and Nekayah are, as we have seen, dilettantes. But behind them is an author who, though not a dilettante, has an aesthetic of non-commitment. It is the problem of observation with extensive view: if life is so to be observed, the observer must not commit himself to any one of its departments, otherwise he loses his capacity for wide survey. And yet a wide survey, on the Princess's own admission, is bound in the most important matters to be based on insufficient data; and, more important, it must of necessity be superficial, because it is founded on observation and not on experience. If you do make your choice, Johnson says, you no longer have the choice of life; if you do not, you will not have the full materials with which to make that choice. It is not surprising that in his art Johnson stresses man's helplessness, says little about his will.[8]

The mediating wisdom of the book is Imlac's, and Imlac refuses to commit himself to any one station. He recognises the absolutism to which the detached inquirer is subject (and even suggests that those who have apparent freedom to choose are in fact doomed to be choosers, just as much as each individual the inquirers meet is shut in his own lot): 'The causes of good and evil . . . are so various and uncertain, so often entangled with each other, so diversified by various relations, and so much subject to accidents which cannot be foreseen, that he who would fix his condition upon incontestable reasons of preference, must live and die inquiring and deliberating' (pp. 46–7; see also p. 17). Imlac is the artist, and, as he portrays it, it is the business of the artist to remain detached. His history is that of one given sufficient money to escape the course of commercial life planned for him by his father, and to assume a stance outside life (and, incidentally, contradicting himself, he has fixed on this condition from incontestable reasons of preference). He has committed himself willingly to non-commitment; Rasselas, Nekayah and Pekuah are doomed to it. Imlac's picture of the artist captures what the Prince and Princess do for most of the story, but, where they look for one thing amid all, he looks always for the all, and for knowledge:

The business of a poet . . . is to examine, not the individual, but the species; to remark general properties and large appearances. . . . His character requires that he estimate the happiness and misery of every condition; observe the power of all the passions in all their combinations, and trace the changes of the human mind as they are modified by various institutions and accidental influences of climate or custom, from the spriteliness of infancy to the despondence of decreptitude. He must divest himself of the prejudices of his age or country; he must consider right and wrong in their abstracted and invariable state; he must disregard present laws and opinions, and rise to general and transcendental truths, which will always be the same. (pp. 28–9)

And Imlac's conclusion after many years of such dedication? It is not far from Nekayah's: 'Human life is every where a state in which much is to be endured, and little to be enjoyed' (p. 33; compare the Princess's 'All that virtue can afford is quietness of conscience, a steady prospect of a happier state; this may enable us to endure calamity with patience; but remember that patience must suppose pain' – p. 72).

This insight, as testified by Imlac and borne out by the narrative, drives *Rasselas* towards the detachment from the world of the devout ascetic. The withdrawal proceeds through the visit to the pyramids, the note of bereavement in Nekayah's loss of Pekuah and the story of the astronomer's desperation in the face of death. The distinction (following this) between the hermit who fled in pique from civilisation and the monks who choose to withdraw themselves from the world for devout reasons is made clear: if earthbound motives drive one forth, they will also pull one back, as the hermit returns to Cairo. In the uniformities of the monkish life Imlac allows more happiness than in the happy valley, because the motives of the monks are 'adequate and reasonable' (p. 126):

> Their labour supplies them with necessaries; it therefore cannot be omitted, and is certainly rewarded. Their devotion prepares them for another state; and reminds them of its approach, while it fits them for it. Their time is regularly distributed; one duty succeeds another, so that they are not left open to the distraction of unguided choice, not lost in the shades of listless inactivity. There is a certain task to be performed at an appropriated hour; and their toils are cheerful, because they consider them as acts of piety, by which they are always advancing towards endless felicity.   (ibid.)

The next and last visit of the travellers is to the catacombs and the mummies. The note is *memento mori*; and the Prince, looking on the bodies, recognises how frail is human choice: 'they were, perhaps, snatched away while they were busy, like us, in the choice of life' (p. 132). But the debate on the real existence of the soul, and on the power of God to destroy it, asks that further withdrawal, not only from life but even from the fact of death, that, following Rasselas's words, is voiced by Nekayah: 'To me . . . the choice of life is become less important; I hope hereafter to think only on the choice of eternity' (ibid). This is the real Conclusion, in which *Everything* is Concluded – the different title of the last chapter points back to this. For in the last chapter all return to the mundane motivation of the search for happiness – and such a search, as Johnson has amply demonstrated, is bound to be frustrated, just as inconclusive as the end of the book itself.

'Those conditions, which flatter hope and attract desire, are so constituted that, as we approach one, we recede from another. . . . Of the blessings set before you make your choice, and be content.' Nekayah's picture of the dividedness of life is also the picture we have from Johnson's *Rasselas* and *The Vanity of Human Wishes* of his own sensibility. On the one hand, Johnson looks to art to provide truths which will command universal assent, and to the artist to rise above his material and survey it: this, we have suggested, is a mid-eighteenth-century and empiricist version of the Augustan need to find values which are permanent and objective. Yet at the same time Johnson knows that the universal and single view is inadequate to the full multiplicity of experience, and he exposes it by his ironic method in *Rasselas*. There, however, he also reveals the division between exposing the single view in his characters while espousing it himself. There, too, he shows a pained awareness of the gap between the artist and life, his knowledge that the artist cannot know life to the full, because, to have the detachment necessary to a comprehensive survey, he cannot commit himself to any one of its departments. In *The Vanity of Human Wishes* Johnson is equally torn between detachment and commitment, but here the division is one between a desire to escape from the painful character of existence by distancing and judging it, and a strong human sympathy for the 'committed' figures he so satirises. The product of similar tensions in Gray's *Elegy* was a giving of himself by the poet to the circumscribed life and death of the rustics; Johnson, however, removes himself, turning finally away from the world.

What we see in Johnson, therefore, is one form of the dividedness of the later eighteenth-century mind, a fissure between uniformity and variety, between the urge to make the world say one thing, and the sense that its true variety escapes such categorisation. In his criticism Johnson was untaxed in taking the balanced double view; but in his art that balance turns into dichotomy, and, at last, flight.

13 Goldsmith and Crabbe

GOLDSMITH: 'THE DESERTED VILLAGE' (1770)

Goldsmith's *Deserted Village*, which describes an ideal rather than an actual village, in terms that are conceptual rather than particular, is part of the conservative literary tradition going back to Sidney.[1] In the destruction of Auburn, Goldsmith is not portraying simply the effects of the Enclosure movement or even inveighing against the luxurious vices of his own day; he is depicting the final departure of the humanist values of grace, proportion and harmony which we saw in the poetry of Jonson and Pope. For Jonson, Penshurst was still an isolated reality; for Pope, Dulness was a terrifying possibility; but for Goldsmith a whole conceptual landscape has been swept away for ever, and, when he paints the final removal of his well-proportioned Arcadia, the painting is not a warning but an account of what he felt to be an event already performed. With Goldsmith the Renaissance humanist tradition is shown losing any 'objective correlative' in nature; when we see it once more, in Jane Austen, the sole landscape remaining to it is that of the human psyche.

Every builded item in Goldsmith's poem serves to contrast the values that were with the non-values which are. The 'sweet society' of Auburn is seen in terms of a *concordia discors*, a marriage of such opposites as civilisation and nature, reason and passion, order and variety, the useful and the sweet. We hear of

> The sheltered cot, the cultivated farm,
> The never-failing brook, the busy mill,
> The decent church that topped the neighbouring hill,
> The hawthorn bush, with seats beneath the shade,
> For talking age and whispering lovers made   (10–14)

and how on holidays

>   toil remitting lent its turn to play,
> And all the village train, from labour free,
> Led up their sports beneath the spreading tree,
> While many a pastime circled in the shade. . . .   (16–19)

The reason why the cot is sheltered and the brook never fails is that man has acted in harmony with nature. The church is a perfect example of what Marvell or the Augustans understood by elevation without pride: it rounds off, or tops, the hill, while rising above it. The hill itself is social ('neighbouring'); and so too is the hawthorn bush: while the seats have been provided by man, they seem also provided by the bush, because they have been made in co-operation with its advantages. On these seats the conversations of age and youth become intertwined. In natural rhythm toil gives place to play; but the freedom of the villagers is not chaotic licence: they form a train, they lead up their sports, and their pastimes circle. And, as always, this is done in marriage with nature, 'beneath the spreading tree' and 'in the shade'. When Goldsmith later describes the village sounds heard from a distance, he does so in terms that make them a musical counterpoint to nature: we hear of 'The watchdog's voice that bayed the whispering wind', and how, when the villagers 'in sweet confusion sought the shade', they 'filled each pause the nightingale had made' (121, 123–4); now, however, 'No cheerful murmurs fluctuate in the gale' (126). All the portraits of the village depend on these and similar contrasts. The village preacher's pride is 'to relieve the wretched' (163); his steadiness controls and orders the chaotic passions of the deathbed sufferer (171–6); he is compared to a parental bird leading the spiritual flight of his parishioners, and to a tall cliff that looks beyond them to heaven (167–70, 188–92); his spiritual aloofness from, is justified by his equal involvement in, the cares of his flock. The schoolmaster is both serious and amusing, severe and kind; though he is 'skilled to rule', his school is 'his noisy mansion' (195). In Auburn there are no discontinuities: in old age and death one

> Bends to the ground with unperceived decay,
> While resignation gently slopes the way;
> And all his prospects brightening to the last,
> His Heaven commences ere the world be past!   (109–12)

The luxury that invades Auburn, and the city and the American wilderness to which its inhabitants are exiled, are characterised in terms of divorce and warfare. Without humanity, the village becomes a wilderness: the brook is choked with sedges, and no longer reflects the day, or man (41–2); the only guest of Auburn's glades is now the 'hollow-sounding bittern', which has to guard its nest (43–4); and

> Amidst thy desert walks the lapwing flies,
> And tires their echoes with unvaried cries.   (45–6)

Identity is lost, 'Sunk are thy bowers in shapeless ruin all' (47). Now, instead of the decent church topping the hill, 'the long grass o'ertops the mouldering wall' (48) – o'ertops it not, like civilisation properly married to nature, to crown it, but to obliterate and eventually destroy it. The implicit irony is that all this dominance of wild nature has occurred because of an excess of civilisation. In place of the 'sweet succession' that characterised the transitions from one activity to another in Auburn, 'trade's unfeeling train / Usurp the land', where now 'vistas strike . . . [and] palaces surprise'; and 'half the convex world intrudes between' home and American exile (32, 63–4, 298, 342). In the city, restlessness is not balanced with rest, and personal identity and even a sense of place and time are lost in a turmoil quite different from the 'sweet confusion' of the village, and in a warfare wholly other than the cheerful competitions of the rustic community (123, 20–34):

> Here, while the courtier glitters in brocade,
> There the pale artist plies the sickly trade;
> Here, while the proud their long-drawn pomps display,
> There the black gibbet glooms beside the way.
> The dome where Pleasure holds her midnight reign
> Here, richly decked, admits the gorgeous train;
> Tumultuous grandeur crowds the blazing square,
> The rattling chariots clash, the torches glare.   (315–22)

This 'rank luxuriance' (351) and confusion are to be found alike in unnatural civilisation and in uncivilised nature, the disjoined poles of the Auburn-metaphor: the regions of the 'wild Altama' are crowded with ferocious scorpions, snakes, tigers and men, 'While oft in whirls the mad tornado flies, / Mingling the ravaged landscape with the skies' (344–58). To one or other of the opposites that were married in Auburn its citizens are scattered, leaving only one poor old woman, 'yon widowed, solitary thing' (129), both to try to eke out a bare existence amid the barren remnants of the village, and to provide an emblem of them.

At the end of the poem Goldsmith makes the conceptual emphasis explicit: he sees 'the rural virtues leave the land' (398),

> Downward they move, a melancholy band,
> Pass from the shore and darken all the strand.
> Contented toil and hospitable care,
> And kind connubial tenderness are there;
> And piety, with wishes placed above,
> And steady loyalty and faithful love.
> And thou, sweet Poetry. . . .   (401–7)

It was not, of course, Goldsmith's farewell to poetry. If there is a weakness in the poem (apart from the typically eighteenth-century failure of logical relation in the image comparing the land to a woman – 287–302), it is that the conservative nostalgia on which it is founded is here a little self-indulgent – a case of 'Returned and wept, and still returned to weep' (370). Goldsmith clearly enjoys the fragrant pain of lamentation for departed bliss. He shares with many Augustans a sense of man's helplessness, and a deterministic view, but he takes a slightly masochistic pleasure in it; so, more emphatically, as we shall see, does Crabbe. His poem does not develop towards any higher certainty, like 'Lycidas', or offer any remedy: it simply oscillates continually between past happiness and present woe.

There is irony here, in that, while Goldsmith excoriates divorce in his poem, he himself exhibits it in his refusal to accommodate in the slightest to the new state of affairs, and in his determination to dye it in the blackest colours; on the subject of luxury he is elsewhere not so harsh.[2] Of course, at the conceptual level, there are certain opposites which cannot be joined; and there is the strong antipathy of good to bad. But, as soon as we try to relate Goldsmith's poem to the historical context and the 'real life' from which it arose, the bias becomes evident. The problem is potentially there in the similar accounts of Jonson and Pope, and surfaces in *The Deserted Village* because here not even a poetic world of value remains, and there is nothing Goldsmith will do but face nothingness, with a pleasurable sense of the elegiac. In short, *The Deserted Village* finally typifies all the one-sidedness of the Augustans, the conservative reluctance to admit contrary facts, opinions and trends. Taking the point further, the poem illustrates a more general tendency in eighteenth-century literature to see all things pointing in one direction rather than to give full weight to the random and the inextricable mixture of good and bad in them: thus Mr B. in Richardson's *Pamela* is either devil or saint; Fielding states, but does not fully show, that his characters are morally mixed; and Johnson's *The Vanity of Human Wishes* and *Rasselas* are in one way lists of examples all proving the same point.

CRABBE: 'THE VILLAGE' (1783)

As a reply to Goldsmith's *Deserted Village*, this poem is rather misconceived; but the misconception is a revealing one. Crabbe thinks Goldsmith set out to portray the actualities of country life, where in fact *The Deserted Village* is concerned finally not with an actual but with an archetypal village, one which contained partial reflections of itself in the various individual villages from which, in the fashion of Reynolds, Goldsmith extracts the ideal.[3] Goldsmith's Auburn is a picture of the kind of village that the spiritual landscape of English rurality *could*, if it did not, sustain, but can no more; but, more than this, his poem speaks finally not of lost actualities but of lost potential because of lost values. That Crabbe seizes on the actualities, considers the poem only as an attempt at a 'real picture of the poor', shows what poetry is now losing – how, to put it barely, the last coverings of late Renaissance literary tradition are giving way to shivering fact, proudly offered here as the sole truth. Metaphysics, in Crabbe at least, has become physics.

Crabbe's poem is best approached from several angles. First, there is the question of his own art. He tells us that he has set out to give us 'the real picture of the poor' (5), and that 'I paint the Cot, / As Truth will paint it, and as Bards will not (53–4)[4] – which fairly raises the question of how far a picture and a painting, however concerned to put over truth, can of their very nature do so – an issue reminiscent of that raised by Herbert's 'Jordan' poems.[5] The question which also arises with this poem is how far it was written as a retort to idealising poets, and how far its inspiration was simply sympathy with the rustics – that is, how far its beginnings were literary or social. Crabbe is uncertain as to the role of art and song: he tells us that 'the Muses sing of happy swains / Because the Muses never know their pains' (21–2), and, while it is obvious that his contempt here is for facile artistic optimism, the attack widens:

> They boast their peasants' pipes; but peasants now
> Resign their pipes and plod behind the plough;
> And few, amid the rural-tribe, have time
> To number syllables, and play with rhyme.   (23–6)

Now it seems all poetry is frippery: the reader is left to wonder what role, even allowing for the avowed need for social protest (1–6), Crabbe has left himself as a poet. (And in order to make this point, Crabbe has put himself in the position of speaking of labour as more important, even more dignified, than poetry – where the whole aim of the poem is to re-count the degrading life and tasks of the peasantry, and to lament their lack of time for the 'poet's rapture'.)

A further point emerges in lines 55 onwards:

> Nor you, ye poor of letter'd scorn complain,
> To you the smoothest song is smooth in vain;
> O'ercome by labour, and bow'd down by time,
> Feel you the barren flattery of a rhyme?

It would seem from the rather clumsy organisation here that, since smooth songs, which is all the rustics are offered, are in vain, they have every right to complain of 'letter'd scorn'. But, since Crabbe has just been saying, 'I paint the Cot / As Truth will paint it, and as Bards will not', it is to be supposed that he rescues poetry from the general curse. What is most significant here is his portrayal of the true function of poetry as expressive, not consolatory: a mirror, not a prism. He will in no way present a 'nature wrought up to an higher pitch' (Dryden) – or even a nature of which any sense may be made or from which any general truth may be drawn, or attemptedly drawn.[6] Here unalloyed empiricism makes its first significant mark on English poetry.[7]

Crabbe allows that there may once have been truth in the pastoral picture of happy swains. There once, he will allow, was a Golden Age, and pastoral idylls were then nearer being statements of fact.

> Fled are those times, when, in harmonious strains,
> The rustic poet praised his native plains:
> No shepherds now, in smooth alternate verse,
> Their country's beauty or their nymphs' rehearse.   (7–10)

First, Crabbe is here in part allowing himself a historical escape from the bleakness of truth (though once again he has mishandled his purpose by making it seem as though earlier times were childish ignorance compared to the – preferred – mature harshness of the present). He escapes physically later in the poem: like the swallows, he tells us after recounting many painful scenes,

> So waited I the favouring hour, and fled;
> Fled from these shores where guilt and famine reign,
> And cried, Ah! hapless they who still remain. . . .   (122–4)

And still later, though there for the sake of pathos, Crabbe can set the miseries of the old man beside the joys he experienced in his rustic youth – at the thought, 'A transient pleasure sparkles in his eyes' (192). Clearly, the country is not all gloom.

In his lines on the lost Golden Age Crabbe is also allowing that present conditions are temporally local – partial, not universal truth. And it is here also revealing that much of his poem is local in its application, in that, speaking as it does of the environs of Aldeburgh, it speaks of a locality where the land is peculiarly ill-equipped to reward peasant labour. This is why, halfway through the poem, Crabbe is forced to move to wider contexts, admitting, as he does so, of those he has so far 'painted', 'But these are scenes where Nature's niggard hand / Gave a spare portion to the famish'd land' (131–2). Even after he has done this, however, he still returns to scenes of nature's niggardliness (150).[8]

Crabbe is concerned with things that were or are, but never with how the 'were' changed into the 'are' – or, indeed, how the 'are', the 'state of things', whether of nature or the social order, may be altered. He is interested only in being, not becoming; it is, one may say, the sentimentalist's worship of actuality, and it misses half the truth. 'They boast their peasants' pipes; but peasants now / Resign their pipes and plod behind the plough' (23–4): the resigning and the plodding are simultaneous.

Crabbe tells us that the pastoral idyll is easy to write, both because 'no deep thought the trifling subjects ask' (revealing ignorance, like Johnson's, of the metaphysical dimension of pastoral, and an almost nominalist approach to experience) and because

> To sing of shepherds is an easy task:
> The happy youth assumes the common strain,
> A nymph his mistress, and himself a swain;
> With no sad scenes he clouds his tuneful prayer,
> But all, to look like her, is painted fair.   (34–8)

Easy to write, he feels, because cliché, but even more because all items point one way: but a similar criticism might equally be applied to Crabbe's monocular concentration on the bad and painful sides of rustic life. Though Crabbe writes to remove the stereotyped view of country pleasures (and indeed deals with the side of peasant life Goldsmith omitted – their labour), he himself produces an equally stereotyped vision of rustic pains.[9] Crabbe is, in common with other eighteenth-century writers, capable only of the single view, and his poem takes on the aspect of a list of tribulations designed simply to force us up against hard fact. And with Crabbe's poem we can learn for future conduct no more than with Goldsmith's: a large part of it is concerned with pains which nature and not man causes, pains therefore (in Crabbe's own view) unrectifiable.

Like Goldsmith in *The Deserted Village* (287 ff.), Crabbe at one point compares the land to a woman, and like Goldsmith's, the comparison does not work; this again illustrates the weakness of eighteenth-century literature in handling logical relations.[10] Crabbe's analogy is longer and, significantly, has much more detail than Goldsmith's: he is concerned much more with an individual scene, not with the typical and the conceptual.

> Lo! where the heath, with withering brake grown o'er,
> Lends the light turf that warms the neighbouring poor;
> From thence a length of burning sand appears,
> Where the thin harvest waves its wither'd ears;

> Rank weeds, that every art and care defy,
> Reign o'er the land, and rob the blighted rye:
> There thistles stretch their prickly arms afar,
> And to the ragged infant threaten war;
> There poppies nodding, mock the hope of toil;
> There the blue bugloss paints the sterile soil;
> Hardy and high, above the slender sheaf,
> The slimy mallow waves her silky leaf;
> O'er the young shoot the charlock throws a shade,
> And clasping tares cling round the sickly blade;
> With mingled tints the rocky coasts abound,
> And a sad splendour vainly shines around.
> So looks the nymph whom wretched arts adorn,
> Betray'd by man, then left for man to scorn;
> Whose cheek in vain assumes the mimic rose,
> While her sad eyes the troubled breast disclose;
> Whose outward splendour is but folly's dress,
> Exposing most, when most it gilds distress.   (63–84)

The beautiful weeds demonstrate by their presence the sterility underneath, but it is the woman's unadorned eyes that disclose her troubled
breast. Crabbe senses this, and tries to force the parallel in the last
line. In no truly related sense is the land 'Betray'd by man, then left for
man to scorn'. Its sterility is inherent in its being poor soil, and one is
to assume that as yet science cannot alter the situation; and the sight
of the weeds amid the corn is one not for scorn but for lamentation.
Again the land has never been any good, but the woman has; stasis is
being compared to flux – the problem with Goldsmith's analogy also,
Beyond this there is, of course, the whole problem of comparing an
involuntary to a voluntary agent – a land, on which beautiful weeds
grow not to conceal the ugliness, but simply because the soil is good
for nothing else, to a woman, who deliberately puts on her weeds to
effect such concealment. The result of such breakdown in the analogy
is that it cannot be taken in any but a very general sense – the common
factor of the two terms becomes only 'Misery cannot be concealed', in
the same way that Goldsmith's analogy dilutes itself.

Crabbe's analogy is, however, unlike Goldsmith's in being far more
specific and detailed, and concerned much more with portraying a scene.
We are far from the point-to-point parallel essayed in Goldsmith's comparison: the description of the land becomes a powerful vignette in its
own right. It has the lack of generality (even while Crabbe insists on its
typicality in his use of the definite article) and the attention to detail
that Johnson and other Augustans might deplore; and yet, as we read it,
we see that its very detail has given the picture a conceptual and meta-

phoric power it might not otherwise have had. The image is a Hobbesian one of nature at war with itself; but, more than this, it grows into a metaphor of England's social fabric as well. The 'rank weeds' that 'reign o'er the land and rob the blighted rye' need small comment in view of what Crabbe has been saying about the lot of the peasant. The poppies which 'nodding, mock the hope of toil', perhaps remind us of the 'sleepy bards' (17). The 'blue bugloss [that] paints the sterile soil' recalls both the 'Can poets soothe you, when you pine for bread, / By winding myrtles round your ruin'd shed?' just previously (59–60), and the earlier,

> I grant indeed that fields and flocks have charms
> For him that grazes or for him that farms;
> But when amid such pleasing scenes I trace
> The poor laborious natives of the place. . . .   (39–42)

The remainder of the picture – the slender sheaf with the high and slimy mallows waving its leaf over it, the charlock throwing a shade over the young shoot, and the clasping tares clinging (in a beautifully mimetic line) round the sickly blade – is a natural mirror of the oppressed lot of the peasant. By itself this scene is a fine metaphor, but it is a mark of the Augustan strain in Crabbe that he should not consciously see this, and that he should try to make it explicit in so inapt a way.

Crabbe's most frequent attack in this poem is levelled at distance from reality. Poets sentimentalise the lot of the peasant by ignoring it: 'thus the Muses sing of happy swains, / Because the Muses never know their pains' (21–2; it is typical of Crabbe that 'know' here should have more of a physical than an intellectual reference). Of farmers, or sheep, he says, 'I grant indeed that fields and flocks have charms / For him that grazes or for him that farms' (39–40). He satirises the rich, who 'trifle . . . with wants you cannot feel' (168), who complain at 'fantastic woes' which 'real pain and that alone can cure' (250, 257) and whose 'slaves advance / With timid eye, to read the distant glance' (252–3). His portrait of the parish doctor's visit to the poor-house, 'In haste he seeks the bed where Misery lies, / Impatience mark'd in his averted eyes' (288–9), is matched in bitterness only by that of the parish priest, who prefers hunting to tending the sick or officiating at the burials of the dead (296–317). Thus it is that the poem contains frequent injunctions to such people to 'Go!' and to 'see' for themselves the miseries they conceal or ignore (142, 174, 175, 182, 200).

Yet there is a real ambivalence in Crabbe's attitude here, for he himself finds proximity depressing in a different way from distance (this is reminiscent of Johnson): close to, the lot of the peasant is so repulsive to him that he longs to escape it. On the one hand he feels that anything which is remote from such life is evanescent, immature and effeminate (there is perhaps something of British sentimentality about the working classes here); and on the other he knows that such life is, far from being a condition to be admired, one which is degrading, stunting and obscene (thus at one point – 119–24 – he flies from the scenes of misery he has traced). This ambivalence ties in with what we know of Crabbe himself, a mixture of fascination and repugnance which can and does turn into fascinated repugnance in this poem.

It might be argued that the teller of this poem is a dramatised narrator, ironically seen by Crabbe himself. Perhaps the only suggestive lines in this respect, however, are those in which he is portrayed, like Goldsmith, as at first deluded: 'Here, wand'ring long, amid these frowning fields, / I sought the simple life that Nature yields' (108–10); but these sentiments are described as having occurred before he developed into the truth-teller he announces himself to be at the outset of the poem. There seems little case for seeing the speaker as other than Crabbe himself.

That said, what we nevertheless watch in his position in the poem is the development of his own masochism beneath the fabric of social protest. Crabbe is fascinated here, as in all his poetry, by the notion of oppression, of enormous weight striking down, of utterly burdened misery; here he conceives of leaving the land in terms of taking wing. When the peasants are described, syntax and sense are commonly confined to couplets, giving a sense of repression; and there is frequent use of imperatives and plosive consonants, with the effect of heavy blows. Twice we see the rustics bowed down by the heat: 'see the mid-day sun, with fervid ray, / On their bare heads and dewy temples play' (43–4); and 'See them beneath the dog-star's raging heat, / When the knees tremble and the temples beat' (144–5). The harvest is crushed by the weeds. The peasants strive to sustain themselves, but fail; the words 'droops', 'drooping', 'declining' recur (2, 161, 165, 176, 269, 292). In the last third of Book I we move to the hoary swain, a symbol of humanity bowed by time and labour, 'propp'd on that rude staff', looking at his 'sad emblem' in the 'bare arms broken from the withering tree', weeping 'beneath the hillock' and murmuring to the winds 'that blow / O'er his white locks and bury them in snow'. He is longing for death, longing for the final oppression which cannot be felt, 'Then let my bones beneath the turf be laid' (184–7, 201–3, 224). Now he is 'oppress'd' by disease and committed to the parish poorhouse, whose 'walls of mud' symbolically 'scarce bear the broken door', and 'where the putrid vapours, flagging, play' (226–30); and, after the failures of doctor and priest, he dies at last.

The movement in the poem has in a sense been one of increasing proximity. Crabbe begins with rural life in general as described by previous poets, moves to a panoramic vision of the miseries of the labouring poor, and thence to the interior of a cottage and family life; then he fixes on one typical old man and his progress, from the outside world of nature, to the parish poor-house and finally the house of death. The development has also been what Crabbe promised in the first lines – 'every care that reigns / O'er youthful peasants and declining swains' – but it is not only as formal as that: it is a picture too of someone being drawn against his will into a vortex of obsessive fascination. And at the bottom of that vortex is both the ultimate reality of, and the answer to, all the scenes of feeble struggle ('the rude turf heaving', as Gray might put it) that we have witnessed in the poem. In death the old man ascends:

> Up yonder hill, behold how sadly slow
> The bier moves winding from the vale below.   (321–2)

The dead are happy: death is for them an escape, and at the same time an oppression devoutly to be wished,

> No more, O Death! thy victim starts to hear
> Churchwarden stern, or kingly overseer;
> No more the farmer claims his humble bow,
> Thou art his lord, the best of tyrants thou!   (325–8)

Irony may be intended, but is lost here. The poem has shrunk in to this one all-embracing fact, as in a sense a poem which sets out to relate fact must finally do; and the imagery of crushing, so clearly native to the poet himself, has moved to this complete prostration. The last image is one of total privacy, but of privacy violated and made public; Crabbe is there in horrified fascination with the village children as the grave is opened –

> While bending low, their eager eyes explore
> The mingled relics of the parish poor.   (339–40)

One is reminded of Tennyson on the yew tree: 'I seem to fail from out my blood / And grow incorporate into thee' (*In Memoriam*, iii); beside this, all vicissitude, movement and life seem evanescent.

This poem is indeed social protest, but only intermittently, for its real drive is towards death. Even at a conscious level it is divided between showing the miseries of the poor as miseries and showing them as functions of social ills; and only half of the sufferings of the poor described can be attributed to man rather than to nature. These ambivalences are reconciled in the imagery and the direction of the poem, which make it into Crabbe's spiritual pilgrimage. The pessimism of the poem is not only oversimplification: it springs from morbidity.

Crabbe is aware enough of some of the contradictions: 'But these are scenes where Nature's niggard hand / Gave a spare portion to the famish'd land' (131–2); 'Yet grant them health' (164); 'I too must yield, that oft amid these woes / Are gleams of transient mirth and hours of sweet repose' (II, 3–4). Nevertheless, the poem sprawls on as social protest into a second book, and Crabbe tries, as in the last quotation, and in the picture of the virtuous (but dead) Manners, to offer some ray of light in a gloom which he knows other people would find too unrelieved. But his heart is not in it, for the poem proper has ended with the first book. Indeed, the continuation is much more radically confused. Crabbe starts by telling us that he will describe exceptions to the general rule of pain in the village, exceptions which he finds in Sunday, the day of rest. He speaks of them as 'gleams of transient mirth and hours of sweet repose' (4) and, indeed, so they are to appear: for the picture of the masters of the peasants grinding their teeth in rage at the thought of this holiday (19–24) gives frailty, indeed almost nonenity, to their freedom. After enjoining the peasants to 'enjoy your hour, / This is your portion, yet unclaim'd of power' (25–6), Crabbe relapses into a portrayal of how the holiday itself relapses into misery:

> But yours, alas! are joys that soon decay;
> Frail joys, begun and ended with the day;
> Or yet, while day permits those joys to reign,
> The village vices drive them from the plain.   (29–32)

There follow the portraits of the 'stout churl' striking his wife in a drunken fury (33–8); of how Slander, 'the city's vice . . . / . . . steals along and taints the Green' (39–48); of the syphilitic nymphs distributing disease to the rustics (49–54); of thefts from the Squire (55–62); of the 'rustic battle' at the tavern (63–72); and of the enforced and doomed marriage of the swain and the nymph (75–86).

At the end of this Crabbe tells us that the object of these portraits has been to show rural crime:

> Yet why, you ask, these humble crimes relate,
> Why make the poor as guilty as the great?
> To show the great, those mightier sons of pride,
> How near in vice the lowest are allied. . . .   (87–90)

This certainly is not what we thought he was doing when he set out to show how even the repose of the peasants is disturbed, or when he blamed the city for the ills of slander and disease that they suffer, or seemed to blame the rigour of the law and the hypocrisy of the local justice for their punishments (71–4, 79–82). Now, it would seem, we are to take the picture of the thefts from the squire at face-value, as reprehensible acts, not as a justifiable removal of excess by the deprived (Crabbe was nearer this latter view in his picture of the smugglers in 1, 101–18):

> Here too the 'Squire, or 'squire-like farmer, talk,
> How round their regions nightly pilferers walk;
> How from their ponds the fish are borne, and all
> The rip'ning treasures from their lofty wall;
> How meaner rivals in their sports delight,
> Just rich enough to claim a doubtful right;
> Who take a licence round their fields to stray,
> A mongrel race! the poachers of the day.   (55–62)

We are no longer speaking of 'The Village life, and ev'ry care that reigns / O'er youthful peasants and declining swains' but of the miseries of the well-to-do. And where in the first book Crabbe saw the pains of the great as imaginary, because distant from real pains, he now argues,

> And you, ye poor, who still lament your fate,
> Forbear to envy those you call the great;
> And know, amid those blessings they posses,
> They are, like you, the victims of distress;
> While sloth with many a pang torments her slave,
> Fear waits on guilt, and danger shakes the brave.   (101–6)

Crabbe is making this contradictory point because his poem is drawing to a conclusion in which he feels he must find some consolation for the miseries of the peasant lot.

But in moving to the great, and in moving finally to Manners as a palliative for the peasantry, Crabbe has left the context which alone could offer anything to the suffering humanity he has portrayed. The last passage quoted has been an attempt to bridge the gap, as Crabbe shifts from the torments that beset the vices of the great to the trials of their virtue ('danger shakes the brave'). He now tries to portray the sufferings of the great and virtuous Manners as far larger and more weighty than anything the peasants experience: the poem has, in short, turned upside-down. Like Christ, Manners includes and transcends the sufferings of the peasants,

> to all you feel or fear resign'd;
> Who gave up joys and hopes to you unknown,
> For pains and dangers greater than your own. . . .   (110–12)

But the picture of Manners is given no connection with rustic life, except in the natural imagery of him as guardian oak (119–26) and as a great river (200 ff.). And we know that his death was 'given' to Crabbe as a way of finding an end for his poem.[11] Its detachment from the issues it is there to answer can be seen in the way Crabbe's shrill grief at his loss is for him alone. When we read

> 'Tis not, I know, the chiming of a song,
> Nor all the powers that to the Muse belong,
> Words aptly cull'd and meanings well express'd,
> Can calm the sorrows of a wounded breast   (157–60)

we recall that just such words were used of the sufferings of the peasants at the beginning of the poem. Now the peasants have been lost – at most, theoretically subsumed in the loss of Manners – and the poem grieves the death of an aristocrat. Now Crabbe can say that

> Life is not measured by the time we live:
> 'Tis not an even course of threescore years,
> A life of narrow views and paltry fears,
> Grey hairs and wrinkles and the cares they bring,
> That take from death the terrors or the sting;
> But 'tis the gen'rous spirit, mounting high
> Above the world, that native of the sky. . . .   (172–8)

Ideally life may not be so measurable; but for the peasants what other view is possible? How can the spirit be generous when it is permanently crushed? Between the abject misery of rustic life that Crabbe has portrayed, and the soaring spirits of those free to soar there can be no meeting-ground. Gray could effect such a junction because his peasants have spirit, in life and in death. Crabbe's can have no other but narrow views, paltry fears, grey hairs and wrinkles. It may be, of course, that Crabbe is here trying to lighten his own gloom rather than that of the society he has portrayed.

The collapse of the poem in this second book, and the contradictory attitudes taken in it, are significant. Crabbe was no Marxist: he was divided between social concern and Augustan conservatism, just as in real life he was the son of a well-to-do family and an 'experiencer' of the hard toil he saw about him, a man who fled Aldeburgh to become patronised by the great, and returned to endure provincial sneers and envy. The two attitudes are unreconciled in this poem: on the one hand there is contempt for the distant rich and sympathy for the suffering poor, and on the other greatness seems to claim its own. When the crunch came – ?: one wonders whether the question finally matters. For the imaginative power of this poem (in Book 1) is not so much its conscious intent, whether of social outcry or praise of greatness, but the fully integrated theme of suppression and of death. It is this that, while it may not make the poem art (if art be the reconciliation of contraries), makes it extremely powerful as literature; this too, once again, that makes this poem a picture of the pre-Romantic strength of Augustan poetry at unconscious, rather than at conscious, levels of organisation.

Although in its method of attack Crabbe's *The Village* has affinities with Pope, there is little that is Augustan in its orientation: the empiricist base of the poem leaves small place for any theme save the injunction to rub one's nose in essential quiddity, an injunction which develops into an obsession with the physical which has nothing to do with its *value* as fact. Crabbe's poem shares the deterministic outlook of much eighteenth-century poetry, and, indeed, in this goes further than Goldsmith: for, where *The Deserted Village* describes a change from happiness to misery, Crabbe's portrays wretchedness as the settled lot of the peasant. Doubtless this was what appealed to Johnson in *The Village*: but Johnson's own gloom was set in a frame of detached philosophic inquiry, while Crabbe's, lacking this conceptual and traditional basis, reveals the lineaments of neurosis and subjectivism all too plainly. With Crabbe, two centuries of the growth of empiricism have brought us to the particular fact and the isolated individual.

The Village is as one-sided as *The Deserted Village*: where Goldsmith gives us in Auburn a nature wrought up to a higher pitch, Crabbe gives us a nature wrought down. There is no remission to the gloom, no escape from its obsessive fascination: the holidays of the rustics are destroyed, the flight to Manners (how appropriately named) and Augustanism is a flight to nowhere. No balance or synthesis is possible: now the rustics are valued above the great, now the reverse. At the same time the reference to the particular is strictly limited. Crabbe is uneasily conscious that his generalisations on rustic misery have no more extensive purview than the environs of Aldeburgh, yet still he makes them. But, despite Crabbe's wishes, what is portrayed cannot finally be moralised, because the facts described are interesting only as facts, not as instructive facts: *The Village* soon loses its pretensions to literary or social protest, and even comparison with other contexts, as in the case of the image of the land and the woman, breaks down. The sole dynamic of the poem becomes the portrayal of a psyche entering a vortex. This subjectivist base of the poem might make it 'pre-Romantic': but it is also to be seen as the consequence of the eighteenth-century view of man as the observer and nature as the observed. Many of the writers of the period are detached from the world, yet seeking roots; much of the literature describes travels and journeys. Crabbe, like Gray, Johnson or Goldsmith before him – and Byron after him – is in search of an 'objective correlative', a certainty. Like Johnson he is pulled by the world he tries impartially to describe: but what, in Johnson, is a strain or tension between the impartial and the partial tips over, in Crabbe, into total immersion. With Crabbe we see the poet no longer able to rise above his material.

We may trace in the development of eighteenth-century poetry an increasing proximity to nature. While Thomson and Johnson range over the whole of life, Gray and Goldsmith fix on one representative village, and Crabbe and Cowper on one special locality; Wordsworth was to find truth in spots of time, Blake the world in a grain of sand. There is a growth of the historical sense that one age is not to be judged by the terms of reference applicable to another, and similarly with the country, one school of poetry, or one scene in nature. Singularity becomes as interesting as likeness. The subject-matter of poetry increasingly nears the particular identity of things, while at the same time developing towards the expression of self rather than society. Indeed, this increasing proximity is true of the very lives of many of the pastoral poets of the eighteenth century. Gray and Goldsmith (if we except Goldsmith's childhood) were occasional visitors to the country; Crabbe divided his life between village-life and the metropolis; Cowper left London in early manhood and spent most of the rest of his life in the village of Olney. Finally, with Wordsworth, we find someone reared not only wholly in the country, but in a countryside almost untouched by man, the uncivilised wilderness so abhorrent to the Augustans.

But with Crabbe the gap between man and his environment is almost closed – even if for him the process was one by which he was drawn out of himself by nature, in fascinated horror, where for Wordsworth the relation was the more gladly reciprocal one of nature pursuing him, and of his welcoming the pursuit, in surprised joy.

14 Cowper

With Cowper, as with Crabbe, nature is, finally, the 'objective correlative': it seems to have more reality and more certainty than anything else, and, having that, to pull the observer in. The conscious, moralising or 'emoting' self is no longer a stable one. Empirical fact is now so large that it has become hypnotic. Nature is ceasing to be simply an observed phenomenon, the datum for mind to survey and admire, and is beginning to be seen as something to enter or be entered by, and that in which one finds by losing oneself.

Yet Cowper is too much of an eighteenth-century poet consciously to admit this. We have to trace the urge in the conflicts of his poetry, and in the places where it catches fire. His late poem 'Yardley Oak' shows both the poetic strengths and the divisions of sensibility which this underlying interest produced.

The opening lines of the poem show that Cowper has no mean poetic ability when it is awakened.

> Survivor sole, and hardly such, of all
> That once liv'd here thy brethren, at my birth
> (Since which I number three-score winters past)
> A shatter'd veteran, hollow-trunk'd perhaps
> As now, and with excoriate forks deform,
> Relicts of ages! Could a mind, imbued
> With truth from heav'n, created thing adore,
> I might with rev'rence kneel and worship thee.   (1–8)

'Survivor sole', three syllables followed by one, imitates the shrunken singularity of the tree, while at the same time the grandiose inverted phrase keeps up the sense of its epic might and resistance. '. . . and hardly such' is a neat pun. The uneven vowel lengths of this line and the clogged consonants of this and the next,

> Survivor sole, and hardly such, of all
> That once liv'd here thy brethren, at my birth,

imitate the struggle of the tree against enormous odds; and together with the broken fragments of syntax enact the 'shatter'd veteran' that now remains. The first line gives the sense that the tree is the sole survivor of all things, before the particularities of the second line localise its longevity in time and place. 'A shatter'd veteran, hollow-trunk'd perhaps' and the later 'excoriate forks deform' are fine renderings in sound of the smashed, the empty and the twisting (the last also brought home in the phrasal inversion). And, if we consider the syntax of the whole stanza, which almost but not quite breaks down, we have a further picture of the sense.

There are other effects, less specifically poetic and less intentional. After reading the first phrase, 'Survivor sole', one is faintly jerked by the 'and hardly such': admiration of strength seems to have turned into pity for weakness. The tree evokes two quite different reactions in the poet, and he has no way here of uniting these into a third, inclusive perception. Much of the poem is indeed the attempt to find such a fusion: 'shatter'd veteran', in this stanza, for instance, or 'Relicts of ages', in which 'Relicts' is both the venerable and the pathetic leavings; but both seem to fall on the admiring side – as is suggested further at the end of the stanza, when the speaker exclaims, 'I might with rev'rence kneel and worship thee.'

There is also a limit to the analogies between himself and the tree: he may be a 'shatter'd veteran', or 'number three-score winters past', but in what sense more than the whimsical or the *voulu* is he 'hollow-trunk'd, or 'with *excoriate* forks deform'? Cowper seems to look at the tree and then at himself, but not to feel a more than fleeting kinship. Like the double feeling of admiration and pity, this points to a fundamental uncertainty of stance: he is divided between an involved and a detached standpoint. In the last line he wants to simplify the dilemma by worshipping the tree, becoming one with it. This division is continued into the next stanza, in his sense that in the Christian view this would be idolatry, or at best pantheism: he knows that nature is one of God's creatures, frail and mortal, and yet he feels drawn to this creature. (The same shifts of standpoint can be seen in *The Task*.) What is more, in this first stanza he feels, and is drawn to, the fact of the tree, while in the next he stands back and thinks; and this alternation is carried on throughout the poem.

The suspended syntax of this first stanza also gives a sense of something continually about to be. When the verb comes in the last line, it comes as a possibility – 'I *might* with rev'rence kneel'. This 'imminence' applies not only to the sensibility of Cowper, pausing before the plunge, as he is to pause throughout the poem, but also to the special interest he shows in this poem (precisely the opposite of Crabbe's in *The Village*) in the category of 'becoming', rather than of 'being'. The tree is chosen as subject not only because of its mixture of grandeur and frailty, but also because it is the product and the expression of change and process. This may here be one reason for Cowper's wanting to become part of it: he wants to escape from the stasis of his reflective self and lose himself in process.

'If it were not that the Christian cannot worship created things . . .'. the first stanza has, in effect, ended. Now, in the second, Cowper continues this thought:

> It seems idolatry with some excuse
> When our fore-father Druids in their oaks
> Imagin'd sanctity.   (9–11)

The first line, with the Druids as yet unmentioned, can be taken as saying, 'There is excuse for my worshipping the tree, even if the act is proscribed.' The 'seems' furthers the link by continuing the present of the first stanza, and the word 'excuse' reduces the sin to a peccadillo. When we come to the second line we find that it is the Druids rather than himself whom he means to excuse; yet even here the description of them as 'fore-fathers' seems to justify a descent of their little errors to later generations (the notion of descent is continued later in this stanza with the analogy with Adam). That 'when', too, taken in conjunction with the tense of 'seems', suggests 'since': that is, the lines mean, 'If our forefathers the Druids could do it, why cannot we?' Only now does the stanza turn to the Christian abrogation of such images, and it does so in curiously inert, legalistic terminology:

> The conscience, yet
> Unpurified by an authentic act
> Of amnesty, the meed of blood divine,
> Lov'd not the light, but gloomy into gloom
> Of thickest shades, like Adam after taste
> Of fruit proscrib'd, as to a refuge, fled.   (11–16)

The mixture of abstract and concrete here is typical of the poem; that Cowper reaches particularity once more in the last lines suggests that he has consolidated the change of viewpoint uncertainly managed before. The implicit idea seems to be that the Druids behaved as did their own forefathers, that it was their sense of sin that drove them to lose themselves: this makes a judgment on the poet's own longing to worship the tree. Here, in short, Cowper is affixing an ethical and spiritual label to a spontaneous longing: the tension between free response and imprisoned valuation, and the jarring shifts from one to the other (mirrored in the movement from concrete to abstract diction), are largely felt in this poem – and in *The Task*.

In this stanza too we see Cowper's addiction to 'time-travelling', to the process of change. Once this was not so; now it is: one can explore the 'then' as well as the 'now' as having almost equal title to present actuality; the constant movements of the poem backwards in time are an aspect of the speaker's desire to escape his present knowing self. Again, the syntax is suspended, with the effects seen in the first stanza.

Now that the speaker has got himself through this stanza, first almost justifying idolatry and eventually gaining its condemnation, he can return to the oak, now no longer admiring, but slightly contemptuous (the other side of the dualism):

> Thou wast a bauble once; a cup and ball,
> Which babes might play with; and the thievish jay
> Seeking her food, with ease might have purloin'd
> The auburn nut that held thee, swallowing down
> Thy yet close-folded latitude of boughs
> And all thine embryo vastness, at a gulp.   (17–22)

The *p*s and *b*s are factors in the playfully derisive note. The poetry is immediately much more sensitive than in the last stanza: the 'close-folded latitude', with its tight-knit syllables and the semi-spondee on 'close-folded', enacts the sense; and the mixture of abstract and concrete, together with the metre and contrasted vowel lengths of 'all thine embryo vastness, at a gulp', is fine. There is attempt to convey strength as well as frailty in the embryo vastness, but here it is the sense of failty that is dominant. Again we are with change, with what was, compared (here to undercut) with what is now. Again, too, the speaker is musing on possibilities.

Having voiced these possibilities the poet bows to fact, which he sees in terms of a scheme, that which limits life to one line of development: 'But Fate thy growth decreed' (23). (Cowper is in this poem split between his desires for such narrow certainty of act and for the free potential of multiple choice – a Johnsonian dichotomy.) There now follows a picture of the tree being nourished in the soil beneath the parent tree, and of a skipping deer that 'With pointed hoof dibbling the glebe, prepar'd / The soft receptacle in which secure / Thy rudiments should sleep the winter through' (26–8). This picture is meant as an accurate portrayal of what may indeed have happened: even if there are overtones of the pathetic fallacy – 'the soil / Design'd thy cradle' (24–5), the deer which 'prepar'd / The soft receptacle' – the facts themselves may well be correct.

Perhaps it is to this picture that Cowper is referring when he now suddenly turns, in what sounds like self-goaded irritation, to say,

> So Fancy dreams – Disprove it, if ye can,
> Ye reas'ners broad awake, whose busy search
> Of argument, employ'd too oft amiss,
> Sifts half the pleasures of short life away.   (29–32)

There was nothing *finally* fanciful in the picture: these lines seem to express a more general sense of nervousness, and to reflect Cowper's larger uncertainties between the pulls on him of truth and fancy; the 'broad awake' unfortunately implies that Cowper is only half so. The passage attacks what receives part of his own allegiance, the sense of actuality, which matters to him as much as possibility, and, apart from the description of reason as sifting '*half* the pleasures of short life away', is an oversimplification. How (the defiant 'if ye can' seems half-aware of this) could reason *disprove* the picture? Nothing that has been said of what might have happened to the tree and what did is beyond possibility. What seems to be revealed here is a distaste on the part of the poet for his own consciousness, which is continually calling him away from his pleasure in the identities of created things to reflect upon them; this is a rare glimpse, though, for elsewhere in the poem he is quite happy to oscillate between contemplation and reflection upon it.

These four lines are typical of Cowper's shifts of attention in the poem. He wants to contemplate the tree for itself, as a physical phenomenon altered by other physical phenomena, and at the same time he wants to make it give moral or other instruction to man: as soon as he concentrates on the one, he shifts awkwardly back to the other. There is in the poem a split between body (physical portrayal) and mind (rational or moral application); and one between the tree as *dulce* or *utile*, as affording pleasure or instruction. We saw much the same in Thomson, but here the division seems much more painfully felt. Cowper hovers on the edge of finding spiritual truth within his pleasurable experience of nature, but his faith, and his Augustan or Renaissance habits of moralising, of emblematising, of reflecting upon experience to *make* it sensible or exemplary, forbid him this fusion of opposites. It is not surprising that Wordsworth and Coleridge felt drawn to Cowper's poetry.[1]

We return in the next stanza to the tree as both mighty and puny:

> Thou fell'st mature, and in the loamy clod
> Swelling, with vegetative force instinct
> Didst burst thine egg, as theirs the fabled Twins
> Now stars; two lobes, protruding, pair'd exact;
> A leaf succeeded, and another leaf,

>   And all elements thy puny growth
>   Fost'ring propitious, thou becam'st a twig.   (33–9)

The verbs at first portray the independent force of purpose in the tree --
'fell'st', 'Swelling', 'burst', 'protruding', 'pair'd', 'succeded' – but then turn
to describing the assistance given to the tree, in the elements' 'Fost'ring
propitious' its 'puny' growth; and the climax of all this energy, 'thou
becam'st a twig', has much of the mockery of mountains labouring over
the birth of a mouse.

Once again, no sooner has the poet considered this physical process
than he jerks aside to try to make some conceptual use of it:

>   Who liv'd when thou wast such? Oh could'st thou speak,
>   As in Dodona once thy kindred trees
>   Oracular, I would not curious ask
>   The future, best unknown, but at thy mouth
>   Inquisitive, the less ambiguous past.   (40–4)

The first sentence seems rather shrill and clumsy. The use of the oaks
of Dodona is rather limited here, except in that they spoke: the poet
does not wish to hear the prophecies they told, but histories. Similarly
restricted is the comparison of the birth of Castor and Pollux to the
oak's inception, where the only likeness is that both burst an egg, and
that at one point the oak has twin leaves; the rest is beautifying, which
could have been accomplished by any number of images. The whole
simile suggests that Cowper is glancing away from the object without
really focusing on the alternatives. Having introduced the Dodona oaks
without sufficient thought, he cannot get rid of them, and has to talk
of them as revealing the past as well as the future. Why the future
should be any more 'best unknown' than the past is not altogether
clear; nor is the difference between 'curious' and 'Inquisitive', even if
Cowper intends it to be that between forbidden and permitted knowledge. The 'Oh could'st thou speak' suggests an urgent desire, a quest
for significant knowledge, even a search for information throwing more
light on the actual growth of the tree (or at least giving the poem a
theme), but the earnestness is empty, for the object would be a merely
pedantic one:

>   By thee I might correct, erroneous oft,
>   The clock of history, facts and events
>   Timing more punctual, unrecorded facts
>   Recov'ring, and misstated setting right –
>   Desp'rate attempt, till trees shall speak again!   (45–9)

The clock analogy is a little inapt, in so far as clocks can be set right only once. The whole purpose of this lengthy aside collapses in the last line, with the 'Desp'rate' suggesting precisely what it has not been – unless the desperation be considered descriptive of the poet's attempts to make the tree meaningful or intelligible.

The next lines return us to his dual apprehension of the tree as both mighty and frail, but here the duality becomes for once bonded:

> Time made thee what thou wast – King of the woods;
> And time hath made thee what thou art – a cave
> For owls to roost in. (50–2)

In a sense these are among the finest lines of the poem: their subject is time, and the account of the oak's growth and its decay are alike re-counted here in monosyllables suggesting the ticking of a clock, or that steady construction and dismantling which are accomplished by the same medium: the rhythm rises and falls, the words build up like bricks, and then come down. This is the apprehension of unity that the poet has been searching for, the notion of piece added to or removed from piece by the same quiet process, 'Noiseless, an atom and an atom more / Dis-joining from the rest' (106–7); or as he elsewhere tries to put it, in clumsy abstract language, phenomena, 'worn by frequent impulse, to the cause / Of their best tone their dissolution owe' (84–5).

Yet there are too many other forces and interests pulling on the poet to allow this sense to give poetic tension to the whole:

> Thought cannot spend itself, comparing still
> The great and little of thy lot, thy growth
> From almost nullity into a state
> Of matchless grandeur, and declension thence
> Slow into such magnificent decay. (86–90)

Thought cannot spend itself because thought cannot more than occa-sionally find a way out: not admiration only, but frustration also is ex-pressed here. Cowper is fascinated by the duality, but he is so concerned with making the tree explicitly meaningful or useful, so concerned with his nervous consciousness, that he cannot get into right relation with the object, like a camera only rarely in focus.

Thus the poem continues, from physical apprehension to moral or intellectual comment, and back again. We have yet another picture of the oak's growth from small to great (60–8; here time only really enters in the destruction of the tree), followed by a long verse-paragraph on change as the force 'on which all subsist' (69–85). Change means much to Cowper – indeed, it fascinates him – and he makes it one of the basic themes of *The Task*; but he cannot make or leave the point implicit in his portrait of the tree. Later, having described how the root of the oak is still 'sincere', holding it erect, he turns aside to draw an analogy with man:

> So stands a kingdom, whose foundations yet
> Fail not, in virtue and in wisdom laid,
> Though all the superstructure, by the tooth
> Pulveriz'd of venality, a shell
> Stands now, and semblance only of itself.
>   (120–4; cf. 56–9)

Intellectual discussion may lead to conflict with physical fact: the poet speaks of the tree as spared by the axe and subject only to time's nibbling power, which removes 'an atom and an atom more' (93–109), but in fact the oak has lost its branches in high winds (125–9). At length, having resorted once more to the physical appearance of the oak, Cowper abandons all attempt at making a relationship between it and man, and recoils upon himself. 'I will perform / Myself the oracle, and will discourse / In my own ear such matter as I may' (141–3).

The performance is certainly interesting. The poet returns to (Milton's) Adam, but this time for another reason – to escape process.

> One man alone, the Father of us all
> Drew not his life from woman; never gaz'd,
> With mute unconsciousness of what he saw
> On all around him; learn'd not by degrees,
> Nor owed articulation to his ear;
> But, moulded by his Maker into Man
> At once, upstood intelligent, survey'd
> All creatures, with precision understood
> Their purport, uses, properties, assign'd
> To each his name significant, and, fill'd
> With love and wisdom, render'd back to heav'n
> In praise harmonious the first air he drew.
> He was excus'd the penalties of dull
> Minority. No tutor charg'd his hand
> With the thought-tracing quill, or task'd his mind
> With problems; history, not wanted yet,
> Lean'd on her elbow, watching Time, whose course,
> Eventful, should supply her with a theme.   (167–84)

Adam was truly independent, because he owed his being to no other created thing; and his intelligence, knowledge and articulacy were inborn.

We perhaps touch here on that theme of freedom so dear to Cowper in *The Task*. But the first important fact about Adam here is that he was an example of pure being, as opposed to becoming: he was part of no process, and 'history [was] not wanted yet'; no course of development made him. He therefore in this sense escapes the category of time and change, which Cowper has hitherto portrayed as the lot of all mortals. Further, Adam was independent of phenomena not only for his being, but for his knowledge: he had an inner light which needed no education from experience. We recall that the poet himself has by this point left consideration of the tree and made himself the oracle; and that Cowper's Calvinist faith (and his terror of damnation) were founded on just such a belief in the inner light of the spirit as the only true guide to certainty.[2] We may conclude that these lines therefore are a palinode in which he rejects the dependence on phenomena and the subjection to time and the process of becoming which he has hitherto made the guiding lights of his poem. It is only process, too, which supplies themes, and that is why 'history, not wanted yet, / Lean'd on her elbow': perhaps we see here a longing in the poet to escape the constant need to make objects significant and meaningful; perhaps equally a picture of that 'waiting for a theme' that in one way has been Cowper's lot throughout the poem.

This concluding passage thus shows a further extension of that irritation of sensibility which has been evident throughout 'Yardley Oak' in the shifts from particularity to general comment, the uncertainties of verse and tone, or the uneasiness of stance in relation to the tree. Cowper's search for a 'right relation to the object' anticipates that quest for the light of imaginative vision which was to cause Wordsworth and Coleridge so much pain. But he falls between Augustan and Romantic stools — his moral perception reduced to febrile reflection, and his sense of the imaginative truths in phenomena only occasionally able to move beyond empirical presentation.

'THE TASK' (1785)

The Task, in common with much of Cowper's poetry, can be considered a retirement poem, but one in which the retirement has not, as the character of the poem reveals, fully been earned by long experience.

The poem has a certain measure of unconscious unity, even if Cowper himself is nervous of his own rambling (III, 1–20; IV, 232–42). Its recurrent subject is change, which is here dialectically understood as a marriage of stillness and movement, rest and restlessness (we are reminded of the interest of Defoe, another Nonconformist, in this theme). In Book I Cowper glorifies process, describing how 'By ceaseless action

all that is subsists', and how the oak owes its stability to the movement caused by storms, 'More fixt below, the more disturb'd above,
(I, 367, 384). Cowper sees activity and repose as fully themselves only
when alternated with one another (I, 385–416); throughout the poem
he now sits and contemplates, now walks and beholds. A constant variety
of scenes is for him the way to avoid spiritual stagnation: 'Not rural
sights alone, but rural sounds, / Exhilarate the spirit, and restore / The
tone of languid Nature' (I, 181–3). The sofa with which he opens the
poem is seen both as this particular static object on which Cowper is
seated, and as the product of a long history in the evolution of the chair.
Similarly, the frozen stream of Book v is described in such a way that
it seems to be mobile rather than fixed, building itself rather than built:

> Here glitt'ring turrets rise, upbearing high
> (Fantastic misarrangement!) on the roof
> Large growth of what may seem the sparkling trees
> And shrubs of fairy land. The crystal drops
> That trickle down the branches, fast congeal'd,
> Shoot into pillars of fantastic length,
> And prop the pile they but adorn'd before.   (110–16)

The poem is scattered with accounts of 'becoming', from the account of
growing cucumbers (III, 446–543) to the picture of the activities of the
prisoner in the Bastille (v, 400–32). God, who conditions all things, is
for Cowper not simply the transcendent static One of the deists, but is
also immanent and ever-working (VI, 118–261): 'The Lord of all, himself
through all diffus'd, / Sustains, and is the life of all that lives' (221–2).

The theme of change is extended and further defined in other areas
of *The Task*. Cowper marks off his notion of change from the 'novelty'
of cities where people struggle to whet their jaded appetites with unnatural titillations; the Augustan basis of the distinction is reminiscent
of that made in *The Deserted Village*:

> Variety's the very spice of life,
> That gives it all its flavour. We have run
> Through ev'ry change that fancy at the loom,
> Exhausted, has had genius to supply;
> And, studious of mutation still, discard
> A real elegance, a little us'd,
> For monstrous novelty and strange disguise.
>   (II, 606–12; see also I, 455–92, and VI, 704–9)

It is true that a little later Cowper can use novelty as a term of commendation: 'The earth was made so various, that the mind / Of desul-

tory man, studious of change, / And pleas'd with novelty, might be indulg'd' (I, 506–8); true too that in Book III he says, of domestic happiness, 'thou art meek and constant, hating change' (55). But though Cowper may occasionally forget his own views, or fail to remember distinctions of meaning which he has established, the material of his poem keeps his basic views clear: indeed, one could almost argue that the mixture of constancy and change in Cowper's own attitudes is an unwitting extension of the poem's subject.

The recurrent subject of human liberty is seen in terms of a marriage of fixity and movement. Liberty does not for Cowper mean unbridled freedom, just as it does not in nature, whose course follows laws and patterns: hence the frequent attacks on profusion, riot and hedonistic ministers, and the praise of discipline (I, 681–90; II, 326–78; III, 51–107, 811–48; IV, 553–612). But it does mean to him the ability to be free of being one continual, fixed thing: he attacks slavish obedience to kings (V, 230–378), and imprisonment, whether just or unjust (V, 379–445). Those, too, without knowledge of Christ, and those who cannot trace the hand of God in nature are slaves; Cowper finds the perfect marriage of liberty and restraint, of motion and constancy, in God, service of whom is perfect freedom (V, 538–906). The frozen waterfall of Book V is truth and beauty, because beneath its ice the stream continues to run, but the ice palace, having no such animating life beneath its 'death', is the more transient as it is durable (166–8, 173–4). Equally, without a central stillness about which to wheel, motion has no reality: this can be seen as expressed in the way the poem follows the seasons in their constant variations about the year.

While there is thus a recurrent theme in the poem, lending it a measure of unity, there are features which reduce its cohesion. First, there is the degree of intensity in Cowper's method. It is significant that he should begin his poem with a history of the sofa and its gradual refinement in the production of ease and comfort, for relaxation and quiet pleasure are his ideals in this poem. His life is one of retirement, and reads as one of holiday: the walk, the reflection, the hobbies of growing cucumbers or tending to the greenhouse, the relaxation over the paper, the happy exchange of conversation with his partner (Mrs Unwin). We would not for a moment think this the work of a man whose life was punctuated by psychological disturbance and the terror of imminent and final damnation – indeed, there are points in the poem where he seems to welcome the idea of Armageddon (II, 48–74; VI, 729–905). Perhaps the poem itself is a holiday – as then is nearly all of Cowper's poetry – from such terrors; but to say this is only to explain, not justify, its lack of profound feeling. And without a sense of pressure, a sense that what Cowper describes is passionately felt, the poem cannot have a more than flabby unity.

That Cowper is often only half-convinced by what he is saying is suggested by his repetitiveness, especially on the subject of city life: he senses that what he claims is an oversimplification, and yet cannot find a way of being more certain than shrill (I, 681–748; III, 811–48; IV, 553–79; VI, 262–94). He recurs nervously to the question of his right to moralise on the actions of men from his rural retreat:

> What chance that I, to fame so little known,
> Nor conversant with men or manners much,
> Should speak to purpose . . . ?
> (III, 23–5; see also 191–220; II, 216–25; IV, 23–87)

He silences such imagined criticisms with irritated defiance:

> What's the world to you? –
> Much. I was born of woman, and drew milk,
> As sweet as charity, from human breasts.
> I think, articulate, I laugh and weep,
> And exercise all functions of a man.
> How then should I and any man that lives
> Be strangers to each other? (III, 195–201)

The flat would-be Shakespearian rhetoric here underlines the falsity of the protestation.[4]

A second feature working against the unity of the book is Cowper's frequent self-contradiction. Like Thomson, he is inconsistent in his attitude to human learning (I, 626–8, 693–724, and III, 137–90). Sometimes, having gone to one extreme in condemnation, he admits exceptions which take him to the other: thus his crudely overwritten lines on cities –

> Thither flow,
> As to a common and most noisome sew'r,
> The dregs and feculence of ev'ry land.
> In cities foul example on most minds
> Begets its likeness. Rank abundance breeds
> In gross and pamper'd cities sloth and lust,
> And wantonness and gluttonous excess (I, 682–8)

– are followed by a praise of London as a focus of culture (700–24); having said which, he returns with a 'She has her praise. Now mark a spot or two' (725), as if no spots had yet been mentioned – and the spots that are described are, as Thersites might have wished, so many as to cover London all over. And, we recall, all this imprecation against cities when it was precisely the values of civility – 'Our palaces, our ladies, and our pomp / Of equipage, our gardens, and our sports' – which the poet thought it right that the ignorant savage Omai, visiting these shores, should miss most on his return to his native land (I, 641–53).[3] Here we see how Cowper can go back on himself within a brief compass. A further striking instance of this is the passage in Book IV where, looking at the snow falling, he talks of how one should compassionate the traveller, and then, in painting the picture of such a man, changes to claim that he is made vigorous and healthy by such weather, 'Oh happy; and, in my account, denied / That sensibility of pain with which / Refinement is endued, thrice happy thou!' (357–9). Less pleasant is his false *laisser-faire* argument that the poor choose to be poor in order to be clear of the rich (407–24), followed by an attack on those, less willing to accept their lot, who become thieves and offend the god of property (429–52); Cowper forces condemnation upon them by claiming, without justification, that their thefts are not for their families, but merely for themselves (452–65). The problem is that, like Thomson, Cowper must always be absolute in his varying judgments: he cannot present and try to reconcile both sides of the truth, but sympathises totally now with one side, now with the other. The further problem is that, unlike Thomson, his tone reveals that he is uneasily aware of this.

The Task, then, has no dynamic unity, and the results are similar to those traced in 'Yardley Oak'. Observation of objects becomes pushed to non-Augustan limits of the peculiar and the minute, while moral comment flies to the opposite pole of the over-general. In his portrait of God's causing the Sicilian earthquake (II, 75–132), Cowper strays from the subject into fascination at the 'upside-down', nature made a creature of fancy: 'What solid was, by transformation strange, / Grows fluid; and the fixt and rooted earth, / Tormented into billows, heaves and swells' (99–101); and

> The sylvan scene
> Migrates uplifted; and, with all its soil
> Alighting in far distant fields, finds out
> A new possessor, and survives the change.   (107–10)

In an attack on profusion, the hortatory assault grows shrill, slips into the desultory, and finally into an irrelevant image:

> It is a hungry vice: – it eats up all
> That gives society its beauty, strength,
> Convenience and security, and use:
> Makes men mere vermin, worthy to be trapp'd
> And gibbeted as fast as catchpole claws
> Can seize the slipp'ry prey.   (II, 680–5; cf. 432–9)

Similarly, after a long general assault on the vices of London he collapses in bathos: 'sabbath rites / Have dwindled into unrespected forms, / And knees and hassocks are well-nigh divorc'd' (I, 746–8). Cowper's portentousness is always subject to such swings to particularity.

He has, too, a feeling for the local and fanciful conceit. Thus the picture of 'The soft settee; one elbow at each end, / And in the midst an elbow it receiv'd / United yet divided, twain at once' (I, 76–7); or of flowers supported by wooden sticks, 'wedded thus, like beauty to old age, / For int'rest sake, the living to the dead' (III, 660–1). Cowper delights in fanciful recreation, such as the images he traces in the cinders of his fire (IV, 272–307), or the grotesque shape of his shadow in the early morning sun (V, 10–20).

Yet it is this very weakness of structure and uncertainty of approach which admits a portrait like that of the mad Kate (I, 534–56). This picture runs counter to much of the drift of the poem, but not intentionally, for Cowper simply happens on it as one more rustic vignette brought to mind during a walk, and it catches his imagination at an unconscious level. It is one of the most powerful descriptions in *The Task*, and shows for a moment a Romantic and profoundly-stirred Cowper quite at odds with the querulous Augustan of much of the rest of the poem. Cowper has just been describing how what delights us in nature may pall if we do not absent ourselves from it for a while, and how the returning sailor is transported with delight at the coarsest rocks of home (518–33); this leads him on to Kate, who once roamed the wild cliffs, waiting in vain for the return of her sailor-lover, and who now wanders the waste in despair. A poetic contrast is thus built up between the sailor, who thinks only of the land, and Kate, whose mind is only on the sea. What is fine in the picture of her is that for once Cowper forgets his preference for cultivated and comfortable nature, and contemplates the harsher truths of life and landscape; for once his poem admits a genuine tension between man's need for security and his knowledge that it may perhaps not be found; for once there is true and not ritual sympathy:

> And now she roams
> The dreary waste; there spends the livelong day,
> And there, unless when charity forbids,
> The livelong night. A tatter'd apron hides,
> Worn as a cloak, and hardly hides, a gown
> More tatter'd still; and both but ill conceal
> A bosom heav'd with never-ceasing sighs.
> She begs an idle pin of all she meets,
> And hoards them in her sleeve; but needful food,
> Though press'd with hunger oft, or comelier clothes,
> Though pinch'd with cold, asks never. – Kate is craz'd!   (546–56)

(The 'hides . . . and hardly hides' reminds us of Wordsworth's 'hedge-rows, hardly hedge-rows' in 'Tintern Abbey', 15). The pin that Kate always asks suggests that, baulked of her true need, everything else is to her but an 'idle pin', which analogy has been made by her into fact. The 'tatter'd apron', the pun on 'Worn' and the gown 'More tatter'd still' are partly symbolic. We may say that what, perhaps, most saddened Cowper in Kate's plight was that for her time had stopped, and she had stopped becoming; but, whatever the reason, here is real sympathy made poetry.[5]

The mood of sympathy, the vision which is able to contain opposed ways of seeing, continues with the picture of the gypsies (I, 557–91) – in which picture Cowper comes his nearest to Wordsworth's view of nature as sustaining its own, even if the emphasis is rather more on the physical rather than the spiritual invigoration given (580–91). But here Cowper is already becoming more condemnatory: the gypsies are 'A vagabond and useless tribe' (559); they steal and cheat (563–4, 570–3); they are rational beings who have 'brutalize[d] by choice' their nature (574–6) and, 'Self-banish'd from society, prefer / Such squalid sloth to honour-able toil' (578–9). Their joys are exceptional, holidays from their own nature. When Cowper moves on, he rejects the portraits of Kate and the gypsies as if they could not exist in England, as if nature in England, and the people in it, were nothing but cultivated and virtuous.

> Blest he, though undistinguish'd from the crowd
> By wealth or dignity, who dwells secure,
> Where man, by nature fierce, has laid aside
> His fierceness, having learnt, though slow to learn,
> The manners and the arts of civil life. . . .
> Here virtue thrives as in her proper soil;
> Not rude and surly, and beset with thorns,
> And terrible to sight, as when she springs
> (If e'er she spring spontaneous) in remote
> And barb'rous climes, where violence prevails,
> And strength is lord of all; but gentle, kind,
> By culture tam'd, by liberty refresh'd,
> And all her fruits by radiant truth matur'd.   (592–6, 600–7)[6]

It is Thomson's vision too, but here it is resisted by the portraits the poem has admitted. Yet such portraits are few, and one may trace in the above passage Cowper's unceasing epitaph on his own poetic sensibility.

With Cowper, eighteenth-century poetry peters into almost total un-certainty. Even where earlier poets revealed tensions in their work, these were never admitted to the point where they overthrew poetic purpose: Thomson, Johnson, Gray, Goldsmith and Crabbe all sound sure of where they are going, even if their poetry often belies this confidence. But Cowper is unable to get into proper relation with his subject-matter, and has lost touch with value. He is aware of being drawn to the identities of things even while he tries to moralise them; he feels uncomfortable with his absolute dicta; he lacks confidence in his credentials as a poetic legislator. Some of this must be put down to his personality; but we then have to ask why such a personality manifested itself when it did. In Goldsmith and Crabbe we see how the gap between 'conceptual' and 'empirical' literature has steadily widened from that which we saw between Pope and Defoe; Cowper is the first poet to sense that neither side is sufficient, even while he is drawn to both, and this renders him uncertain both as moralist and as painter.

15 Conclusion

What we have been concerned with throughout this book could be broadly termed 'inclusiveness' – that is, the amount of reality that the writers of the period 1600–1800 were able or prepared to admit into their work, at a time when the world was beginning to be seen to be far more various, and was also *becoming* far more various (in terms of the multiplicity of opinions) than ever before.

Most of the writers we have considered are absolutists, in a world where absolutism is no longer the condition of truth: that is, they are not consciously prepared to see truth in any moral, political or religious positions opposed to their own. The renascence of satire expresses the polarisations of seventeenth-century beliefs and attitudes. Particularly in the eighteenth century, this dividedness forces its way into the individual human mind. Many authors, while still writing from an Augustan standpoint, admit into their work features sheerly in conflict with that standpoint. With the possible exception of Gray, not one of them admits to this: they all write as if what they mean to say and what they in fact do say are one and the same thing. As we have seen, in the unconscious meanings of Milton, Pope and Crabbe, or the tensions and inconsistencies in Thomson, Johnson or Cowper, this leads to startling differences between 'official doctrine' and actual presentation. Writers were drawn both to finding general truths, and to particulars which defied their formulations. The law works both ways: those who strive for the single and one-sided view become self-divided; those who, like Fielding, make some attempt to cater for the multiple nature of truth, slip in practice into type-characterisation and moral simplification.

During the eighteenth century, the method of establishing general truths does move from *a priori* towards *a posteriori*: significance is less imposed on the world by a cultural priesthood than, at least apparently, derived from it after investigation of phenomena. Of course, in *Rasselas* Johnson found the truths he expected to find, but he makes his statements appear to grow from impartial and unprejudiced inquiry into as many different walks of life as possible. Johnson, however, still looks for the 'typical' in the human condition: other writers, such as Gray,

Crabbe or Cowper, move much closer to the experience of the single and idiosyncratic datum. In Gray we consider the rustics for themselves rather than as representatives; in Crabbe the exceptional environs of Aldeburgh refuse the generalisations about all pastoral life which he tries to make from them; in Cowper we come against the limiting idiosyncrasies of the poet himself. The broad movement from 1600 to 1800 is from a symbolic to a typical to an individual account of phenomena, and from objective to generally-agreed to personally-based truth systems.[1] The certainties of poets thus become increasingly febrile and ill-defined in the eighteenth century: it was for the, Romantics to take the process a step further and find truth inherent *in* the experience rather than imposed on or deduced from it by a separate act of mind.

The 'separateness' of the act of mind is a besetting feature in the literature of the seventeenth and eighteenth centuries. The disappearance early in the seventeenth century of the Christian symbolist picture of the universe, wherein each item in creation could be seen as instinct with conferred meaning, led to a divorce between the perceptions of objects and of concepts by the human mind. We find writers from Herrick to Crabbe preoccupied with phenomena to the exclusion of significance; and others, from Donne to Goldsmith, who are at an intellectual and 'conceptualising' extreme. Others still bring both urges into conflict in one work: particularly in Thomson and Cowper we see a fascination with phenomena for themselves existing uneasily beside the desire to draw rational and moral laws and lessons from them. Increasingly in the eighteenth century, apprehension of objects is so divided from their comprehension, experience from reflection, as to inhibit creativity.

The constant and growing interest, scientific and otherwise, in the manifold nature of the world throughout this period, the vogue of the doctrine of plenitude, and the unpicturable, irregular and infinite nature of the universe, also had clear impact on the literature of the age. The encyclopaedic approaches of Pope, Thomson, Fielding and Johnson, even of Milton and Spenser, whereby general truths are traced in as many areas of existence as possible, can be seen not only as an expression of empiricism and scientific method, but also as an attempt to capture and sum up a universe fast becoming unclassifiable and unintelligible. The system of universal correspondence which disappeared in the seventeenth century had made it possible for the microcosm, whether the individual person or the single lyric poem, to figure the macrocosm: when the unit became merely a unit, the only way in which the universal could be captured was by adding as many individuals together as possible. This, and the departure of the circular image of the universe, were largely responsible for the additive and architectural method of structuring literature, and for the disappearance of formal shape as an aesthetic criterion. When the only organising structure of the cosmos is the infinitely great chain of being, the mode of internal development in the literary work moves from that of the circle to the ladder, whereby the work mounts to a pitch of intensity, and descants upon rather than develops a theme. Such a structure is inherently unstable: without any organic informing principle, or a clear picture of the universe to provide the ground of artistic order, literature tends increasingly towards fragmentation and disunity as the period advances.

In Milton, Defoe, Thomson and particularly Cowper, we see an interest in the idea of change, energy and movement which is in contrast to the predominantly conservative and 'static' essence of the literature of the time, and in conflict with that side of the authors themselves. (Indeed, time as a theme or as a structural principle has small part to play in Augustan literature.) This interest in evolution and dynamism, which was to be the foundation of Romantic and nineteenth-century thought, began to give back to poetry an organic principle founded on the notion of self-realisation through growth. If the idea of architecture is fundamental to an understanding of the poets of the seventeenth and eighteenth centuries, the image of the developing plant is so for the Romantics;[2] Cowper is drawn to write about the growth and decline of an oak tree, and in almost the very terms in which the universe was at that time being conceived — that is, as the gradual rather than the once-for-all realisation of an infinity of possibilities.[3] At the same time, feeble in spirit and paralysed by guilt himself, he portrays the capacity for change and free choice which the deterministic world-views of most of the writers before him could not admit. Donne saw the disappearance of one circular notion of being; Cowper, his descendant, even while he marks the bankruptcy of eighteenth-century literature, registers the beginnings of another.

Notes

Abbreviations of academic journals used:

EC	*Essays in Criticism*
ELH	*Journal of English Literary History*
HLQ	*Huntingdon Library Quarterly*
MP	*Modern Philology*
PMLA	*Publications of the Modern Language Association*
PQ	*Philological Quarterly*
SEL	*Studies in English Literature*
SP	*Studies in Philology*

Publication details of works (excluding main texts – see List of Editions Used, following Preface) and articles cited are given in the Bibliography. Throughout the Notes, authors generally are identified by surname only.

PREFACE
1 Eliot, *Selected Essays*, 3rd edition; p. 288. Effective refutation of wholesale acceptance of this idea is given by Frank Kermode, 'Dissociation of Sensibility', *Kenyon Review*, xix, pp. 169–94.

CHAPTER 1
1 See particularly Willey, *The Seventeenth-Century Background* and *The Eighteenth-Century Background*; Lovejoy, *The Great Chain of Being: A Study of the History of an Idea*; and Nicolson, *The Breaking of the Circle: Studies in the Effect of the 'New Science' upon Seventeenth-Century Poetry*, revised edition.
2 This phrase is Lovejoy's from *The Great Chain of Being*, p. 116.
3 Hence perhaps the miniaturism and the theme of *multum in parvo* in seventeenth-century poetry (for instance in Marvell). See also Nicolson, *The Breaking of the Circle*, pp. 174–82.
4 Mazzeo, 'A Critique of Some Modern Theories of Metaphysical Poetry', *MP*, L, pp. 88–96, argues that the object of the conceit was to make poetic sense of an increasingly diverse world by fusing widely-opposed contexts.
5 Empson, 'Donne the Space Man', *Kenyon Review*, xix, pp. 342–5.
6 Nicolson, *The Breaking of the Circle*, pp. 80, 116–22, 146–8, 155–6.

1   The basis of the argument advanced here is close to that in Lewis, 'Donne and Love Poetry in the Seventeenth Century', in *Seventeenth Century Studies Presented to Sir Herbert Grierson*, pp. 64–84.

2   Much of this method of reading may be traced back to William Empson: his paraphrase, in *Seven Types of Ambiguity*, p. 176, of the first stanza of 'A Valediction: of Weeping' is a classic instance of mistaking a largely 'conceptual' poem for a simply personal one. While Professor Empson may have been right ('Donne and the Rhetoricians', *Kenyon Review*, XI, pp. 571–87) to say that Rosemond Tuve's insistence, in her *Elizabethan and Metaphysical Imagery*, on the conceptual orientation of metaphysical poetry lacked sufficient argument from, and sensitivity to, texts, her argument can readily be demonstrated from many of Donne's poems.

3   Martz, *The Poetry of Meditation: A Study in English Religious Literature of the Seventeenth Century*, pp. 228–33.

4   Eliot, 'Andrew Marvell', in *Selected Essays*, p. 303.

1   See also Parfitt, 'The Poetry of Ben Jonson', *EC*, XVIII, pp. 18–31.

2   See also Nicolson, *The Breaking of the Circle*, pp. 7–8.

3   Fussell, *The Rhetorical World of Augustan Humanism: Ethics and Imagery from Swift to Burke*, ch. 8.

4   Eliot, 'Ben Jonson', in *Elizabeth Dramatists: Essays by T. S. Eliot*, p. 74.

5   *Conversations with William Drummond of Hawthornden*, pp. 381–3.

6   Nicolson, *The Breaking of the Circle*, pp. 28–32, 113–15, 189–92; Lovejoy, *The Great Chain of Being*, pp. 101, 109.

7   Notably the portrait of Faustinus's Baian farm in *Epigrams*, III, 58; the sources for the fish betraying themselves are *Epigrams*, X, 30, and Juvenal, *Satire* IV, 69; and, for the woodland divinities, *Epigrams*, IX, 61.

8   See Hibbard, 'The Country House Poem of the Seventeenth Century', *Journal of the Courtauld and Warburg Institutes*, XIX, pp. 159–74.

9   Røstvig, *The Happy Man: Studies in the Metamorphoses of a Classical Ideal*.

10 See also Cubeta, 'A Jonsonian Ideal: "To Penshurst" ', *PQ*, XLII, pp. 17–24.

11 See also Wilson, 'Jonson's Use of the Bible and the Great Chain of Being in "To Penshurst" ', *SEL*, VIII, pp. 78–89, on this and other biblical references.

12 Anthony Mortimer, in 'The Feigned Commonwealth in the Poetry of Ben Jonson', *SEL*, XIII, p. 75, suggests that the poem has a rough circularity because it begins and ends with attacks on 'prodigy' houses: but in mathematical fact returning to a point of origin need not imply that a circle has been traversed any more than that a straight line has been retraced; and Jonson refers to other houses during the course of the poem also (61–75). It is more reasonable to see the opening and closing lines as simply marking Penshurst off, making a closed world. A. D. S. Fowler's fine 'The Locality of Jonson's *To Penshurst*', *Conceitful Thought: The Interpretation of English Renaissance Poems*, pp. 127–8, argues the pres-

ence of a broad numerological sequence symbolising the construction both of a building instinct with values and of regenerate human nature.

13 Cohen, 'The Augustan Mode in English Poetry', in *Studies in the Eighteenth Century: Papers Presented at the David Nichol Smith Memorial Seminar, Canberra 1966*, ed. Brissenden, pp. 171–92.

14 Jonson, *Discoveries*, 2194–2836.

15 *Moral Essays*, Epistle IV (*To Burlington*), 66. The theme of proper subordination of parts is central to the *Essay on Criticism*, and is implicit in all Pope's poetry.

16 See also Parfitt, 'Compromise Classicism: Language and Rhythm in Ben Jonson's Poetry', *SEL*, XI, pp. 112–15.

17 Miner, *The Cavalier Mode from Jonson to Cotton*, p. 159.

18 See also his 'Julia's *Petticoat*' and '*Upon* Julia's *Clothes*'. Nicolson, *The Breaking of the Circle*, p. 191, draws analogy with courageous delight in the new-found disorder of the stars.

19 Elsewhere also these opposites are divided. In '*Art above Nature, to* Julia', Herrick, though he claims a wild civility in Julia's dress, describes that which is completely organised and civil: he says, 'when I see thy Tresses bound / Into an Ovall, square, or round; / And knit in knots far more then I / Can tell by tongue; or true-love tie', that 'I must confesse, mine eye and heart / Dotes less on Nature, then on Art.' On the other hand, in '*Upon* Julia's *haire, bundled up in a golden net*', he asks, 'what needs those rich deceits' and demands that Julia set her tresses naturally free, 'let them flow / As aires do breathe, or winds doe blow', to catch him the more surely.

20 cf. also Herrick's '*Upon the Nipples of* Julia's *Breast*' with its source, the third stanza of the fourth piece ('Her Triumph') of Jonson's 'A Celebration of Charis in Ten Lyric Pieces': Charis's whiteness, softness and sweetness are sensuous and conceptual at once. Herrick's comparison of roses, cherries, lilies, strawberries in cream, rubies and orient pearl to 'each neate Niplet of her breast' is one not of extracting essences but simply of putting object beside object. Herrick is fascinated by objects for themselves, as the introductory poem of *Hesperides* announces.

CHAPTER 4

1 Tuve, *Images and Themes in Five Poems by Milton*, pp. 24–7.

2 See also Brooks and Hardy, *Poems of Mr. John Milton: The 1645 Edition, with Essays in Analysis*, p. 137.

3 The Elder Brother in the poem envisions the final victory of virtue, when 'evil on itself shall back recoil, / And mix no more with goodness' (*Comus*, 592–3).

4 For an approach similar in method to the one used here, see Brooks and Hardy, *Poems of Mr. John Milton*, pp. 215–23; placing less emphasis on the Renaissance meanings of 'nature', however, they maintain that Comus's inconsistencies do not demolish his case, and that the Lady does not answer his arguments. Contrast on 'nature' Tuve, *Images and Themes*, pp. 126–8, 133, 141–2, 144–5.

5 See also Wallerstein, *Studies in Seventeenth-Century Poetic*, p. 110.

6   For example, by Charles Williams, who argues that men may, through Christ's bearing of their burdens on the Cross, become him by re-enacting that task; Williams's belief springs from his idea of a 'coinher-ent' Godhead, in relation with whom the categories of time, space and personal identity may be abrogated. See Williams's *The Image of the City and Other Essays*, ed. Ridler, pp. 152–3, 158; and 'The Practice of Sub-stituted Love', *He Came Down from Heaven*, ch. 4.

7   For a fuller account of the dialectical progress of the poem, see, for ex-ample, Lawry, ' "Eager Thought": Dialectic in *Lycidas*', *PMLA*, LXXVII, pp. 27–32.

8   See Lloyd, 'The Fatal Bark', *Modern Language Notes*, LXXV.

9   However, both of these heavenly glimpses are of justice. It is the last, with Christ, that is of mercy and love. This metamorphosis of justice into mercy figures the shift of Old Testament into New and parallels the change from pagan into Christian in the poem.

10   Tuve, *Images and Themes*, p. 96.

11   At IV, 375–8, Satan contemplates 'league . . . / And mutual amity so strait, so close' with man that 'I with you must dwell, or you with me / Henceforth.'

12   See also the comparisons of Eve to the pursued virgins Pales, Pomona and Ceres (IX, 393–6).

13   See also his seductive speech (parodying Adam at V, 17–25) ₋o Eve in her dream (V, 38–48): 'with ravishment / Attracted by thy beauty still to gaze. / I rose' (pp. 46–8).

14   Cf. John 3: 14, on Christ as Serpent.

15   See Jung, *The Archetypes and the Collective Unconscious*, in *The Col-lected Works of C. G. Jung*, vol. 9, Part I, pp. 35, 312–90. On the general subject of the marriage of opposites, Jung's *Mysterium Coniunctionis, An Inquiry into the Separation and Synthesis of Psychic Opposites in Alchemy* (*Collected Works*, vol. 14) is most illuminating, particularly on the alchem-ist's propagation of the ideal of quaternity (trinity $+$ 1; see, for example, pp. 187–8) and on the origin and double aspect of the serpent (pp. 340–3).

16   See, for example, Augustine, *City of God*, XII, 7.

17   Lewis, *A Preface to 'Paradise Lost'*, p. 95.

18   Ibid., p. 94.

19   In the light of this, the frequent similarities in the poem between events and features in Hell, on the one hand, and in Heaven and Earth, on the other, cannot be considered as serving only to heighten contrast.

CHAPTER 5

1   See Kernan, *The Cankered Muse: Satire of the English Renaissance*, chs 1, 2; and Paulson, *The Fictions of Satire*, p. 97.

2   See Paulson, *The Fictions of Satire*, p. 96.

3   For a fine account of the different contexts and aims of Dryden's and Pope's poetry, see Rivers, *The Poetry of Conservatism 1600–1745: A Study of Poets and Public Affairs from Jonson to Pope*, esp. pp. 174–6.

4   As may be clearly seen in his 'A Discourse Concerning the Original and Progress of Satire' (1693); he is divided between the high moral direction

and style of Juvenal, on the one hand, and the Horatian method of witty raillery at follies, on the other; the issue is not that Juvenal is moral where Horace is not, but one of how relaxed and detached from their creations they are. For Dryden's shifts of preference, see his *Of Dramatic Poesy, and Other Critical Essays*, ed. Watson, vol. 2, pp. 122, 130, 136.

5 Ibid., pp. 136–7.

6 For Dryden's (late) dislike of antithesis and all forms of violent wit, and his preference for the elegance of the 'turn', see *Of Dramatic Poesy*, vol. 1, pp. 95–9; and vol. 2, pp. 150–2. This bias is traceable in part to the influence on the aesthetic thought of the time of Bishop Sprat and the Royal Society, of which from 1662 Dryden was himself a member.

7 *Of Dramatic Poesy*, vol. 2, p. 137.

8 See for example the fully human portraits at the end of Epistle I of the *Moral Essays*.

9 For his distinctions between 'metaphrase', 'paraphrase' and 'imitation' in translation, see *Of Dramatic Poesy*, vol. 1, p. 268.

10 On this see Frost, *Dryden and the Art of Translation*, pp. 74–6. Frost suggests that the alterations are a product of Dryden's feelings concerning the monarchy under the militarist William and his own loss of favour after long and loyal service to the throne; in this light 'Palamon and Arcite' becomes a fictional compensation.

11 Cf. Miner, 'Chaucer in Dryden's *Fables*', in *Studies in Criticism and Aesthetics 1660–1800: Essays in Honor of Samuel Holt Monk*, ed. Anderson and Shea, p. 65: 'the terms of the metaphor . . . often fuse or exchange dominant roles.'

12 Chanticleer's regality has been adduced in support of a *roman a clef* reading of the tale in which the bird is seen as a covert portrayal of Louis XIV; see Hinant, 'Dryden's Gallic Rooster', *SP*, LXV, pp. 649–56.

13 On the static and iconic mode in Dryden's poetry, see Jean H. Hagstrum, *The Sister Arts*, pp. 178–90.

14 See Preface to the *Fables*, 453–62; 'I have confin'd my Choice to such Tales of *Chaucer*, as savour nothing of Immodesty. . . . I will no more offend against Good Manners: I am sensible as I ought to be of the Scandal I have given by my loose Writings; and make what Reparation I am able, by this Publick Acknowledgment. If any thing of this Nature or of Profaneness, be crept into these Poems, I am so far from defending it, that I disown it.'

15 On Dryden's interest in the theme of rustic retirement, and the more homely language in his later poetry, see Brower, 'Dryden and the "Invention" of Pope', in *Restoration and Eighteenth-Century Literature: Essays in Honor of Alan Dugald McKillop*, ed. Camden, pp. 211–33.

16 See Brower, 'Dryden and the "Invention" of Pope', pp. 222–4.

CHAPTER 6

1 Lovejoy, *The Great Chain of Being*, pp. 183–6, 231

2 Ibid., pp. 110–11, 115–19, 124–5, 130, 183; and ch. 8.

3 See also Allison, *Toward an Augustan Poetic: Edmund Waller's 'Reform' of English Poetry*, p. 21.

4   Goldberg, 'Alexander Pope', *Melbourne Critical Review*, VII, p. 50.

5   T. S. Eliot, in 'The Metaphysical Poets' (*Selected Essays*, p. 288), writes, 'The [eighteenth-century] poets revolted against the ratiocinative, the descriptive; they thought and felt by fits, unbalanced; they reflected.' The diagnosis is correct; the causes wider.

6   Rosenblum, 'Pope's Illusive Temple of Infamy', in *The Satirist's Art*, ed. Jensen and Zirker, p. 54, points out the danger to Pope of his predominantly negative vision sucking him, by a kind of fascination, into the very objects he attacks, and leaving no sense that the forms of true civilisation his satire recommends are possible.

7   *Essay on Man*, II, 39–42, 53–204. Pope's determinism is a function of his complete endorsement of the conservative implications of the principles of plenitude and of the chain of being: man must accept what he is made and given.

8   Edwards, *This Dark Estate: A Reading of Pope*, p. 60.

9   Exactly as happens to the Puritans in Jonson's *The Alchemist* under the mocking analysis of Subtle (III, ii, 1 ff.).

10 Undercut by Pope's 'The well-bred cuckolds in St. James's air' (388).

11 See Curtius, *European Literature and the Latin Middle Ages*, pp. 94–8.

12 On this see Edwards, *This Dark Estate*, pp. 51–63. Edwards argues that the basic theme of the *Moral Essays* is 'tragic alienation from things as they are' (p. 50). Though this theme can be made to fit much of the material, it seems doubtful that the reader would be aware of it before Epistle III, which most answers to it; and it is possible, since an enormous body of literature could be subsumed under this theme, that Edwards has reduced Pope's individuality as a poet too far. The theme itself seems rather to be one aspect of Pope's preoccupation with 'proportion'.

13 Mack, *The Garden and the City: Retirement and Politics in the Later Poetry of Pope, 1731–1743*, pp. 60–9.

14 For previous accounts of the unity of the poem, see Olson, 'Rhetoric and the Appreciation of Pope', *MP*, XXXVII, pp. 21–33 (of particular value); Mengel 'Patterns of Imagery in Pope's *Arbuthnot*', *PMLA*, LXIX, pp. 189–97; Maresca, *Pope's Horatian Poems*; Hardy, *Reinterpretations: Essays on Poems by Milton, Pope and Johnson*.

15 The first version of this, in the 'Fragment of a Satire' (1727), 39–41, was of a single tense, and couched as a hypothesis: 'Should modest Satire bid [*sic*] all these *translate*, / And own that nine such Poets make a *Tate*; / How would they fume, and stamp, and roar, and chafe!'

16 See 281–2, 'can I chuse but smile, / When ev'ry Coxcomb knows me by my *Style*?' 'Style' here is not merely the literary, but the more general public image.

CHAPTER 7

1   What Crusoe's father recommends is not to do with one's appointed station so much as with comfort, going smoothly through life and out of it (pp. 4–6). He enjoins a life of simple comfort, without conflict: Crusoe, like all of Defoe's heroes, needs a more dialectical existence, in which comfort and discomfort are the two poles.

2 Defoe oscillates throughout his writings between viewing defiance of one's calling or settled condition as a sin and viewing it as an evolutionary imperative. See, for example, *The Farther Adventures . . . of Robinson Crusoe* (1719), in *Romances and Narratives by Daniel Defoe*, ed. Aitken, vol. 2, pp. 142, 149–50, 183–6, 211, 213, 214, 216, 249; or cf. *Serious Reflections . . . of Robinson Crusoe* (1720), in *Romances and Narratives*, vol. 3, pp. 63–6, with *The Complete English Tradesman* (1725), Letter III, in *Selected Writings of Daniel Defoe*, ed. Boulton, p. 238, or *Madagascar; or, Robert Drury's Journal*, ed. Oliver, Preface, and pp. 1–3. Crusoe shifts his view of what his calling is, from staying with his father, to staying in Brazil and to staying on the island, with contradictory results: cf. *Robinson Crusoe*, pp. 35–6 with p. 38 or p. 40; or pp. 156–7 with pp. 194–5.

3 It has been argued that Crusoe's disobedience of his father involves a sin against 'a specific religious–economic doctrine' (Novak, *Economics and the Fiction of Daniel Defoe*, p. 40; see also Hunter, *The Reluctant Pilgrim: Defoe's Emblematic Method and the Quest for Form in 'Robinson Crusoe'*, chs 2, 6). It is certain that part of Defoe believed this to be the case, but equally true that part of him did not. The split here must be traced to the two strands of Puritan thinking, one conservative and cautionary, the other dynamic and self-advancing, which Novak admits to have existed together in Defoe's time (*Economics and the Fiction of Defoe*, pp. 40–3; Hunter's dismissal of Weber's and Tawney's views of the dynamic capitalism – *The Reluctant Pilgrim*, pp. 34–6 – is too sweeping here). Novak has also shown how in his economic thinking Defoe was both a conservative and an admirer of Hobbes (*Economics and the Fiction of Defoe*, pp. 33–6). Neither the background evidence nor the novel itself will support any single view of the matter.

4 Hunter, *The Reluctant Pilgrim*, passim; see also G. A. Starr, *Defoe and Spiritual Autobiography*.

5 Not the least reason for *Robinson Crusoe*'s possession of more of a spiritual theme than any other of Defoe's novels is the fact that Crusoe has to stay in one place, and therefore has more scope for introspection.

6 *Moll Flanders*, p. 98; *Roxana: The Fortunate Mistress*, ed. Jack, pp. 49, 133.

7 See, for example, *Moll Flanders*, pp. 226, 280, 281; also *Roxana*, pp. 43, 79, 132, 300–1.

8 It is impossible to take seriously a supposed final repentance on Moll's part which involves the kind of stupid moral vanity, especially towards her former companions of Newgate, with which she comports herself on board the ship bound for Virginia; or to see any real reform in a life raised on the hoardings from her former crimes (pp. 290, 295, 312, 314–6).

9 See, for example, Columbus, 'Conscious Artistry in *Moll Flanders*', *SEL*, III, pp. 415–32; Koonce, 'Moll's Muddle: Defoe's Use of Irony in *Moll Flanders*', *ELH*, xxx, pp. 377–94.

10 Watt, *The Rise of the Novel: Studies in Defoe, Richardson and Fielding*, pp. 118–30.

11 See also, for example, pp. 194–5, 226–8, 252.

12 Columbus, 'Conscious Artistry'.

13   Often the old Moll so directly berates herself on what she ought to have done that we feel the self-recrimination to have been made at the time of her folly: indeed, that in a sense the folly becomes a mere function of the object lesson – see for example, pp. 25–6. Nor should we forget that Moll shows just as many romantic failures of 'policy' when older, and criticises herself for them too (falling in love with Jemmy, thieving for the mere love of it).

14   The clumsinesses of the narration, which are not envisaged by Defoe in any way, and in any case often occur in non-moral contexts (contrast Swift's narrators), also reduce the possibility of subtle ironic intent: see the inconsistencies at pp. 7–10, 63 (on her husband's escape), or between p. 98 and p. 124 (on the linen-draper); or the style at pp. 74, 222–3, 306. The case is similar with *Robinson Crusoe*: for example, the repetitions at pp. 16–17, 68 and 115 (on board-making), 102–3 and 148 (on cats), 275–6 (the mutineer hanged); the inconsistency between terming the seafaring life the most godless (p. 131) and ending by packing his son off to sea (p. 305); or even the way Crusoe inadvertently falls into Friday's idiom at p. 296, 'when the Bear see his Enemy gone . . .'.

15   *A Journal of the Plague Year*, ed. Landa, pp. 47–8, 69–71, 158, 161–2, 166–7.

16   G. A. Starr, in *Defoe and Casuistry*, argues, with some of these inconsistencies, that they are a function of a casuistic method, whereby one view of the narrator is played off against another, leaving us to find a point of balance: 'Whenever the narrator's judgments verge on the peremptory, something is added to restore a more tentative atmosphere' (p. 73). But such a reading involves making the shadowy H. F. a dramatised narrator; and the fact that the opposed views are widely separated in the novel rather than brought together in one place as in some of Defoe's potentially casuistic treatises – *The Family Instructor* (1715–18), *Religious Courtship* (1722), *A New Family Instructor* (1727) – works against any sense that they are deliberate.

17   Watt, *The Rise of the Novel*, p. 65; see also his chs 3 and 4.

18   Ibid., p. 69.

19   Ibid.

20   Before his rescue of Friday Crusoe says, 'It came now very warmly upon my Thoughts, and indeed irresistibly, that now was my Time to get me a Servant, and perhaps a Companion, or Assistant; and that I was call'd plainly by Providence to save this poor Creature's Life' (p. 202). Cynics will reject the second as mere 'gilt on the gingerbread'; yet, though it comes second, it still has some small part of the motive power.

21   *Roxana*, pp. 157–61.

22   *The History . . . of Colonel Jacque* (1722), in *Romances and Narratives*, vol. 10, pp. 180–2, 199; see also vol. 11, pp. 71–2.

23   Watt, *The Rise of the Novel*, p. 73.

24   There is a similar collapse of the sociological intent of *Colonel Jacque* (Author's Preface, p. xv). Dickens, in writing *Oliver Twist*, which is heavily indebted to Defoe's novel, learnt much from this failure.

25   This theme is present in *Roxana* even though the heroine is for most of

the story comfortably off: for her potential for ruin increases the more as she rises in fortune, and is accentuated by her being pursued throughout the story, whether by an avenging Jew who knows part of the ruinous truth about her, or by a cast-off daughter harrying her to the limit.

26 *The Farther Adventures . . . of Robinson Crusoe*, in *Romances and Narratives*, vol. 2, p. 211.

27 This is said by Crusoe of his shifting attitudes to the island, now liking it, now loathing it, now seeing it as a place to stay, now as one to escape, now as the scene of divine punishment of him, now as one of divine favour: see pp. 62–3, 65–7, 111, 112–13, 128–32, 135–6, 143–4, 156–7, 171, 187–8, 194–5, 210, 220, 229.

28 It is this self-division which marks off Defoe from Bunyan, who, unlike Defoe, was wholly given over to religion in his life: there is little such tension between sacred and secular impulses in Bunyan's work.

29 Wyndham, *The Chrysalids*, p. 234.

30 Ibid., p. 217.

31 *Moll Flanders*, p. 191. See also Defoe, *The Review*, VIII, no. 75 (15 Sep 1711), quoted in *Selected Writings*, p. 131: 'Distress removes from the Soul, all R[e]lation, Affection, Sense of Justice, and all the Obligations, either Moral or Religious, that secure one Man against another.'

32 Both Defoe and Wyndham's Coker argue that there is no real difference between the temperaments and mental abilities of men and women (Defoe, 'An Academy for Women', *An Essay Upon Projects* (1697), in *Selected Writings*, pp. 32–4; Wyndham, *The Day of the Triffids*, pp. 193–9).

33 In *The Farther Adventures . . . of Robinson Crusoe*, Defoe's portrayals of feeling are reduced to grotesquerie (see, for example, pp. 17–19, 34–5, 113, 231).

34 Defoe wrote in *The Complete English Tradesman*, Letter III ('Of the Trading Stile'), 'If any man was to ask me, which would be supposed to be a perfect stile, or language, I would answer, that in which a man speaking to five hundred people, of all common and various capacities, idiots or lunaticks excepted, should be understood by them all in the same manner with one another, and in the same sense which the speaker intended to be understood, this would certainly be a most perfect stile' (*Selected Writings*, p. 227. See also, ibid., p. 229; *Serious Reflections . . . of Robinson Crusoe*, in *Romances and Narratives*, vol. 3, p. 23; and Payne, *Mr. Review: Daniel Defoe as Author of 'The Review'*, pp. 20–36.)

35 See, for example, *Selected Writings*, pp. 130–1, 242; Defoe, *A General History of the Pyrates*, ed. Schonhorn, pp. 43, 389–404.

36 See Defoe's remarks on man's essential solitude in *Serious Reflections . . . of Robinson Crusoe*, in *Romances and Narratives*, vol. 3, pp. 2–3.

37 See on this Ross, *Swift and Defoe: A Study in Relationship*, esp. 125–37.

CHAPTER 8

1 See also Leavis, 'The Irony of Swift', in *The Common Pursuit*, pp. 80–4.

2 See Crane, 'The Houyhnhnms, the Yahoos and the History of Ideas', repr. in *Jonathan Swift: A Critical Anthology*, ed. Donoghue, pp. 379–80; Wind, *Pagan Mysteries in the Renaissance*, pp. 145–7.

CHAPTER 9

1   Ralph Cohen, in *The Unfolding of the Seasons*, p. 136, finds even his powers of Thomson-justifying ingenuity taxed by this passage. First to give extended treatment to its contradictions was R. D. Havens' 'Primitivism and the Idea of Progress in Thomson' *SP*, xxix, pp. 41–51, though his tracing of the cause to a mixture in Thomson of nationalist and commercial fervour with world-renouncing nostalgia is different from the one proposed here. John Chalker, in *The English Georgic: A Study in the Development of a Form*, pp. 100–9, argues that this inconsistency may be resolved by seeing the poem as an attempt to be emotionally comprehensive, allowing as much weight to the Ovidian nostalgia for a simple Golden Age and the Lucretian involvement with a progressivist Iron Age that he finds blended in Virgil's *Georgics*. There is in fact only occasionally a double view in Virgil, and where it does occur (particularly *Georgics* i, 121–59) Virgil sees the limitations of both Ages, the 'lethargy' of the Golden and the painful toil of the Iron, *at the same time* as being drawn to both. Thomson, however, veers between being wholly for, and wholly against. Thomson's use of the Georgic genre is an attempt common in eighteenth-century poets to give their work form and their increasingly frail philosophies authority within the armour of classical precedent. Most of them write within 'informal' genres – satire (progressively less organised by epic analogy), epistle, Georgic or ode.

2   It is significant that, of all biblical worthies, Milton should have chosen the morally recalcitrant Samson: the choice is a consequence of his fascination for strength and energy.

CHAPTER 10

1   See, for example, *The Champion*, 5 Jan 1740; quoted in Battestin, *The Moral Basis of Fielding's Art: A Study of 'Joseph Andrews'*, p. 150.

2   Richardson, *Pamela*, ed. Kinkead-Weeks, vol. 1, p. 57.

3   Ecclesiastes 7:16.

4   See also Paulson, *Satire and the Novel in Eighteenth-Century England*, p. 109.

5   See, for instance, Fielding, 'An Essay on the Knowledge of the Characters of Men' (1743), in *The Complete Works of Henry Fielding*, ed. Roscoe, p. 645, col. i; *Tom Jones*, pp. 783–4; or the ironic *Covent-Garden Journal*, ed. Jensen, vol. 1, pp. 233–6 (no. 16, 25 Feb 1752). Hence, in part, Fielding's castigations of the work-shy poor and beggars (see *An Inquiry into the Causes of the Late Increase of Robbers Etc.* (1751), in *Works*, pp. 773–5; and *Covent-Garden Journal*, vol. 2, pp. 10–11 (no. 44, 2 June 1752)). But compare *Covent-Garden Journal*, vol. 1, p. 278 (no. 24, 24 Mar 1752), where Fielding warns against excessive busyness.

6   See also pp. 95–6, 728, 765, 783–4, 815–6; 'A Journey from This World to the Next' (1743), in *Works*, p. 601, col. i; *Covent-Garden Journal*, vol. 1, pp. 308–9 (no. 29, 11 Apr 1752).

7   See also Paulson, *Satire and the Novel*, pp. 101–3.

8   This is carried to exhaustive lengths in the metempsychotic history of Julian the Apostate in 'A Journey from This World to the Next', chs

10–15. See also the encyclopaedic method of Fielding's similes, in, for example, *Joseph Andrews*, pp. 149, 278–9, and *Tom Jones*, pp. 593, 658.

9   It is therefore inevitably ironic that Fielding married his former wife's maid, Sarah Daniel, in 1747.

10   *Pamela*, vol. 1, p. 98.

11   Remarked by Ian Watt in *'Shamela'*, in *Fielding: A Collection of Critical Essays*, ed. Paulson, p. 50.

12   For an account of Fielding's more secular views on rank, see Rawson, *Henry Fielding and the Augustan Ideal Under Stress*, ch. 1. Rawson does not, however, mention the Christian complication, and this allows him to find Fielding's views more consistent than they are: contrast, for example, p. 636, col. i, and p. 708, col. i, in *Works*.

13   There are exceptions – for example, *Tom Jones*, pp. 370, 494.

14   Fielding exposes the suspicious temper in *Tom Jones*, pp. 427–8, 615–16, and in *Amelia*, Bk viii, ch. 9 (*Works*, p. 479, col. ii), yet knows that the kind of straightforward inference from appearances and actions that he recommends in *Tom Jones*, pp. 615–16, and in 'An Essay on the Knowledge of the Characters of Men' (*Works*, pp. 643–50, esp. pp. 644, col. i, 646, col. i, and 649–50; p. 647, col. ii, swings back to suspicion) will rarely suffice to expose a Blifil – as the ignorance concerning him of Tom, Allworthy and Sophia alike indicate. When, having revealed the true nature of Thwackum to us, Fielding bids us not, from our privileged insight, condemn the imperceptiveness of Allworthy for not so seeing (*Tom Jones*, p. 135), he underlines the whole weakness of his own doctrine of watchfulness (some critics have preferred to see Allworthy as gently criticised for his supposed gullibility).

15   See, for example, pp. 37, 39–40, 171, 320, 625, 768, 818.

16   Even if we do just recall that he uttered the same cries much earlier to Blifil (pp. 344, 345).

17   See also Fielding's last work, *The Journal of a Voyage to Lisbon* (1755), which in parts could almost have been written by the Man of the Hill; allowance, but not sufficient, must be made for Fielding's illness at the time.

18   Fielding recognises the contradiction (Preface, p. 8), but in attempting to reduce it can find only tenuous arguments.

19   In *Amelia* there is a disturbing tendency for characters (particularly Mrs James, Mrs Atkinson and Colonel Trent) to be presented as now good, now bad, without psychological or other links.

CHAPTER 11

1   For earlier scattered occurrences of the theme, see Lonsdale (ed.), *The Poems of Gray, Collins and Goldsmith*, pp. 123, 125, 126. It is not to be found in the contemporary graveyard poetry or elegy (of Blair, Young, Hammond or Shenstone), of which Gray's poem is in part an expression.

2   Certainly the Augustans saw man as a frustrated species, but for them that frustration was inherent in his nature – essential, not accidental: the only necessity which governed it was that, in a universe of total plenitude (as it expresses God, the universe must be the best of all

universes, and fullness of creation is a concomitant of this) there must at some point in the scale of being be such a creature of ambitious thoughts and limited abilities. See Pope, *Essay on Man*, i, 35–76; and Lovejoy, *The Great Chain of Being*, pp. 198–9, 204–5, 214–6.

3   See Jones, *Thomas Gray, Scholar*.

4   Ibid., pp. 47–8.

5   On these friendships see Ketton-Cremer, *Thomas Gray: A Biography*, pp. 15–16, 26–7, 54–5; Jack, 'Gray's *Elegy* Reconsidered', in *From Sensibility to Romanticism: Essays Presented to Frederick A. Pottle*, ed. Hilles and Bloom, pp. 149–50.

6   For previous accounts of the structure of the poem, see Ellis, 'Gray's *Elegy*: The Biographical Problem in Literary Criticism', *PMLA*, LXVI, pp. 998–9; Brooks, 'Gray's Storied Urn', in *The Well Wrought Urn: Studies in the Structure of Poetry*, pp. 85–100; Brady, 'Structure and Meaning in Gray's *Elegy*', in *From Sensibility to Romanticism*, pp. 177–89. None of these deals with the problem of the subject-changes.

7   See H. W. Starr, *Gray as a Literary Critic*, pp. 58–9, 86, 95–9.

8   Empson, *Some Versions of Pastoral*, p. 4.

9   Brooks, 'Gray's Storied Urn', p. 93.

10   On the whole Gray was antipathetic to moralising or philosophising in poetry. Moral reflections he accepted 'if they are well joined with the character'. If not, 'they had better be left to the audience, than put into the mouths of a set of professed moralists, who keep a shop of sentences and reflections . . . whether they be sages . . . or young girls that learnt them by heart, out of their sample and primers' (*The Correspondence of Thomas Gray*, ed. Toynbee and Whibley, vol. 1, pp. 359–60; see also p. 183). Incidentally, Gray disliked Thomson 'when he attempted to be moral, in which attempt he always became verbose' (ibid., vol. 3, Appendix Z, p. 1291). See also the ironic treatment of morals and moralising in the 'Ode on the Spring' and the 'Ode on the Death of a Favourite Cat'.

11   *Correspondence*, vol. 1, p. 289.

CHAPTER 12

1   See, for example, Gifford, '*The Vanity of Human Wishes*', *Review of English Studies*, n.s. 6, pp. 157–65, and Lascelles, 'Johnson and Juvenal', in *New Light on Dr. Johnson: Essays on the Occasion of his 250th Birthday*, ed. Hilles, pp. 35–55. Both, however, tend to see Johnson as too simply sympathetic; Leopold Damrosch Jr, in *Samuel Johnson and the Tragic Sense*, pp. 139–59 recognises both the tragic and satiric elements, terming the whole 'tragical satire' in Dryden's sense, but admits that the two impulses are not often or evidently reconcilable.

2   On preying, see 36, 166, 257; on firing and burning, 17, 20, 74, 76, 136, 141, 191, 229; on warring, 15, 22, 41, 45, 140, 142, 149–50, 151, 157, 205–6, 281–2, 329–30, 335–40, 352, 362; on diseasing, 23, 46, 135–6; on crowding, 4, 24, 80, 248, 253, 271, 281, 335–6; on falling, 13, 22, 79, 83, 125, 339; on transience, 99, 249–50, 304. See also Bloom, '*The Vanity of Human Wishes*: Reason's Images', *EC*, xv, pp. 181–92.

3   Juvenal does not have this sense of fate: he has contempt for the activity

of wishing (see particularly *Satire* x, 346 ff.) and supposes that man could by choice dispense with it; this is the basis of the satiric rather than the tragic vision.

4   Juvenal, on the other hand, prefers such caution (99–102).

5   Juvenal, 61–90, sees the fickleness of lackeys and the rabble as expressing the folly of ambitious men, more than as a subject for scorn in its own right.

6   Juvenal, 19–22, sees this man much more conventionally, as unhappy with spoils, happy without.

7   This phrase recurs (37, 44, 45, 46, 56, 79, 132); it was Johnson's original title for *Rasselas*.

8   Outside such a context, he can give more weight to choice: see Fussell, *The Rhetorical World of Augustan Humanism*, pp. 45–8, citing *Rambler*, no. 41.

CHAPTER 13

1   See Miner, 'The Making of *The Deserted Village*', HLQ, xxii, pp. 137–8; Storm, 'Literary Convention in Goldsmith's *Deserted Village*', HLQ, xxxiii, pp. 252–6; and, particularly, Jaarsma, 'Ethics in the Wasteland: Image and Structure in Goldsmith's *The Deserted Village*', *Texas Studies in Literature and Language*, xiii, pp. 447–59. Similar conclusions are advanced here, but with different materials.

2   On this, and the degree of consistency of Goldsmith's views on the subject throughout his writings, see Crane (ed.), *New Essays by Oliver Goldsmith*, pp. xxxviii–xl, 28–9, 81–4, 116–24; Bell, 'The Deserted Village and Goldsmith's Social Doctrines', *PMLA*, lix, pp. 747–72; Miner, 'The Making of *The Deserted Village*', pp. 125–41.

3   It is a strange fact that Crabbe and Reynolds became close friends.

4   See also Crabbe's distinction between poetry which addresses itself to the 'fancy and imagination' and that which speaks to the 'plain sense and sober judgment' – Preface to *Tales* (1812), in *Poems by George Crabbe*, ed. Ward, vol. 2, pp. 9–10.

5   Crabbe clearly thought of his art in terms of photographic verisimilitude and accuracy of depiction (ibid., p. 8); he speaks of 'this nudity of description, and poetry without an atmosphere' (ibid., p. 10).

6   In his preface to the *Tales* Crabbe discards the possibility of a unifying theme for 'greater variety of incident and more minute display of character, by accuracy of description and diversity of scene' (pp. 6–8).

7   On eighteenth-century forerunners of Crabbe's pastoral realism, see Tinker, *Nature's Simple Plan: A Phase of Radical Thought in the Mid-Eighteenth Century*, pp. 90–111; Lang, 'Crabbe and the Eighteenth Century', *ELH*, v, pp. 305–33.

8   See also the perceptive (unsigned) notice by Edmund Cartwright in *Monthly Review*, lxix (Nov 1783), pp. 418–21; repr. in Pollard (ed.), *Crabbe: The Critical Heritage*, pp. 42–4. Crabbe admitted his preference for singularities rather than types: see his Preface to *The Borough* (1810), p. xxix.

9   See also Cartwright, in *Monthly Review*, lxix, pp. 418–19 (see previous

note); and unsigned notice in *Anti-Jacobin Review and Magazine*, XXVIII (Dec 1807), repr. in Pollard (ed.), *Crabbe: The Critical Heritage*, p. 52.

10 On this see Greene, 'Logical Structure in Eighteenth-Century Poetry', *PQ*, XXXI, pp. 315–36.

11 George Crabbe (the younger), *The Life of George Crabbe*, p. 103.

CHAPTER 14

1 Wordsworth was so taken by 'Yardley Oak' that on its first pubication (1804) he copied it into his commonplace book.

2 See, for example, the attack on deism in *The Task*, v, 779–906. It is arguable, incidentally, that it is as much Cowper's religion as any eighteenth-century development in aesthetic thought that makes him more a 'pre-Romantic' than previous poets: his insistence on the 'inner light' makes him bound to stress the seer before the seen, and to approximate in the workings of his imagination to the Romantic 'auxiliar light' which animates the world. See, however, Spacks, *The Poetry of Vision: Five Eighteenth-Century Poets*, p. 194, for the contrary view.

3 And in order to make this point Cowper has to portray Omai's native pleasures as simple, where previously he has described his people as 'victims of luxurious ease' (625).

4 Cowper is sometimes nervous too of the 'non-Augustan' specificity of his poem, and the quaintness or reconditeness of its vignettes: see, for example, his defence of the account of cucumber-growing (III, 446–62, 562–5).

5 It has been claimed (Spacks, *The Poetry of Vision*, p. 183) that Cowper is exposing Kate's excessive 'fancy' here; but within a few paragraphs he himself is to produce as fanciful a picture, of the savage Omai pining for England (654–71); and he delights in fancy elsewhere in the poem (I, 402; IV, 232–42, 272–307, 691–703; v, 6–20).

6 Thereafter the fierceness he has portrayed is relegated to the Arctic and Antarctic regions (I, 608–20).

CHAPTER 15

1 For a fine account of the expression of this in Sterne, see Wasserman, *The Subtler Language: Critical Readings of Neoclassic and Romantic Poems*, pp. 169–72.

2 See Abrams, *The Mirror and the Lamp: Romantic Theory and the Critical Tradition*, ch. 8.

3 Lovejoy, *The Great Chain of Being*, ch. 9; pp. 265–6, describing the new conception of the universe, could almost be an account of Cowper's oak.

Bibliography

Abbreviations of journal titles are as given at the beginning of the Notes. Place of publication is London, unless otherwise stated. The editions used of the main texts referred to are listed following the Preface, and are not detailed here.

Abrams, M. H., *The Mirror and the Lamp: Romantic Theory and the Critical Tradition* (Oxford University Press, 1953).

Allison, Alexander Ward, *Toward an Augustan Poetic: Edmund Waller's 'Reform' of English Poetry* (Lexington, Ky: University of Kentucky Press, 1962).

Auerbach, Erich, *Mimesis: The Representation of Reality in Western Literature*, trans. Willard Trask (Garden City, NY: Doubleday and Co., 1957).

Augustine, St, *Concerning the City of God against the Pagans*, ed. David Knowles (Harmondsworth: Penguin Books, 1972).

Battestin, Martin C., *The Moral Basis of Fielding's Art: A Study of 'Joseph Andrews'* (Middletown, Conn.: Wesleyan University Press, 1959).

Bell, Howard J., Jr, 'The Deserted Village and Goldsmith's Social Doctrines', *PMLA*, LIX (1944).

Bloom, Edward A., 'The Vanity of Human Wishes: Reason's Images', *EC*, xv (1965).

Brady, Frank, 'Structure and Meaning in Gray's Elegy', in *From Sensibility to Romanticism: Essays Presented to Frederick A. Pottle*, ed. Frederick W. Hilles and Harold Bloom (Oxford University Press, 1965).

Brooks, Cleanth, 'Gray's Storied Urn', in *The Well Wrought Urn: Studies in the Structure of Poetry* (Methuen, 1968).

Brooks, Cleanth, and Hardy, John E., *Poems of Mr. John Milton: The 1645 Edition, with Essays in Analysis* (New York: Harcourt, Brace and Co., 1952).

Brower, Reuben A., 'Dryden and the "Invention" of Pope', *Restoration and Eighteenth-Century Literature: Essays in Honor of Alan Dugald McKillop*, ed. Carroll Camden (Chicago: University of Chicago Press, 1963).

Chalker, John, *The English Georgic: A Study in the Development of a Form* (Routledge and Kegan Paul, 1969).

Cohen, Ralph, 'The Augustan Mode in English Poetry', *Studies in the Eighteenth Century: Papers Presented at the David Nichol Smith Memorial Seminar, Canberra, 1966*, ed. R. F. Brissenden (Canberra: Australian National University Press, 1968).

Cohen, Ralph, *The Unfolding of the Seasons* (Routledge and Kegan Paul, 1970).

Columbus, Robert L., 'Conscious Artistry in *Moll Flanders*', *SEL*, III (1963).

Crabbe, George, *The Borough* (1810).

Crabbe, George, *Poems by George Crabbe*, ed. A. W. Ward (Cambridge: Cambridge University Press, 1906).

Crabbe, George (the younger), *The Life of George Crabbe* (Cresset Press, 1947).

Crane, Ronald S. (ed.), *New Essays by Oliver Goldsmith* (Chicago: University of Chicago Press, 1927).

Crane, Ronald S., 'The Houyhnhnms, the Yahoos and the History of Ideas' (1959), repr. in *Jonathan Swift: A Critical Anthology*, ed. Denis Donoghue (Harmondsworth: Penguin Books, 1971).

Cubeta, Paul M., 'A Jonsonian Ideal: "To Penshurst"', *PQ*, XLII (1963).

Curtius, Ernst R., *European Literature and the Latin Middle Ages*, trans. Willard R. Trask, Bollingen Series, no. 36 (New York: Pantheon Books, 1953).

Damrosch, Leopold, Jr, *Samuel Johnson and the Tragic Sense* (Princeton, NJ: Princeton University Press, 1972).

Defoe, Daniel, *Madagascar; or, Robert Drury's Journal*, ed. Capt. Pasfield Oliver (T. Fisher Unwin, 1890).

Defoe, Daniel, *Romances and Narratives by Daniel Defoe*, ed. George A. Aitken, 16 vols (J. M. Dent, 1895).

Defoe, Daniel, *Roxana: The Fortunate Mistress*, ed. Jane Jack (Oxford University Press, 1964).

Defoe, Daniel, *A Journal of the Plague Year*, ed. Louis Landa (Oxford University Press, 1969).

Defoe, Daniel, *A General History of the Pyrates*, ed. Manuel Schonhorn (Columbia, SC: University of South Carolina Press, 1972).

Defoe, Daniel, *Selected Writings of Daniel Defoe*, ed. James T. Boulton (Cambridge: Cambridge University Press, 1975).

Dryden, John, *Of Dramatic Poesy, and Other Critical Essays*, ed. G. Watson (J. M. Dent, 1962).

Edwards, Thomas R., Jr, *This Dark Estate: A Reading of Pope* (Berkeley, Calif.: University of California Press, 1963).

Eliot, T. S., *Selected Essays*, 3rd edition (Faber and Faber, 1951).

Eliot, T. S., *Elizabethan Dramatists: Essays by T. S. Eliot* (Faber and Faber, 1963).

Ellis, F. H., 'Gray's *Elegy*: The Biographical Problem in Literary Criticism', *PMLA*, LXVI (1951).

Empson, William, *Seven Types of Ambiguity* (Chatto and Windus, 1930).

Empson, William, *Some Versions of Pastoral* (Chatto and Windus, 1935).

Empson, William, 'Donne and the Rhetoricians', *Kenyon Review*, XI (1949).

Empson, William, 'Donne the Space Man', *Kenyon Review*, XIX (1957).

Fielding, Henry, *The Complete Works of Henry Fielding*, ed. Thomas Roscoe (Bell and Daldy, 1869).

Fielding, Henry (Sir Alexander Drawcansit), *The Covent-Garden Journal*, ed. George E. Jensen, 2 vols (New Haven, Conn.: Yale University Press, 1915).

Fowler, A. D. S., 'The Locality of Jonson's *To Penshurst*', *Conceitful Thought*:

The Interpretation of English Renaissance Poems (Edinburgh: Edinburgh University Press, 1975).

Frost, William, *Dryden and the Art of Translation*, Yale Studies in English, no. 128 (New Haven, Conn.: Yale University Press, 1955).

Fussell, Paul, *The Rhetorical World of Augustan Humanism: Ethics and Imagery from Swift to Burke* (Oxford: Clarendon Press, 1965).

Gifford, Henry, 'The Vanity of Human Wishes', *Review of English Studies*, n.s. 6 (1955).

Goldberg, S. L., 'Alexander Pope', *Melbourne Critical Review*, VII (1964).

Gray, Thomas, *The Correspondence of Thomas Gray*, ed. Paget Toynbee and Leonard Whibley, 3 vols (Oxford: Clarendon Press, 1935).

Greene, Donald J., 'Logical Structure in Eighteenth-Century Poetry', *PQ*, XXXI (1952).

Hagstrum, Jean H., *The Sister Arts: The Tradition of Literary Pictorialism and English Poetry from Dryden to Gray* (Chicago: University of Chicago Press, 1958).

Hardy, J. P., *Reinterpretations: Essays on Poems by Milton, Pope and Johnson* (Routledge and Kegan Paul, 1971).

Havens, R. D., 'Primitivism and the Idea of Progress in Thomson', *SP*, XXIX (1932).

Hibbard, G. R., 'The Country House Poem of the Seventeenth-Century', *Journal of the Courtauld and Warburg Institutes*, XIX (1956).

Hinant, C. H., 'Dryden's Gallic Rooster', *Studies in Philology*, LXV (1968).

Hunter, J. Paul, *The Reluctant Pilgrim: Defoe's Emblematic Method and the Quest for Form in 'Robinson Crusoe'* (Baltimore: Johns Hopkins Press, 1966).

Jaarsma, Richard J., 'Ethics in the Wasteland: Image and Structure in Goldsmith's *The Deserted Village*', *Texas Studies in Literature and Language*, XIII (1971–2).

Jack, Ian, 'Gray's *Elegy* Reconsidered', in *From Sensibility to Romanticism: Essays Presented to Frederick A. Pottle*, ed. Frederick W. Hilles and Harold Bloom (Oxford University Press, 1965).

Jones, William P., *Thomas Gray, Scholar* (Cambridge, Mass.: Harvard University Press, 1937).

Jung, C. G., *The Collected Works of C. G. Jung*, trans. R. F. C. Hull, 17 vols (Routledge and Kegan Paul, 1957–73).

Juvenal (Decimus Junius Juvenalis), *Juvenal and Persius*, trans. G. G. Ramsay, Loeb Classics Series, revised edition (Heinemann, 1969).

Kermode, Frank, 'Dissociation of Sensibility', *Kenyon Review*, XIX (1957).

Kernan, Alvin B., *The Cankered Muse: Satire of the English Renaissance* (New Haven, Conn.: Yale University Press, 1959).

Ketton-Cremer, R. W., *Thomas Gray: A Biography* (Cambridge: Cambridge University Press, 1955).

Koonce, Howard L., 'Moll's Muddle: Defoe's Use of Irony in *Moll Flanders*', *ELH*, XXX (1963).

Lang, Varley, 'Crabbe and the Eighteenth Century', *ELH*, V (1938).

Lascelles, Mary, 'Johnson and Juvenal', in *New Light on Dr. Johnson: Essays on the Occasion of his 250th Birthday*, ed. Frederick W. Hilles (New Haven, Conn.: Yale University Press, 1959).

Lawry, Jon S., ' "Eager Thought": Dialectic in *Lycidas*', *PMLA*, LXXVII (1962).

Leavis, F. R., *The Common Pursuit* (Harmondsworth: Penguin Books, 1962).

Lewis, C. S., 'Donne and Love Poetry in the Seventeenth Century', in *Seventeenth Century Studies Presented to Sir Herbert Grierson* (Oxford: Clarendon Press, 1938).

Lewis, C. S., *A Preface to 'Paradise Lost'* (Oxford University Press, 1942).

Lewis, C. S., *Perelandra* (John Lane, The Bodley Head, 1943).

Lloyd, Michael, 'The Fatal Bark', *Modern Language Notes*, LXXV (1960).

Lovejoy, Arthur O., *The Great Chain of Being: A Study of the History of an Idea* (New York: Harper and Brothers, 1960).

Mack, Maynard, *The Garden and the City: Retirement and Politics in the Later Poetry of Pope, 1731–1743* (Toronto: University of Toronto Press, 1969).

Maresca, Thomas E., *Pope's Horatian Poems* (Columbus, Ohio: Ohio State University Press, 1966).

Martial (Marcus Valerius Martialis), *Epigrams*, trans. Walter C. A. Kerr, 2 vols, Loeb Classics Series (Heinemann, 1919–20).

Martz, Louis, *The Poetry of Meditation: A Study in English Religious Literature of the Seventeenth Century*, 2nd edition (New Haven, Conn.: Yale University Press, 1962).

Mazzeo, J. A., 'A Critique of Some Modern Theories of Metaphysical Poetry', *MP*, L (1952).

Mengel, Elias, F., Jr, 'Patterns of Imagery in Pope's *Arbuthnot*', *PMLA*, LXIX (1954).

Miner, Earl, 'The Making of *The Deserted Village*', *HLQ*, XXII (1958–9).

Miner, Earl, 'Chaucer in Dryden's *Fables*', *Studies in Criticism and Aesthetics 1660–1800: Essays in Honor of Samuel Holt Monk*, ed. Howard Anderson and John S. Shea (Minneapolis: University of Minnesota Press, 1967).

Miner, Earl, *The Cavalier Mode from Jonson to Cotton* (Princeton, NJ: Princeton University Press, 1971).

Mortimer, Anthony, 'The Feigned Commonwealth in the Poetry of Ben Jonson', *SEL*, XIII (1973).

Nicolson, Marjorie Hope, *The Breaking of the Circle: Studies in the Effect of the 'New Science' upon Seventeenth-Century Poetry*, revised edition (New York: Columbia University Press, 1960).

Novak, Maximilian E., *Economics and the Fiction of Daniel Defoe* (Berkeley, Calif.: University of California Press, 1962).

Olson, Elder, 'Rhetoric and the Appreciation of Pope', *MP*, XXXVII (1939–40).

Parfitt, G. A. E., 'The Poetry of Ben Jonson', *EC*, XVIII (1968).

Parfitt, G. A. E., 'Compromise Classicism: Language and Rhythm in Ben Jonson's Poetry', *SEL*, XI (1971).

Paulson, Ronald, *The Fictions of Satire* (Baltimore: Johns Hopkins Press, 1967).

Paulson, Ronald, *Satire and the Novel in Eighteenth-Century England* (New Haven, Conn.: Yale University Press, 1967).

Payne, William L., *Mr. Review: Daniel Defoe as Author of 'The Review'* (Morningside Heights, NY: King's Crown Press, 1947).

Pollard, A. W. (ed.), *Crabbe: The Critical Heritage* (Routledge and Kegan Paul, 1972).

Price, Martin, *To the Palace of Wisdom: Studies in Order and Energy from Dryden to Blake* (Garden City, NY: Doubleday and Co., 1964).

Rawson, C. J., *Henry Fielding and the Augustan Ideal Under Stress* (Routledge and Kegan Paul, 1972).

Richardson, Samuel, *Pamela*, ed. M. Kinkead-Weekes, 2 vols (J. M. Dent, 1962).

Rivers, Isabel, *The Poetry of Conservatism 1660–1745: A Study of Poets and Public Affairs from Jonson to Pope* (Cambridge: Rivers Press, 1973).

Røstvig, Maren-Sofie, *The Happy Man: Studies in the Metamorphoses of a Classical Ideal*, Oslo Studies in English, no. 2 (Oslo: Akademisk Forlag, 1954).

Rosenblum, Michael, 'Pope's Illusive Temple of Infamy', in *The Satirist's Art*, ed. H. James Jensen and Malvin R. Zirker Jr (Bloomington, Ind.: Indiana University Press, 1972).

Ross, John F., *Swift and Defoe: A Study in Relationship* (Berkeley, Calif.: University of California Press, 1941).

Roston, Murray, *The Soul of Wit: A Study of John Donne* (Oxford: Clarendon Press, 1974).

Sanders, Wilbur, *John Donne's Poetry* (Cambridge: Cambridge University Press, 1971).

Spacks, Patricia M., *The Poetry of Vision: Five Eighteenth-Century Poets* (Cambridge, Mass.: Harvard University Press, 1967).

Starr, George A., *Defoe and Spiritual Autobiography* (Princeton, NJ: Princeton University Press, 1965.

Starr, George A., *Defoe and Casuistry* (Princeton, NJ: Princeton University Press, 1971).

Starr, Herbert W., *Gray as a Literary Critic* (Philadelphia: University of Pennsylvania Press, 1941).

Storm, Leo F., 'Literary Convention in Goldsmith's *Deserted Village*', HLQ, XXXIII (1969–70).

Tinker, Chauncey B., *Nature's Simple Plan: A Phase of Radical Thought in the Mid-Eighteenth Century* (Oxford University Press, 1922).

Tuve, Rosemond, *Elizabethan and Metaphysical Imagery* (Chicago: University of Chicago Press, 1947).

Tuve, Rosemond, *Images and Themes in Five Poems by Milton* (Cambridge, Mass.: Harvard University Press, 1957).

Wallerstein, Ruth, *Studies in Seventeenth-Century Poetic* (Madison, Wisc.: University of Wisconsin Press, 1950).

Wasserman, Earl R., *The Subtler Language: Critical Readings of Neoclassic and Romantic Poems* (Baltimore: Johns Hopkins Press, 1959).

Watt, Ian, *The Rise of the Novel: Studies in Defoe, Richardson and Fielding* (Chatto and Windus, 1957).

Watt, Ian, 'Shamela', in *Fielding: A Collection of Critical Essays*, ed. Ronald Paulson (Englewood Cliffs, NJ: Prentice-Hall, 1962).

Willey, Basil, *The Seventeenth-Century Background* (Chatto and Windus, 1934).

Willey, Basil, *The Eighteenth-Century Background* (Chatto and Windus, 1940).

Williams, Charles, *He Came Down from Heaven* (Heinemann, 1938).

Williams, Charles, *The Image of the City and Other Essays*, ed. Anne Ridler (Oxford University Press, 1958).

Wilson, G. E., 'Jonson's Use of the Bible and the Great Chain of Being in "To Penshurst" ', *SEL*, VIII (1968).

Wind, Edgar, *Pagan Mysteries in the Renaissance* (Harmondsworth: Penguin Books, 1967).

Wyndham, John, *The Chrysalids* (Michael Joseph, 1955).

Wyndham, John, *The Midwich Cuckoos* (Michael Joseph, 1957).

Index